Hollywood
Confidential

Hollywood Confidential

HOW THE STUDIOS BEAT THE MOB AT THEIR OWN GAME

TED SCHWARZ

TAYLOR TRADE PUBLISHING
Lanham • New York • Boulder • Toronto • Plymouth, UK

Published by Taylor Trade Publishing
An imprint of The Rowman & Littlefield Publishing Group, Inc.
4501 Forbes Boulevard, Suite 200, Lanham, Maryland 20706

Estover Road, Plymouth PL6 7PY, United Kingdom

Distributed by NATIONAL BOOK NETWORK

Library of Congress Cataloging-in-Publication Data

Schwarz, Ted, 1945–
  Hollywood confidential : how the studios beat the mob at their own game / Ted Schwarz.—1st Taylor Trade Publishing ed.
     p.   cm.
  Includes bibliographical references and index.
  ISBN-13: 978-1-58979-320-0 (cloth : alk. paper)
  ISBN-10: 1-58979-320-X (cloth : alk. paper)
    1. Organized crime—California—Los Angeles—History—20th century.
  2. Motion picture industry—California—Los Angeles—History.   3. Hollywood (Los Angeles, Calif.)—History.   I. Title.
  HV6793.C2S39   2007
  364.106′0979494—dc22

                                                                    2006031321

∞ ™ The paper used in this publication meets the minimum requirements of American National Standard for Information Sciences—Permanence of Paper for Printed Library Materials, ANSI/NISO Z39.48-1992.

Manufactured in the United States of America.

Contents

Act III

Preview of Coming Attractions

I t was 1980 when the young men came together to talk about their legacy. Each was in his forties. Each had been through the decades-old ceremony that began with the pricking of a finger, the blood smeared on a holy card bearing the image of the crime family's patron saint, the card burned with a candle flame. "I," each had said, giving his full name, "want to enter into this organization to protect my family and to protect my friends. I swear not to divulge this secret and to obey with love and *omertà*. As burns this saint, so will burn my soul. I enter alive into this organization and leave it dead."

These men had survived wars with rival families, tests of loyalty that sometimes meant they had shot and buried a friend, and through which they gained trust for their supervision of loan sharking, gambling, prostitution, extortion, or whatever specialty their godfathers had assigned them. They had achieved the mob equivalent of mid-level management and were in a position to move swiftly to the top.

It bothered these men, however, that they had only done in their careers the same type of work as the fathers, uncles, or mentors who brought them into the organization. And they knew from the old men that that generation had mirrored the men who had come before them. They had all prospered by catering to the greed, the lust, the addictions, and the business miscalculations of the general public. They supplied the women, ran the casinos, made the loans that could never be repaid, and otherwise functioned outside the law, just as generations before them had done. Now, they wanted to bring something new to the business of organized crime. They wanted to introduce a unique business model that would be as remembered for its sophistication as was the crudeness of past generations for their torturing and killing of their enemies.

The older men mostly ignored what the youths were suggesting.

1

They were satisfied with tradition. The Gambino family businesses alone were believed to generate $4 billion a year, and the Gambinos were one of an estimated twenty-six crime families operating alone or in conjunction with one another throughout the United States.

The younger men honored the past but felt that they should establish their own legacy. They had proved themselves as capable of arson, kneecapping, and murder as their respected predecessors, but they thought they could be innovative in the creation of a new business model that would allow unlimited wealth without legal scrutiny. They wanted to buy an island, one of many in existence that are both uninhabited by humans and unclaimed by any nation. And on that island, they would place a bank where all the crime families in America, and any others in the world, that wanted to participate could place their money. Laundering illegal earnings through legitimate businesses, an established practice that entailed the loss of millions of dollars to the Internal Revenue Service (IRS) in order to have "legal" working capital, would be a thing of the past. Legitimate business investments could be made with everyone sharing in the profits.

The island would also maintain apartments, hotels, and such retail businesses as necessary. There would be no extradition agreements with other countries, so anyone mob connected who was fleeing the law would find a safe haven. And because the island would be neutral territory, gang wars and targeted hits would not be permitted. The island would at once increase mob wealth while providing a safe escape from a world otherwise filled with betrayal, distrust, and fear of strangers. The mob would own everyone and everything.

The men who created the idea of the island, men who were connected with the Gambino family, the Genovese family, and others, thought they were being original. They did not realize that two generations earlier another group of ruthless, power-hungry men had amassed great wealth and achieved a variation of the island dream. The "island" was actually on the mainland of the West Coast, though the area was sparsely populated and without any business interests other than agriculture.

The men of that earlier generation were rivals in business and in pleasure. They trained, bought, and sold a variety of beautiful women, and each employed as many as ten thousand people at any given time. They had their own police and fire departments on their vast corporate holdings, ensuring that no crime was called a crime until they said so.

They had their own drug dealers supplying stimulants and sleeping medications to their employees so that the hours worked matched the desires of the all-powerful bosses.

Not that anyone visiting the area noticed what was taking place; perhaps that was why the youths were unaware that they were reinventing a concept from the past. The men in charge made certain that the city at large had all the trappings of an independent community. There was a mayor they kept happy by giving him a share of the $20 million a year spent on recreational gambling. There was a police force, the chief of which was so thoroughly corrupt that he was able to post openly the cost of buying positions of authority within his department. There was a district attorney who was told when to call a scene of violence a crime, when to prosecute an innocent man because his contract had become too expensive, and when to look the other way. And there was an equally corrupt coroner who announced that a major star, who had been battered into unconsciousness, dragged down concrete steps, and tossed into a running car, had committed suicide. The tourists saw the trappings of a normal city, felt the safety of armed police patrols, and experienced the "sting" of traffic cops when they drove too fast or parked too long in the wrong locations. They did not see that perhaps the majority of adult citizens, feeling they could not rely on anyone else for protection, carried handguns. This was the island dream of the young mob members who had not been born at the time of its creation and were mere toddlers when the men who achieved the dream had died of old age.

That "island" was the movie colony of Los Angeles, California, and more specifically the communities of Hollywood and Beverly Hills, where the movie industry ruled. The men who controlled every aspect of life for the thousands who lived and worked there were not part of organized crime; they were the moguls, the producers who owned the studios, made the films, and controlled the news as it affected their business. They were the ultimate tough guys, so powerful in their day that when organized crime made forays into the movie capital, then launched an all-out assault for control, it discovered it was not corrupt enough to win.

Act I

In which the rebels become the establishment and the immigrants become the moguls. As for the nice Methodist Prohibitionists of the little town of Hollywood. . . . It's just too horrible to tell.

CHAPTER One

An ''Island'' of Their Own

''

I always thought of Hollywood like a principality of its own. It was like a sort of a Luxembourg or a Lichtenstein. And the people who ran it really had that attitude. They weren't only running a studio; they were running a whole little world. Their power was absolutely enormous, and it wasn't only the power to make movies or to anoint someone or make someone a movie star or pick an unknown director and make him famous overnight. They could cover up a murder. Buron Fitts, the district attorney, was completely in the pocket of the producers. You could literally have somebody killed, and it wouldn't be in the papers. They ran this place.

> —writer Budd Schulberg, when speaking at a University of Southern California seminar on F. Scott Fitzgerald, many years after the moguls established their fiefdom

''

The outlaws came first, riding in from the east by rail and by horseback. They were armed with revolvers, rifles, and motion picture cameras. They took up guerrilla positions amid the citrus groves, keeping tabs on their pursuers through messages that came by mail and telegraph.

The good people of Hollywood tolerated the outlaws because the men who made a lam to the west knew to keep their distance. Hollywood, after all, was an idyllic development of homes built by good

Christian Prohibitionists on acreage given away by Horace Henderson Wilcox and his wife, Daeida. The Wilcoxes had purchased the former Spanish land of Rancho La Brea back in 1886. Then they laid out a community for the righteous, giving every plot away for free, provided that the new residents also built a Methodist Church on each street. There was no drinking, of course, and there was no gambling, including in private homes. These were proper people, like-minded people, folks who observed the Sabbath as God intended. As for the name of the development, Hollywood, it honored a Midwestern friend of great piety whose Ohio estate was known by that name.

There were neither movies nor moviemakers when Hollywood was planned. There were no actors or theaters in the area where a play could be seen. However, anyone familiar with the attitudes of the church could have predicted that the Wilcoxes would be hostile to anyone connected with such work. Nine years earlier, in 1877, the Methodist Episcopal Church became so concerned about the corrupting influence of plays—any play in any theater, presumably including Easter passion plays presented outside the church—that all members were ordered never to enter a theater or to see a play. The propriety of the subject matter and its presentation made no difference: Evil was present and the members were to avoid it.

The outlaws did not care about Hollywood when they arrived in the Los Angeles area a decade or more later. They probably could not have afforded to live there had they chosen to do so.

The outlaws might have liked to have committed a few "crimes" by making movies on their streets and in the minimal business district—a general store, a small hotel, and a barbershop—but there were other locations, equally interesting, all around. Besides, with the U.S. marshals regularly in pursuit, it mattered most that they had a clear escape route down to Mexico.

The outlaws—counterculture artists and mechanical geeks—felt that the new movie cameras should be used by anyone interested in expressing himself and that the resulting product should be shared with any theater that would pay to use it. One man might have invented the equipment, and that man might have deserved royalties, but his power should have stopped there. At least, that was how outlaws saw the growing business of supplying movies—usually from sixty seconds to four or five minutes long—for the peep shows, the nickelodeons, and the cinematographs.

The independent producers' problems stemmed from controversial patent-law enforcement. Thomas Alva Edison invented the peephole kinetoscope, which he displayed in 1893 at the Columbian Exposition. A year earlier, he had created the kinetograph, the first camera that could take moving pictures, which were then viewed through a peephole. The concept was a popular one, and by January 1894 Edison was manufacturing his equipment in West Orange, New Jersey. The viewing machines were offered for sale at $250 each. The films to be shown on them were prepared and duplicated by employees of the Edison Manufacturing Company. Edison hoped that by patenting every aspect of the process, he could get rich controlling everything except who bought his equipment and where the films made by his businesses could be shown.

With further refinements, increased production, and more aggressive selling, bars, restaurants, hotels, and other public locations were adding a variation of the kinetoscope parlor to entice more money from their customers. Projection equipment followed, further increasing revenue because several people could view the same film at the same time with a single machine in operation. All of this meant growing wealth for the inventor.

Business rivals of Edison began making and marketing their own films, their actions allegedly violating the inventor's patents. The legal battles proved expensive, and the largest rivals in the New York/New Jersey, Philadelphia, and Chicago areas decided to unite with Edison. Soon, a trust of nine production companies, the leading motion picture distributor, and Eastman Kodak, the major manufacturer of film stock, was created as the Motion Picture Patents Company (MPPC). The MPPC dominated the industry, using its combined wealth to sue any independent who they claimed infringed on their patents and failed to pay licensing fees.

The outlaws ignored the court actions as much as possible. They could not ignore, however, the goon squads sent to smash heads and equipment. Edison had a public image as an eccentric, benign, beloved genius making life better for Americans. He was also a ruthless, greedy businessman who sought total control of every aspect of the film industry, including the artists fascinated with making moving pictures.

Finally, the cost of replacing equipment grew too great. Lawyers were fighting the court battles, and so long as the outlaws could avoid the U.S. marshals, they did not have to appear or risk arrest. They took their equipment and went to a region of the country where the sun shone an average of 355 days a year, the terrain was varied, the railroad brought supplies, mail warned of marshals' arrival, and enough businesses existed for them to work. And when the worst occurred, when a telegram or letter alerted the men to yet another planned foray by the marshals, they packed everything they had and rode south into Mexico, where movie making was not an extraditable "crime."

The producers came next—men who either had worked with the Edison Trust until 1915, when the U.S. Supreme Court ruled against its patent claims, or came to the storytelling side of the industry in a roundabout manner. The latter consisted mostly of theater owners who decided they should be creating product, not just showing it, and men who were financial successes in other business and liked the idea of making movies. William Randolph Hearst, the enormously wealthy publishing magnate, was among the latter. Yet, whether the men came from money, like Hearst, or from poverty prior to entering businesses that brought them wealth, such as Sam Goldwyn, Adolph Zukor, Carl Laemmle, Louis B. Mayer, Marcus Loew, and brothers Joe and Nick Schenck, they wanted to create films that were sensitive to the working classes in America. They understood, often from personal experience, the tenement world, where hard-working families never had quite enough money to get ahead. Nineteenth-century New York City, for example, was notorious for providing immigrant housing that was constantly being divided. An apartment building's original suites were divided into single-room apartments for families. Then, the room might be divided again, often by hanging a blanket as a partition, so that two families could share the quarters. Sanitation was limited. Disease was rampant. Violence was all-too familiar, both within the families living in overcrowded conditions and on the streets, where children fought one another to sell newspapers and work in physically demanding adult jobs that frequently left them crippled. Yet, despite the harsh conditions and the existence of numerous ethnic gangs, most of the people were honest, hard working, and concerned with finding a way to get ahead. They had no idea how others lived or what life was like in places other than the streets they walked and the villages from which they had emigrated. It was the new moving-picture experience that enabled them to escape for the first time in their lives. They embraced it and spent as much time as possible viewing the images that the wealthy and well educated scorned as a short-lived fad.

The people lower on the socioeconomic ladder through the country embraced the nickelodeon. Through the moving pictures, short as they were, the audience entered the great museums of the world. They attended prize fights, watched auto races, witnessed an industrial fire, took a train through wilderness areas and into big cities, saw concerts, viewed the sights of Rome, London, and Paris, and witnessed the splendor of the mansions of the wealthy. The movies were crude by today's standards and always in black and white, yet they had a reality to them that amazed the public and brought them back for more.

One of the most famous shorts of those early years was a movie called *The Kiss*. It was exactly what the title indicated, a few seconds of a man kissing a woman. The public found it so real, they "knew" that an actor and an actress were behind the screen on which it was shown, and many viewers sneaked a look.

There were shorts that told brief stories, the best known of those early days being *The Great Train Robbery*, and news films. These were the forerunners of the newsreels, which eventually provided the public with film footage of the major events of the day, from the crowning of the new Miss America to battle footage taken in the midst of whatever war was raging in an area of concern to the viewers. Newsreels continued well into the 1950s, always a staple of movies, along with a cartoon and previews of coming attractions. It was only when the public demanded greater immediacy that the newsreel concept was adapted to television and presented in the constantly repeated, constantly updated format that appears today on the Cable News Network's Headline News. It was also the news footage that led amateur moviemaker William Randolph Hearst not only to start his own motion picture company but also to combine the movies and news with advertising.

The movies created a national base of cultural literacy that had never before been possible. People who did not read English and who had possibly been illiterate in the languages of their countries of origin, shared with the educated elite the visual experience of travelogues, fashion trends, new inventions, and other topics that could be filmed. People in big cities and rural farming communities knew the same films, the same stories, and the same actors and actresses. The nickelodeons unified Americans and created a national experience in a way that nothing else would until the construction of the interstate highway system allowed Americans to visit all parts of the nation easily by car a half-century later.

Statistics demonstrate the popularity of the nickelodeon. A 1907 study of New York City alone showed that two hundred thousand residents a day were spending the 5 cents needed to attend one of the movie houses. That figure doubled on Sunday, when most people had the day off from work.

Three years later, in 1910, there were 10,000 places to see movies in communities across the United States, 407 in Chicago alone. Some were theaters built either for vaudeville or specifically to show the new movies. Many were makeshift locations, such as an unused back room in a general store, where a sheet was hung on the wall and chairs were borrowed from the local funeral home. All were open to the public, without the racial, ethnic, religious, or sexual strictures that existed everywhere from nightclubs to vaudeville houses to social clubs and restaurants. A woman could go to the nickelodeons without an escort, for example, a fact that lured many a tired shop girl at the end of her workday. Other public forms of entertainment, including some restaurants, required that a woman come only escorted by a man. Couples, families, and even unaccompanied children attended the nickelodeons.

Perhaps most surprisingly in an era that would soon see the revival of the Ku Klux Klan, a black, an immigrant, or a Jew might find himself sitting side by side with a white person, who might otherwise avoid such contact. Almost every place that showed this new form of entertainment was more welcoming than most churches.

Perhaps it was the sudden, widespread interest in the movies that caused a backlash against them. Perhaps it was a fear of the unknown. Perhaps it was the fact that the movies were so new that they were unpredictable. Would the stories uphold the values of the local religious community? Would the stories provide ideas that could be harmful to women or children or that would transgress the local standards of decency? And what should be done about the moviemakers who created scenes of great titillation prior to a properly moral ending? For example, was a graphic depiction of the seduction of Sampson by Delilah, with Delilah scantily clad and undulating in ways that made it clear she was not a nice girl, acceptable if Sampson, with the special strength God gave him, crushed her under the pillars he pulled down around himself. Certainly Cecil B. DeMille, one of the earliest directors, thought so, and his earliest Bible stories, shot during the silent film era, are examples of naughty eroticism justified by the revelers' deaths at the end.

The issue was a constant concern, though letters exchanged by some of the early screenwriters show that they saw the problem in a humorous light. They noted that villains were the only people in movies allowed to have fun. They could get into barroom brawls, commit adultery with a bevy of beautiful girls, drink as much booze as they liked, drive expensive cars, and live lives of overstated luxury, provided they died alone at the end of the film. The hero, by contrast, usually had few possessions, was often battered and beaten throughout the film, and, when he finally won the heroine, was allowed only a chaste kiss before the movie ended. In a morally uplifting movie, the bad guys had all the fun.

Censorship issues were such that in 1907, the same year that some of the major studies of the industry were taking place, Chicago's superintendent of police was required to spend time each week reviewing and approving the films the city's theater managers wanted to show. Thirty years had passed since the Methodist Episcopal Church's condemnation of all theaters, and a new generation was growing up with the movies as a routine choice for entertainment, but the theater owners were still constantly made aware of parental and community concerns.

Regional and national groups worried about the impact the film industry might have on the morals of the public. Men such as Louis B. Mayer discovered that when they began opening their own theaters, they had to appear before such organizations as the Independent Order of B'rith Abraham, the Ladies Helping Hand Society, and individual churches whose congregations frequently walked by the area where the new theater was being opened. A new wave of church censorship began when Presbyterian minister Wilbur Crafts became the head of the International Reform Bureau tasked with censoring films. Catholic priests were also concerned, but it was not until the 1930s that a national effort was made to ensure the preservation of the moral purity of those who wanted to see this form of entertainment. The Legion of Decency was established to view the films, then list those that were appropriate for Catholic families and those that were not. This group proved more extreme than the Presbyterians when it stated that a good Catholic should not even go into a theater that was showing an approved film if it had previously shown unapproved films.

Politicians became wary of films when they realized that many movies either ridiculed the excesses of those in power or created tragedies in which the working class was shown sympathetically. Early comedies often showed the wealthy as lecherous buffoons trying to seduce noble shop clerks and serving girls, then taking slapstick pratfalls as their comeuppances. Business leaders and politicians were corrupt, lecherous, and greedy. And the police either took bribes or stole fruit from pushcarts.

There were pure entertainments, such as *The Hold-up of the Rocky Mountain Express* and the trick photography film *Smashing a Jersey Mosquito*, in which a mosquito grew to mammoth proportions and killed the man trying to swat it. There was the proper *The Life of Christ from the Annunciation to the Ascension in 27 Beautiful Scenes* (though some might have questioned whether it was meant to be accompanied by an all-girl orchestra) and the historical *Bluebeard, the Man with Many Wives*. More serious popular films dealt with the working-class struggle for dignity, such as *The Molly Maguires,* or *The Labor Wars in the Coal Mines* and *Suffragettes' Revenge*.

The movies came to dominate American popular culture with a speed that would not be exceeded until the end of the twentieth century, when the invention of the search engine, the inexpensive dial-up modem, and the affordable home computer made the Internet a vehicle for entertainment, not just business. A growing number of companies were creating product, and some of the men who owned the theaters, and who would soon become producers themselves, sought a way to ensure ever-larger amounts of business.

Future moguls like Marcus Loew and Adolph Zukor decided to make the theaters destinations unto themselves. They created worlds of opulence that would make the laborer, the farmer, the shop girl, the store clerk, and other blue-collar Americans feel that, for the price of a movie, they could spend a few hours in surroundings only the wealthy had previously experienced. As Zukor, quoted in Neal Gabler's *An Empire of Their Own*, said of the theater he built around what had once been a penny arcade,

> We had this empty floor over the arcade about forty feet by two hundred and fifty feet. We put in two hundred seats and then began to worry because it seemed like an awful lot, especially as most of our customers didn't know what moving pictures were and were used to paying one cent, not five. So we put in it a wonderful glass staircase. Under the glass was a metal trough of running water, like a waterfall, with red, green, and blue lights shining

through. We called it Crystal Hall, and people paid their five cents mainly on account of the staircase, not the movies. It was a big success.

Other moguls emulated this action: The movie theater was often the most unusual building in smaller communities, as well as the first to have the new air conditioning installed to combat summer heat. The new theaters held anywhere from a few hundred to a thousand or more people, especially in cities like New York, where the Paramount and other theaters offered up to eight shows a day, with a singer, a comic, an orchestra, and a feature film, along with a newsreel and often a serial.

The serial itself was an innovation embraced by William Randolph Hearst as his way of ensuring a continued viewing audience. The theaters were draws. The quality of the movies would bring in the public. And the popularity of a star could increase box-office receipts. But nothing overcame a potential downturn in attendance (due to the occasional second-rate feature film or out-of-favor star) like a "cliff-hanger" serial.

Hearst's idea was to do what became a twenty-episode serial called *The Perils of Pauline*. The title, one of the best known of all the early movies, was all he had developed when he turned to Morrill Goddard, the Sunday Supplement editor of Hearst's *New York Journal*, to arrange a meeting between Hearst and Morrill's brother, Charles, a successful playwright. Charles was to create twenty separate, interconnected stories, each of which would be complete but also end with the start of a new adventure. Each ending was to be a cliff-hanger; that could mean that the star was literally hanging from a cliff, perhaps her grip slipping and certain death waiting below. Or she might be in a run-away balloon, kidnapped by villains about to tie her to a railroad track, lost in a jungle, or otherwise in a situation "impossible" to escape. The audience would be so involved with the adventure, horrified by the fate awaiting Pauline and eager to see if this time she would actually escape, that they would return the following week to see the new episode that would resolve the problem, take her on a new adventure, and then leave her dangling again. And in case such excitement was not compelling enough, Hearst newspapers all ran a contest in which the reader who could predict what would happen to enable Pauline to live one more week would receive a $1,000 prize.

Pearl White, the actress who played Pauline Marvin, was perfect for the role, a fact recognized only in hindsight. She was a delightful woman who could charm both reporters when appearing in person and audiences when projected on the screen. She was originally a circus performer, then she worked as a stewardess on an ocean liner traveling to and from Cuba. She had been a café entertainer and made both one- and two-reel films. She was physically able to handle the rigors of the role, and her life experiences, all provided to the press, indicated that she, too, had a love of adventure. She was the perfect, independent woman at a time when the Victorian era constrained women from having, at least for a time, active, productive lives that did not include marriage.

The character Charles Goddard created was not unlike the daughters of some wealthy New Yorkers, who demonstrated for the right to vote and sought such adventures as working for the Fred Harvey Corporation as tour guides at the Grand Canyon. Pauline Marvin is the ward of wealthy automobile manufacturer Stanford Marvin, a man who feels Pauline should marry his son, Harry. The youth is fine, upstanding, intelligent, and rich—a great catch for any woman.

Pauline agrees with Stanford's appraisal of his son, but she wants to be a writer, and in order for her to have the adventures she will write about, romance will have to wait. She also makes certain that Stanford understands how good a writer she is by pulling out *Cosmopolitan* magazine to show him, in close-up, her article (with the magazine name prominent) and her byline. She is not planning to travel unprepared. She has already mastered her craft well enough to sell to the best.

Cosmopolitan is used once again as the camera moves in for a close-up of an illustration of an ocean liner burning in the water. Then, the movie seems to burst from the illustration, with Pauline on the ship embarking on her first perilous adventure.

The sales of *Cosmopolitan* were said to have dramatically increased with the showing of *The Perils of Pauline*. Both Pearl White and the magazine became instant symbols of independent young womanhood. It went unsaid by Hearst that he owned *Cosmopolitan* and was drumming up as much crossover publicity as he could. At the urging of Carl Florian Zittel, his *New York Journal* drama editor, Hearst invented the use of product placement in his films. Always one to think big, that first "product" was a popular New York amusement park.

Zittel had come to his job with Hearst from a mixed background that included work in his family's real estate business, retail business promotion, and writing for the *New York Morning Telegraph*, where former Dodge City sheriff William "Bat" Masterson, by then a sports and feature writer, sometimes had a shoot-out with an old enemy who tracked him to the big city. Zittel made a deal with Hearst that allowed him to publicize private clients, provided he used the Hearst papers. This often led to multiple payoffs: Zittel, an editorial writer trusted for his accurate portrayal of local, regional, national, and world events, received his salary for turning out a column praising whatever client he was promoting in the *Journal* or another Hearst paper. So long as the client benefited through an increase in business, there were no complaints.

In 1909, two years after joining the *Journal*, Zittel was hired by Nicholas Schenck to find new ways to promote the Palisades Amusement Park, which he co-owned with his brother, Joseph, and other investors. It was a seemingly minor side venture, though that would change over time.

The Schenck brothers were born in the village of Rybinsk on the Volga River. They arrived in the United States in 1893, living in a Lower East Side tenement. The brothers went to work selling newspapers, then running errands for a drugstore. They saved their money, bought the drugstore, and then looked for other businesses.

They found their next commercial venture by chance. During the hot summer days, the Schenck brothers joined other Manhattan residents in taking the trolley to Fort George in the northern part of Manhattan Island. It was a popular recreation area, and the Schencks realized that on any given day thousands of people waited for the return trolley. They opened a beer concession, then added vaudeville acts.

The Schenck operation grew annually and was noticed by Marcus Loew. When the brothers told him of their desire to open a larger amusement location to be called Paradise Park, where the relatively new Ferris wheel and other rides could be enjoyed, Loew advanced them the money. The *New York Journal* began to editorialize about the wonderful changes that had come to the amusement park under the Schenck operation. Then, in 1911, the brothers also bought Palisade Amusement Park, the largest amusement park on the East Coast, and made $80,000 in profit that year. In 1913, looking to increase exposure even more, Zittel and Hearst used the product placement idea in *The Perils of Pauline*. During one of Pauline's adventures, the villain colludes with an amusement park worker to sabotage a balloon on which Pauline is riding. The camera takes different close-ups of the park's gateway sign, which reads, "THE SCHENCK BROS.—PALISADE AMUSE-MENT PARK." Zittel and the *New York Journal* both profited greatly as a result.

The more the producers experimented with ways to increase box-office receipts and their income from movies, product placements, and other ventures, the more important the stars became. Just as many people snuck a peak behind the screen, convinced they would spot the actors performing *The Kiss*, so they believed that the actors were exactly like their screen characters. An actor who played roles in which he was the noble, monogamous, true love of the heroine could never be shown at home if home was littered with empty whiskey bottles, failed marriages, neglected children, and a temper that caused him periodically to smash whatever personal object his latest love treasured most. An actress known behind the scenes for providing doses of sexually trans-mitted diseases to every man working on every picture in which she appeared might have to be pictured as the daughter of a minister, dedi-cated to missionary work among the poor, and too busy to try to find Mr. Right. Otherwise, audiences would hate such people and refuse to pay to see them in their newest pictures.

Many magazine publishers were protective of the motion picture industry because they owed their existence to the public's fascination with films, actors, and production. In 1915, *Motion Picture* went so far as to declare that movie actors were as good and upright as the average reader, something the writer could not say for theater people. The arti-cle writer noted that theater people lived by night and slept during the day, clear proof that they were likely to be disreputable. Stage shows were performed in the evening. Then, the actors often had to get out of makeup and costume, eat, and travel to the next town; thus, men and women were together in close quarters at an hour when decent people were in bed. The publication never told of scandalous activities among the stage actors and actresses, but the implication was clear that such unnatural living led to all manner of outrages. Exactly how stage people were morally repugnant was left to the imaginations of the readers.

The *Motion Picture* article made clear that movie actors, by contrast, were decent people with no need to travel, except with their spouses, presumably on vacations. They lived in the cities where the studios were located, were good neighbors, and kept regular hours since they worked during the day. They were as moral and as integral to the success of their communities as the banker, the baker, the school teacher, and other upright citizens. The public could be proud to live among movie actors. And to add to the wholesome image, many columnists refused to answer questions about an actor's love life and marital history because decent, monogamous people didn't need their fans intruding on their healthy private lives.

The trouble was that none of the producers—neither the outlaws nor the new moguls—had considered what would happen when the success or failure of a movie depended on how the public viewed the "real lives" of the actors. The New York media was not concerned with the business of Hollywood, and most of the writers were as willing to talk about a scandal as they were to talk about the quiet home life of a popular actor. The only exceptions were with the papers controlled by Hearst since his investments in Hollywood made him sensitive to the need to protect his investment.

The West Coast was different. When the moguls moved west to take advantage of the sun and cheap land, thousands of people—actors, extras, technicians, and the like—were beholden to them for work. Thus, it was not long before the moguls controlled Los Angeles in ways organized criminals would take a half-century to imagine. And even then, they would only envision part of the picture.

CHAPTER TWO

Lawdy, Lawdy, They Got Bawdy!

I t was the irony of the New York theater business that both the promoters and the reformers focused on whatever was being presented, from stage shows in the nineteenth century to movies at the start of the twentieth. Few members of the public bothered to mention how many New York theaters were constructed so that audience members could engage in participatory theatrics of their own. This was because the business of theaters, whether showing the classics to an audience of educated swells or contemporary comedies appealing to people with all levels of education and financial success, included the toleration (some say promotion) of what might best be called "illicit activity."

The entertainment industry's open secret was the result of the corruption of the political leadership of the city in the form of Tammany Hall, the name for the group of powerful men who controlled the city's government. Vice was the key to political power, whether it be to achieve office or to stay in power.

Young men of integrity and promise were scouted by politicians and hired by a district leader just before Election Day. They would be handed the forms needed to register voters, men who would show up at the polls, identify themselves by name, and cast a ballot. Each new voter would be registered for more than one voting location, and to keep things honest, each man would be given a different name for each

20

location. The moment the polls opened, Joe Smith might cast his vote, then walk to the next location and cast his vote as Joe O'Malley, then move on to where Joe Reilly voted, then vote as Joe Mantino, and so on. Each man would vote early and often, and no one could say that the same man voted more than once . . . at least not under the same name.

The pay for the young men who arranged for the voters to be registered was $2 per vote cast. Many had worked in the rough-and-tumble world of newspaper circulation, and the $2 for each vote equaled pay for a week's worth of loading newspapers onto delivery vehicles. This was also a far better deal than existed in the neighboring Boston, Massachusetts, where a candidate or his representative stood on the steps of each polling place and gave each voter a cigar wrapped in a dollar bill. One of the candidate's men was inside to make certain that the prepaid vote was properly cast.

The youths looking to move up in politics went from registering voters to buying or opening a saloon. Each saloon was a gathering place for politicians and potential supporters. The saloon keeper could influence his clientele, arrange for meetings with politicians and candidates, spy on the actions of those who might be challenging the status quo, and act as a conduit for payoffs. It was not unusual for quantities of money meant as kickbacks, extortion payments, or bribes to pass through the saloons favored by the men of Tammany Hall. In return, many of the men who became politically powerful were elevated to their positions as a reward for how they ran their saloon activities.

Exposés of corruption were rare because most of the newsmen were sympathetic to the system, even as it spilled over into the theater world. The newsmen found nothing wrong with drinking, gambling, and indulging in sexual activity with a willing professional woman. If these vices—which, though illegal, were certainly not hurtful in the manner of muggings, robberies, and crimes of violence—were being encouraged in a saloon and its backroom, where was the harm? And if the saloon keeper was also a bit of a philanthropist, perhaps supporting soup kitchens for the unemployed, clothing drives for the unfortunate, and the like, there certainly was no reason to hurt him.

With such attitudes in place, Tammany Hall encouraged the construction and operation of theaters throughout the city such that prurient activities could be handled discretely and thus tolerated.

Single men and women, strangers to one another, were allowed to sit together in the theater, an arrangement not approved by various clubs and saloons in the more respectable areas of the city. Liquor was sold during performances, and drinking was permitted among the audience.

The theaters themselves were designed for three tiers of audience, each scrupulously separated from the others so that, if anyone had a complaint, he obviously had chosen to go to the wrong location. The best seats in the house were for watching plays while being seen. This was the area known as the dress circle, where men and women both wore formal clothing and were chauffeured in style. They were usually connected with Tammany Hall, and they were always pleased to know that if a play was about contemporary politics and Tammany Hall was mentioned, it would be with respect.

The second tier of seats was for families. They were less expensive, and the people who attended wore proper business attire, though not the formal wear of the dress circle. Children might be present, making the night on the town too expensive to purchase better seats.

The third and highest tier, sometimes accessed from a different part of the building than the dress circle and the family level, was for prostitutes and their customers. There would usually be a private bar in the back of the third tier exclusively for the use of the ladies and gentlemen at that level. And there would always be hotels of different quality nearby for extra entertainment after the show.

The third tier was not the raucous place of the Bowery theaters. The men and women would dress properly for a night on the town, wearing anything from formal to proper business attire. Ideally, if the audiences from different tiers mingled during the intermission, wives and prostitutes could not be differentiated one from another. However, such intermingling was avoided by placing a bar at the back of the third tier and encouraging professional women who would be meeting their "dates" at the theater to arrive an hour early. This was an especially important rule for women who came alone or with their coworkers from the brothel, and made their business arrangements after they were at the theater.

Men who came to the theater with prostitutes on their arms were not restricted to an early arrival. They mingled with everyone and often sat in the dress circle. Anything else they were inclined to do was enjoyed in one of the hotels or brothels nearby.

Once the show was underway, the third tier, like movie theater balconies a few decades later, might be the site of foreplay. Let the action on stage draw the audience's attention, and couples in the darker sections of the third tier would likely treat each other as teenagers might in similar circumstances.

A reform movement had been taking place when the stage shows were mostly replaced by movies in many of the theaters. The third tier and the private liquor arrangements were no longer considered proper. Instead, only the highest priced, most sophisticated, and most beautiful of the "professional women" could attend the shows with their escorts for the evening. A slightly less desirable woman, though still better than a street-walking prostitute, would be allowed to use either the actors' dressing rooms or the large room where outdoor scenery flats were stored. These were painted trees, flowers, and grass used as backdrops and stored until needed on stage. Their presence resulted in the location being called the Green Room. Years later, when television shows had no need to store "green" scenery but did need a place to store guests, the room in which they were placed, although it contained chairs, tables, a monitor, and other amenities, was again called the Green Room. Guests and scenery had both become the backdrop to enhance the show's stars.

The other term that we use today that evolved from such practices, *behind the scenes*, referred to activity that was a hidden part of what was obviously a more interesting story than the publicly viewed production. Back then, it also meant engaging in paid sex. Today, it refers to any secret machinations, legal or otherwise.

The gang leaders who oversaw prostitution in their territory thus looked upon the theaters as no different from hotels, apartments, and brothels. They were a part of the business: overhead as opposed to potential moneymakers in their own right. These leaders focused on the sex business. They did not try to learn the business of the movies. This decision would cost them dearly as movies changed the entertainment scene of America.

The Really Bad Guys Were Clueless

The moviemakers took over the streets of New York almost as quickly as their product changed the theaters; yet, the bad guys still did not understand the potential for ill-gotten gains. The moviemakers were proud that their full-length films were often "authentic" depictions of the city at its grittiest as well as at its best, or so the producers often claimed. In truth, they were constantly looking to find light and save money. They could do both by creating stories that took place in open areas or in locations wired for high-powered lights. They could also save by using real people in their films, limiting the number of actors. The problem came because, like the concept of the contemporary docudrama, reality was bent to fit a story that might have nothing to do with the way life happened on the streets. And sometimes the results were unexpectedly humorous, at least in hindsight.

Big Brother was a good example. The writer had an idea for a story that would take place in a large, well-lighted, popular dance hall near Harlem. There was adequate power for the large carbon arc lights, called broads, needed to boost the interior light to the approximate strength of daylight in order for the film to capture an evening scene.

The story involved two different gangs attending the dance with their girlfriends. Since the Gas House Gang and the Hudson Dusters were near at hand, the producer went to the leaders of each and offered them money to appear in the dance scene. They all agreed, even though the gangs were normally mortal enemies. This was business, and they both wanted the money that came from pretending they would routinely share an evening in such a manner.

This does not mean that the gangs fully trusted the situation. The boys went armed, with a few carrying revolvers. They slipped their weapons to their girlfriends before they went inside, where the New York Police Department's Hard-Arm Squad awaited them. The Hard-Arm Squad was a group of tough guys experienced with violence and comfortable handling any situation that threatened to get out of hand without the use of excessive force. They searched each male, never thinking that one of the girlfriends might be holding a weapon. Young ladies simply didn't travel armed in those days, and even if one did, no gentlemen—and the Hard-Arm Squad's members were certainly that, albeit on the level of Neanderthals—would ever search one.

The camera was placed in position (film companies used one camera in one position in order to save the cost of multiple cameras simultaneously shooting film from different angles to be spliced together into the final movie as would happen later). The cameraman studied the lighting, then requested that the scrims, called "silks," be removed in order to provide better light.

The scrims were translucent cloth covers that softened the light and made it even. They also cut the brightness just enough that they had to be removed when the goal was to illuminate a large area adequately.

On the day of the dance-hall scene, the cameraman ordered the lighting crew to remove the scrims by shouting a command in technical jargon that had a quite different meaning in the street slang of the gangs: "Take the silks off the broads."

With the shout, the lighting techs removed the scrims, and the male gang members started taking the clothing (silks) off their girlfriends (broads). The girls panicked and started running. The boys, mindful that they were being paid, ran after them, bumping into rivals, throwing punches, and if they could catch their girlfriends, getting the weapons the girls had secreted as the fight became more important than the movie.

The Hard-Arm Squad waded into the fray, not caring who was struck or how badly he or she was hurt. Their job was to stop the battle, whatever the cost to the others. And when they were done, when peace was restored, seemingly every ambulance in the area was busy making trips from the dance hall to the hospital, then back to the dance hall to pick up another battered gang member.

All the while, the cameraman kept cranking the film through. The screenwriter would later rewrite the script to fit the events that occurred. And all of it would be promoted as portraying the true story of the raw underbelly of the city's gangs, even though the fight never would have happened had the deal not been made.

Some of the smaller street gangs might be used in the movies, and the city streets, many of which were controlled by one ethnic youth gang or another, were commonly filmed. But the gangs themselves, especially the larger ones, which were the forerunners of the organized-crime families that would evolve over the next few years, had no use for the movies. They could make no money. You couldn't threaten to destroy a production company's business when all they had to do was pick up their equipment and move into another gang's territory. As for beatings and other forms of violence, even those companies willing to work with the Edison Trust employed men who had had run-ins with the goons to act as field enforcers. One had to be tough to make movies in New York, and taking on tough guys whose business they didn't understand, whose income didn't come immediately, and who asked for no favors seemed like a waste of time. This was especially true for the

Five Pointers, the gang that trained two of the most vicious and successful gangsters of that era.

Charlie and Al

Alphonse Capone and Salvatore Lucania didn't know from movies growing up on the streets of New York, didn't know from nickelodeons and the cinematograph. Not that they didn't hear about them. They could see them on what seemed like every street corner. But they were bimbooms as kids, looking to join the Five Pointers when they were teens, and the Five Pointers thought the movies were brought to their neighborhood to destroy the bad character they had carefully nurtured. If you went to the movies, and probably some of them did from time to time, you didn't talk about it, didn't see it as anything other than satisfying your curiosity.

The gangs of New York staked out their territories long before Salvatore and Alphonse were born. The Five Pointers, fifteen hundred men strong, dominated an area that included the Bowery live-theater district which, when Alphonse and Salvatore were in diapers, had ninety-nine different entertainment establishments, eighty-four of which were declared dangerously disreputable by the police. And the police force at that time—between the end of the nineteenth and start of the twentieth centuries—was arguably one of the most corrupt in the city's history.

Charles Dickens wrote of the area in his *American Notes*: "Let us go on again, and plunge into the Five Points. This is the place; these narrow ways diverging to the right and left, and reeking everywhere with dirt and filth. . . . Debauchery has made the very houses prematurely old." The theater was an escape from such a place, and many of the plays put on in the different locations were considered "Bowery plays," a type of noisy, violent melodrama unique to the area. Shows such as *The Boy Detective* and *Si Slocum* do not sound provocative or inappropriate for "nice" audiences when we hear the titles today, and the Bowery theaters entertained families in the more respectable dress circle seats. But when first performed, these plays often incited the moral indignation that occasionally greets R-rated material today. And though families did attend, the more common audience at the end of the nineteenth century, as noted by an author who visited the area following the Civil War, then was quoted in the 1927 study *The Gangs of New York*, included the less reputable: "Newsboys, street sweepers, rag-pickers, begging girls, collectors of cinders, all who can beg or steal a sixpence, fill the galleries of these corrupt places of amusement. There is not a dance-hall, a free-and-easy, a concert saloon, or a vile drinking-place that presents such a view of the depravity and degradation of New York as the gallery of a Bowery theater."

And the locals, including the gang members, loved it. This was entertainment on their level. This was theater for the masses, much as Shakespeare wrote portions of his plays for the illiterate groundlings, and contemporary cable and satellite companies bring "tits and ass" TV to those viewers who shun PBS's *Masterpiece Theater*.

The gang members, long known for being rowdy and often "aromatic" (Wild Maggie Carson took great pride in having avoided bath water in any form until she was nine years old) included the likes of Googy Corcoran, Hoggy Walsh, Slops Connolly, Pretty Kitty McGown, and Lizzie the Dove. The street friends were of a background that caused them to watch the melodramas, sometimes cheering the heroes and sometimes rooting for the triumph of the murderous villains.

But movies? The simple stories, the travel features, the films of news events were all seen as the work of do-gooders who were trying to corrupt the Five Pointers by keeping them from enjoying the half-century-old tradition of the Bowery theater district. And that was why when Salvatore—later known as Charles Luciano because he found that his friends could neither spell nor say Lucania—and Alphonse—later called Al Capone—were learning how to operate criminal enterprises, the movie producers and theaters were ignored. Their teachers, like Paul Kelly and Terrible John Torrio, focused on the traditional gambling, prostitution, liquor, extortion, and loan sharking. Capone and Luciano had no idea that there would come a time when, with their own organizations, they would lead an assault on the film world.

And Johnny

Filippo Sacco knew the movies but not the gangs or the streets of New York. He had come to America from Esperia, a tiny, poverty-ridden Italian village halfway between Rome and Naples.

It was 1905 when Vincenzo Sacco journeyed to the United States, leaving behind his wife, Maria Antoinette DiPascuale Sacco, and their newborn son, Filippo. He was a shoemaker, a respected, relatively well-paid profession in the larger cities of Italy, and he thought he would instantly find such work in America. Instead, he ended up in North Boston, working for one of several manufacturers that mass-produced footwear. Still, he was able to save his money by living frugally near the plant. By 1911 he could afford to bring his wife, son, and widowed father, a tailor also named Filippo, to live with him. He found a house in East Boston, leaving the overcrowded North Boston tenement where he had survived in the intervening years.

The six-year lag between Vincenzo's arrival and his bringing his family over was not unusual. The cost for each passenger, including the child, was $35. Since wages in Italy were 35 cents a day, the trip cost almost a year's gross pay.

The Sacco family, relying on incomes from both the elder Filippo and Vincenzo, moved to Somerville, a relatively new bedroom community linked to Boston by a new commuter railroad. The younger Filippo had reached seventh grade when the family was suddenly hit by crisis. The elder Filippo died from tuberculosis and what was noted as senile dementia on December 8, 1917. Less than a year later, on October 13, 1918, Vincenzo Sacco died during the influenza epidemic that killed more than 220 Somerville residents and sickened many thousands more. Maria and the children returned to East Boston, where the close Italian community assured their survival.

The suddenly impoverished Saccos lived in a cold-water apartment with no heat. The kitchen stove was used throughout the winter to supply warmth, the family huddling in the small room whenever they were home.

Filippo, at twelve the oldest of the children by six years, was also of an age to begin working for a living. He became a milkman, a job that enabled him to be on the streets late at night and early in the morning.

At this stage of his life, Filippo's history becomes murky, the stories having been amended as the years passed. It is certain that Maria Sacco, at the age of thirty-four a widow with five children, moved in with Liberato Cianciulli, a butcher who owned a two-story house.

Legally, the couple had several problems. Liberato was a man who enjoyed marriage and family no matter what form it might take. He was married, probably in the United States, and either he had divorced his wife, or the marriage had been annulled.

A second marriage ended in a more troublesome manner. Liberato lived the life of a womanizing bachelor in the United States. His wife maintained a home in Italy, having little or no contact with her husband. Neither filed for a divorce, and if an annulment was pursued, the details are unknown today. It seems certain that they chose to live their lives as though the marriage was over.

Between the Italian wife and Maria, Liberato had another dalliance that lasted long enough for two children to be born. This time there was no attempt at marriage, and Cianciulli, a doting father who loved kids, took both children to raise on his own.

By the time Maria and Cianciulli were living and loving together, they shared eight children in all, including their daughter, Maria. Filippo considered the man his stepfather and the man's children to be his step-siblings.

Filippo was involved with petty street crime, using the milk wagon as a cover. The older street criminals recognized the delivery route as the perfect cover for having Filippo deliver small quantities of morphine for the gang leaders.

In 1920, when Filippo was fifteen, Liberato Cianciulli and his wife/mistress/lover Maria were no longer living together. Liberato thought he would like to return to Italy to visit the woman who had been his second wife. The only problem was the cost of such a trip.

In a partnership with Filippo that the youth apparently thought was the start of a closer relationship with his stepfather, Filippo agreed to torch Cianciulli's home, which was well covered by insurance. The action was to be taken during the day when no one was at home. Wet laundry was routinely hung inside the house near the stove to dry. Liberato thought that if Sacco torched the dried laundry, the fire would be presumed an accident caused by the cloth's being too near the heat and it would also spread fast enough to destroy the house.

The arson was only partially successful. Years later, in a story in the August 23, 1976, *Miami Herald*, Sacco, by then calling himself Johnny Rosselli, wrote, "I went across the street and sat on the curbstone to watch it burn. I thought it took hold because smoke and fire was coming out of the roof, but to my surprise, the firemen were there in about three minutes to put it out."*

---

*The vast majority of books and articles mentioning the name by which Filippo Sacco would be known over the years use the spelling "Roselli" for Johnny's last name. However, the business card he carried in 1975 spelled his name "Rosselli." Either "Rosselli" was correct or it was the spelling of choice near the end of Rosselli's life. It is the spelling that will be used in this book.

A deal had apparently been made with the insurance agent so that Cianciulli was paid immediately and could afford to flee the country. Sacco/Rosselli was never paid and fled west ahead of the police. He planned to make his fortune in Los Angeles, but first there was a layover in Chicago that would ultimately have an impact on the film industry for years to come.

CHAPTER Three

The Movies Discover the Bad Guys, but Only John Dillinger Discovers the Movies

Maybe the New York–based gangs were clueless about the movies even when they were paid to be in them, but the producers who worked in New York understood the bad guys. The punk kid sons of immigrants and the youths just fighting to survive long enough to get a job that might pay for a better tomorrow all knew from gangs. They joined some, fought some, and were victimized by some, and when they got a little older, some of them wrote scenarios about their experiences. The movies might tell the story of gang life or focus on a single gang leader, though he would not be based on a real person. Not yet. Such films would not be made for another decade.

D. W. Griffith, who gave the world the classic motion picture that everyone loved, hated, or took as gospel, *The Birth of a Nation*, which portrayed the Ku Klux Klan as heroic, was also interested in the gangs of Manhattan. He created *The Musketeers of Pig Alley* in 1912, a film that tells the story of a slum girl who marries a struggling, but honest, musician. The story presents the Snapper Kid as a gang leader who decides he wants this virtuous wife. He comes close to seducing her, resorting to drugs, but before he can have his way with her or destroy her marriage, he is killed during gang warfare. The wife's marriage is saved, and the future remains honorable, but the film makes clear that the menace of gangs remains.

The story arc is like that of some alien-invasion science fiction movies of a half-century later. Always the menace is thwarted, often at great cost to both sides, but the end of the film cautions the viewer to remain on guard against the continuing menace.

Other gangster stories of the era were urban versions of the cowboy movie. Some of the cowboy movies were about two factions, usually the sheepherders versus the cattlemen at war over grazing rights, in need of someone to stand heroically in the middle. Sometimes the daughter of the rancher head of the cattlemen is in love with the son of the head of the sheepherders. Sometimes a lawman is in the middle of it all; he is usually honest, but sometimes corrupt and trying to restore his honor. Whatever the arrangements, they were mimicked in gangster movies that pitted corrupt police, a prosecutor, and the gangs against one another in various combinations, often with either a gang leader or a prosecutor sacrificing himself for the love of a woman and a better man.

Another Western movie plot, that in which a decent, simple man alienated by forces outside his control seeks vengeance through criminal action, was also emulated. In a Western, the cowboy might once have been an honorable Southern lad raised on a struggling farm where he, his brothers, and parents all worked the land themselves. When the Civil War began, he had done what his neighbors told him was right and gone off to fight for what proved to be the losing side. (Note: His family was never rich, never owned a plantation, and never had slaves.) The soldier returns to find a farm whose crops have been destroyed, his family home burned to the ground, his father murdered, his widowed mother barely getting by working in town at some menial job, and his brothers scattered, perhaps killed in the war. He vows revenge against the society that so devastated a decent family, turning to crimes that seem almost noble. He might become a bank robber or hold up passenger trains, usually giving some of the money to those in need. Or he might find that the man who caused the destruction of his innocent family has become a prominent politician or banker, both of which professions were looked upon with disdain by low-income moviegoers. He eventually destroys this man or his reputation, and though he either dies or goes to jail at the end, he is portrayed sympathetically throughout.

The hurting-good-guy-turned-bad scenario was also used by the film industry in the urban gangster movie. Lon Chaney appeared in several such movies, including *The Big City*, in which his character has risen to become a crime boss with a sympathetic girlfriend. His gang specializes in jewel robberies, again a crime that does not touch the lives of most of the people in his audience. A rival gang muscles in, Chaney and his men (and girlfriend) fight back, and when they triumph, not only is the other gang destroyed, but Chaney, his girl, and those closest to him decide to become honest citizens.

Possibly because the world of New York and Chicago's street life was beyond their experience, the criminals most affected by the movies themselves were small-town thugs trying to be professional criminals. They learned to walk, talk, and handle their enemies by imitating what they saw on the screen. First came the movie; then came the gangster. And the most outrageous of all would be John Dillinger, a man who never took on Hollywood but was, in a sense, created by the film industry.

I Don't Play a Killer in the Movies. I Am One in Real Life

The death that hot, humid night of July 21, 1934, should have been prophetic for both the Hollywood moguls who created the dark world of film noir and the Chicago mobsters who tried to make it their reality. The Biograph Theater was the focus of the violence, but in true noir fashion, the death took place in the adjoining alley.

The victim of both the movie industry and the bullets of federal agents was bank-robbing gangster John Dillinger, who had started his career eleven years earlier with the knowledge gained from repeated Saturday afternoon viewings of the film *Jesse James under the Black Flag*. The silent film, made in 1921, starred Jesse James Jr., the son of the rogue Confederate Army soldier turned killer and thief. It told the romanticized story of a man who was a violent misfit in any era, not just the turbulent period at the end of the Civil War.

Hollywood knew how to capitalize on the myth of the outlaw and had the wisdom to hire the son of the man who was the subject of the film. Dillinger, too, was being scouted by the studios, with offers of money coming in even to Dillinger's father. The older man was offered $500 a week to speak about his son on both the vaudeville stage and in a Coney Island sideshow. The Universal Newsreel Company offered $5,000 for a chance to make a film of Dillinger's arrest. And when still photographs of Dillinger were projected onto movie theater screens throughout the Midwest, the audiences burst into applause. His life represented the epitome of counterculture glamour to a nation in crisis during the early days of the Great Depression.

The movie industry executives, had they thought about it, would have known that Dillinger understood Hollywood no better than the more organized killers based in Chicago, who were planning an assault on the film industry. The bank robber/killer gleaned from hours spent sitting in the Idle Time Theater near Martinsville, Indiana, how to wear a sideways tilt to his hat, how to swagger when he walked, and how to carry a gun. The night of July 21, sitting through a single showing of the movie *Manhattan Melodrama*, taught him how to die.

Myth and reality all came together at Chicago's Biograph in what was a veiled omen for the future of organized crime and its planned assault on Hollywood. There they all were—Blackie Gallagher and John Dillinger, Jim Wade and Melvin Purvis, "Eleanor," Polly Hamilton, and Ana Campanas Sage. The story, which won an Academy Award for screenwriter Arthur Caesar, and three members of that night's audience epitomized classic film noir. Lives on- and offscreen were experienced in the shadows where good, evil, ambition, greed, honor, betrayal, justice, and death all ended the evening melded into one.

On the screen, Blackie and Jim are former childhood friends orphaned in 1904 when their parents were killed during a fire that engulfed the excursion boat *General Slocum*. A Jewish man reaches out to them, taking them into his home, only to be killed by police during a protest rally.

Offscreen, Dillinger's mother died when he was three, and his Indianapolis grocer father, a loving man but a harsh disciplinarian, remarried when John was six. At odds with his stepmother, John quit school to work in a machine shop. His father, worried about his son's lack of interest in education and fearing he would fall into the wrong company, moved the family to a farm in Mooresville, Indiana. Bored and frustrated, young John stole a car and embarked on what would become a life of crime.

On-screen, Blackie (played as a boy by Mickey Rooney, as an adult by Clark Gable) is also a rebel, hating the police and seeking to make whatever money he can by whatever means he chooses. Jim, played by William Powell, sees that the law transcends the evil that men can do, attends law school, and becomes a district attorney.

Offscreen, Ana Campanas Sage, a Romanian immigrant who entered the United States in 1914, became a citizen and pursued the American dream of success through hard personal work. She started as a prostitute, saving her money and choosing one special customer, East Chicago police detective Martin Zarkovich, to be her lover/protector. Their relationship was obvious enough that Zarkovich's wife named Ana in her 1920 divorce proceedings against her husband.

Ana opened her first brothel in Gary, Indiana, in 1921. Two years later, she bought the forty-six-room Kostur Hotel, adopted the business name of Katie Brown, and was known as "Kostur House Kate." Her detective/lover still protected her when she was repeatedly arrested; eventually, however, concerns exceeded his influence, and the government closed the Kostur House and considered deporting Ana.

Ana moved back to Chicago, where she went respectable long enough to marry a fellow Romanian immigrant named Alexander Suciu. They changed their last name to Sage, bought an apartment building in Chicago's Uptown, then separated, with Ana keeping the proceeds from the sale of the building. She eventually invested in a new location in North Halstead in June 1934, using some of the rooms for prostitution and renting the rest so that she would look halfway respectable while fighting deportation. It was to one of the "legitimate" rooms that a longtime friend and former part-time employee named Polly Hamilton came to stay. Through Polly, and allegedly through Detective Zarkovich, who was comfortable having friends on both sides of the law, Ana met John Dillinger.

On-screen, Myrna Loy was Eleanor, a woman of ideals who falls in love with Blackie but hates his involvement with the rackets. He wins a yacht and $40,000, seemingly enough to last a lifetime with frugal spending, and she asks to sail away with him and escape the world of crime. He refuses. She means less to him than money and the power that crime can bring.

Offscreen, John Dillinger complicated his life when he and a partner robbed a police station in Warsaw, Indiana, for guns and bulletproof vests. He tried to hide in the Little Bohemia Lodge fifty miles north of Rhinelander, Wisconsin, but the weather was bad, and when he learned that the authorities were after him, he fled to Gary, Indiana, then to Chicago with Polly Hamilton. They both moved into Ana Sage's apartment, not knowing that she was being threatened with deportation. Ana called the FBI, asking about both a cash reward and the chance to avoid deportation. She was about to betray both Polly and Dillinger.

On-screen, the story becomes more complicated. Blackie and Jim are reunited at the Dempsey-Firpo boxing match shortly before Jim is elected district attorney, and Blackie threatens Manny Arnold, who is avoiding paying a gambling debt. Eleanor meets Jim that night, is impressed with his idealism, and lets him take her home at 5 a.m., knowing she no longer loves Blackie and that she is safe with Jim.

As the movie races to its climax, Blackie shoots Manny Arnold. Jim Wade decides to give up being district attorney to run for governor. A corrupt attorney wants to run for district attorney in Jim's place, but Wade refuses to allow him, and the rival's attempt to destroy Jim is stopped when Blackie kills the man.

Blackie is arrested, and Jim Wade sees that he is convicted for his crimes. He is taken to death row while Eleanor marries Jim, only to leave him when he becomes governor and refuses to commute Blackie's death sentence.

Jim, torn by his love for Eleanor, longtime friendship with Blackie, and adherence to the law goes to Sing-Sing. He ponders what is right as Blackie leaves his cell, accompanied by a priest, the warden, and guards, and begins the walk to the room housing the electric chair.

Blackie stops at the cell of another death row inmate and says, "Die the way you lived, all of a sudden. Don't drag it out. Living like that doesn't mean a thing." Then, as Blackie is about to enter the chamber, he encounters Wade. "Don't, Jim," he says, knowing that Wade wants to save his life. "You're going to ruin your career? For what? Say, listen, if I can't live the way I want, at least let me die the way I want. So long, Jim." Blackie enters the death chamber. The prison lights dim because of the sudden rush of electricity, and an inmate calls out, "They're givin' it to him."

Offscreen, John Dillinger, his girlfriend Polly, and their friend Ana had arrived at the Biograph at 8:36 p.m., six minutes late for the opening of *Manhattan Melodrama*. They never noticed the special agent in charge of the FBI Chicago office, Melvin Purvis, sitting in a car twenty feet away.

Dillinger and the two women took seats in the third row, surrounded by an almost full house of moviegoers. When Purvis bought a ticket and followed them inside, hoping to make an arrest in the theater, he could not spot them. He went back outside, knowing that the movie, a cartoon, and other features would take two hours. The FBI agents who had quietly surrounded the Biograph would have to wait for Blackie to die, Eleanor to return to Jim, and the credits to roll before they could stop the man FBI director J. Edgar Hoover had designated a public enemy.

The necessary delay in making the arrest created problems for the officers, who had tried to look inconspicuous. Passersby knew that no one just stands around the outside of a movie theater on a Saturday night. As a result, at least one unknowing observer called the local police to report what appeared to be impending trouble.

At 10:20 p.m., two carloads of armed East Chicago police officers, one holding a sawed-off shotgun, rolled up to the men in suits who seemed to be loitering near the Biograph. Special Agent E. J. Conroy identified the group and explained that they were on a stakeout, but he would say nothing about their quarry. The officers left, but at 10:30 p.m., when the movie was scheduled to end, two more officers rolled up. These were Chicago police detectives who had also been called about the FBI agents.

Dillinger never considered that there might be armed men standing outside during the movie or even that he might be in danger that night. He carried a gun, but that was habit, as much a part of his style as the straw hat he was wearing.

Ironically, the same entertainment industry that helped Dillinger create his gangster persona also awarded him popular-culture celebrity status and a reputation for high living and adventure.

In reality, during his ten years of robbing and killing his way to public enemy status, Dillinger had fast cars, a massive arsenal of weapons, amoral friends, and willing women, but little else. He and his various gang members lived in hiding, never able to enjoy the money they stole for constant fear of arrest. They slept wherever they thought they wouldn't be seen, whether in filthy rooms or inside one of their getaway vehicles. In the latter instance, three of his men drove the car onto a freight elevator and raised it between floors where no one could see the men inside. "Out of Order" signs prevented any passersby from calling the elevator and discovering them.

The same financial success in a straight life would have enabled the entire gang to enjoy the finest hotels and restaurants. Instead, Dillinger's almost mythic notoriety forced them to live in third-rate locations and rooms provided by friends who they hoped would not betray them. The approach worked for a while, but he and Polly made a major mistake in taking a room in Ana's building. She had a choice between deportation and turning in her friend. There was no question as to which way she would go, and so, while Dillinger remained comfortably transfixed by the movie screen, the tension was building outside even more than it was for the audience inside awaiting Blackie Gallagher's last walk.

Dillinger silently watched the death of Blackie, Eleanor's forgiveness of Jim, and the rolling of the credits. He had no idea that his waiting until the theater was empty and the houselights had been turned back on was worrying not only Special Agent Purvis but also Special Agent Samuel A. Cowley, the hand-picked head of Hoover's "Get Dillinger" squad. Both were concerned that Dillinger might have somehow slipped past them, escaping capture once again.

At 10:40 p.m., Dillinger emerged with Polly on his left arm and Ana Sage, in a readily recognized orange dress, walking near her friends. Purvis stood by the exiting theater crowd, holding a cigar in his mouth. The moment he saw Dillinger, he struck a match and lit the cigar, the signal that Dillinger was there.

Most of the agents saw nothing. The crowd was too big to pick out the target. Instead, just a handful of men were aware that Dillinger had been spotted.

At first, Dillinger was as clueless about what was happening as most of the agents watching for him. Then, a frustrated Purvis struck a second match, and enough movement erupted for Dillinger to realize that something was wrong. He passed a doorway in which Special Agents Ed Hollis and Charles Winstead were standing.

Suddenly, Dillinger crouched slightly, pulling out his .38 caliber revolver. Winstead pulled his .45 caliber automatic, and Special Agents Hollis and Clarence Hurt pulled their guns. Winstead fired first, letting off three rounds as Dillinger was drawing his weapon. A total of three more rounds were fired by the other two FBI men.

When it was over, two bullets had grazed Dillinger, a third had struck his side, and a fourth had entered the back of his neck, severed his spinal cord and smashed through his brain, then exited through his right eye.

The close-quarters shooting with such a high-powered weapon had been a risk to passersby. Dillinger's falling body bumped against a terrified woman movie patron before he fell dead, face down on the pavement by the alley that adjoined the theater. Theresa Paulus, a housemaid who had also escaped the heat by going to the movie, lay beside the alley, her dress bloody, her knee having been struck by a ricochet. Erta Natalsky was hit in the leg by other shrapnel, though she was still standing, hopping on one foot to ease the pain. Neither woman's wounds proved serious.

An ambulance rolled up, along with police responding to calls of shots having been fired. Dillinger's corpse was loaded into an ambulance and raced away from the Biograph. Twenty minutes after he had watched Blackie Gallagher die with dignity, his own death was officially recorded by doctors at the nearby Alexian Brothers Hospital.

CHAPTER Four

Liquor, Loose Women, and Gambling (Oh, My!)

"

No person shall manufacture, sell, barter, transport, import, export, deliver, furnish or possess any intoxicating liquor except as authorized in this act.

—From the Eighteenth Amendment to the United States
  Constitution

"

Exceptions included the use of alcohol for industrial, medicinal, and sacramental purposes. The amendment was effective as of midnight, January 17, 1920, at which time all saloons had to close. For the first time in American history, the liquor industry was the most profitable, albeit officially almost "nonexistent," business in the nation. One barrel of beer that had cost $5 to produce before Prohibition and that sold for a few dollars more still cost $5 to make, but following Prohibition, the cheapest retail available was $55 a barrel. Anyone willing to turn a dishonest dollar through the production, distribution, and sale of illicit alcohol was assured the greatest prosperity of his or her life.

Prohibition may have been the best friend the alcoholic-beverage industry ever had, increasing the consumption of liquor dramatically in the United States, but it also caused a radical change in the film industry. The 1920s were considered a wild and lawless era, but the speakeasies, the illicit nightclubs, and the gambling operations were not put into place overnight. The moment the Eighteenth Amendment became law, the instant reaction was the shutting down of existing bars—five thousand in Los Angeles and fifteen thousand in New York. Many of these featured singers, dancers, comedians, and other entertainers who were suddenly out of work. They had no other skills, and there weren't enough jobs in live theater to warrant their seeing if they could make it on the stage. The result was a rush to the movie studios where hiring was constantly on the rise and jobs were plentiful, even if they did not use the talents from their past careers. Perhaps more importantly, there were men like Charlie Chaplin who had come before them, making a transition that seemed almost miraculous.

Chaplin had been a "legitimate" actor with the traveling Karno troupe of touring actors. He had enough of a following that he was able to make $75 a week for his stage work because his name was a draw for the public. Keystone pictures took a chance that his live-theater success could translate to the screen, offering him $150 a week to start in 1913.

Chaplin not only held the fledgling movie industry in disdain as a career, an attitude shared by many "legitimate" actors, including some who were relegated to locations such as the Bowery theater district, he also did not think he could succeed on the screen. He figured that he would take advantage of the high pay for a few pictures, and then return to what he felt was his future. Instead, the growing film industry and rising salaries for successful actors saw him earning $10,000 a week by 1915.

Most of the people who found work in Hollywood when Prohibition went into effect did not have the talent or the on-screen appeal to have anywhere near the success of a Chaplin. What they did experience was a pay scale far greater than they could have earned in any other business with their educational and vocational backgrounds.

Men and women arriving in Hollywood, whether with an entertainment background or just a desire to be seen on the silver screen, encountered two levels of movie making. There were the big studios, as they would be known for the next sixty years, and there were the tiny independents, not much different from the companies the outlaws had created, though they were permanently based along Beachwood Drive near Sunset Boulevard. The latter stretch of production companies, with budgets so low that the producer might be the only full-time employee, was called Poverty Row.

The pictures were silent, and the vast acreage the production companies had acquired at little expense meant that multiple side-by-side sound stages could be utilized. A damsel in distress might be bound, gagged, and tied to a powder keg inside an old mine on one stage, while on the next, God in His wrath might slaughter all but the faithful at a pagan revel in a biblical epic. And on the stage next to that, a slapstick comedy might be filmed. The sets were close together, and if anyone had seen the arrangement from above, it would have looked like an office filled with cubicles or a maze designed to teach tricks to laboratory rats.

Experienced actors, who were both familiar to audiences and popular enough to bring in box-office receipts when one of their films was shown, usually handled the leading roles under contracts that guaranteed weekly pay. Most others, including rising stars, began as little more than day labor.

Each morning actors would line up at a special entrance to a studio. The ones who knew the type of movie being filmed would be dressed appropriately when possible, wearing a tuxedo or top hat and tails for a formal ballroom scene, cowboy gear for a Western, and so forth. Others would rely on the wardrobe department or buy appropriate clothes with each new job until they had an adequate closet to assure they could dress for any film.

Those chosen as extras simply to fill the screen were paid $5 a day. It was not unusual for an American family of four to get by on approximately $1,300 per year, which was essentially the same income. When a small group of extras were to be filmed together, such as four friends watching a football game, the pay went to $10 per day, double the national average. Someone lucky enough to earn a close-up alone earned $25 a day. And all of this was for nonspeaking parts, where the casting was done based on physical appearance alone. Speaking roles—even silent films were scripted so that the actors on screen would obviously be talking to one another—paid far more. And an actor who was both a star and nationally popular could become rich beyond his or her dreams, though not necessarily on the scale of a Chaplin.

Poverty Row studios had a somewhat similar approach to hiring, though they used as few people and maintained as little overhead as possible. The large studios were willing to rent their sound stages to the low-budget operators the moment a big-money film had been shot. This meant that scenarios were written to match the existing facility. An elaborate ballroom set that was extremely expensive to make, but was the high point of a film about the lives of the wealthy, would be rented cheaply to a Poverty Row producer, who would use a story created just for the rental space. Most films were made outdoors, and mostly men were hired to avoid the cost of a makeup expert to help the actresses.

Costs were carefully planned. In addition to the studio rentals and the occasional location fee for a place such as the Lasky Ranch, stagecoaches cost $15 per day, horses $5 each if purchased from a discounter such as Fat Jones, and cowboys, who hung around the drugstore at Gower Street and Sunset Boulevard, were given $7.50 a day. Where possible, stock footage was used, as were such filming tricks as having everyone connected with the project wear costumes to appear in crowd scenes and keeping a camera low to the ground while the same few horseback riders went round and round to make it look as though a posse of hundreds was riding off to chase a bad guy.

Poverty Row also had a sound stage unconnected with any single production company. This was rentable by the day or week for the shooting of a movie, but required the creation of a set. Many of the sets were painted backdrops, and eventually some of the producers began painting one scene on one side of a backdrop, another scene on the other side, dividing the sound stage with the drop, and filming two different movies simultaneously.

Whether the studios were large or small, cash was always tight. Men such as A. P. Giannini, who ran the Bank of Italy, would back some of the studios and their films, and partnerships were sometimes created to finance specific movies. A successful partnership encouraged the partners to try another film and another. If a first movie did not earn back more than it cost, further funding would not be forthcoming.

Financial needs made the film industry ripe for loan sharking, and had it stayed centered in the East and Midwest, perhaps organized criminals would have realized this. But with the industry mostly centered in Los Angeles, they remained unaware of the possibilities for exploiting filmmakers. By 1920, independent gangsters and organized criminals were focused on bootlegging and providing alcohol to their customers.

❝

To place in the limelight a great number of people who ordinarily would be chambermaids and chauffeurs, give them unlimited power and instant wealth is bound to produce a lively result.

—Screenwriter Anita Loos

❞

The 1920s also brought changes in the movie colony's nightlife. An entire generation had grown into adulthood in the community of Hollywood, for example, and like a new generation anywhere, they rebelled to a certain extent against the values and strictures of their parents. In addition, actors and others connected with the various film studios were frequently using drugs like cocaine, morphine, heroin, and opium.

The drug use was partially the result of naivety and partially the result of the need to work for as many daylight hours as possible. Patent medicines had high alcohol and/or drug contents. The popular soft drink Coca-Cola was introduced with cocaine (the "Coca") being a primary ingredient. Thousands of Americans were likely addicted to the soft drink to some degree without realizing it, but not until 1914 was the danger so recognized that cocaine was outlawed as an ingredient in Coke.

The increase in alcohol consumption resulted in many stars having trouble getting over their hangovers in time to perform in the morning. They experimented with taking drugs as a way to overcome the headache and make them alert enough to act.

Studio executives, working with studio doctors who knew little about the dangers of both short- and long-term pharmaceutical use, began having all their employees take stimulants in the morning and sleeping pills at night. This was meant to assure that the actors could put in the longest possible hours. The fact that they were endangering their healths and their lives was not clearly understood until they collapsed or died. While today we think of such high-profile stars as Judy Garland and Elizabeth Taylor as victims of drug and alcohol abuse, the industry first confronted the problem when in 1920 Jack Pickford, the brother of Mary Pickford, married Olive Thomas, an actress who had gained her greatest fame as both a star in the Ziegfield Follies and as the first woman painted by Alberto Vargas for his series of images of beautiful women collectively known as the Vargas Girls. She was on her honeymoon in Paris when she was discovered dead from an overdose of bichloride of mercury.

Despite the occasional scandal or death, drug use was not seen as a problem. It was illegal to sell or possess most of the drugs, but Prohibition gave license to pick and choose among the laws controlling "recreational" substances. That was why the movie industry took a trilevel approach to keeping actors and crew indulging their habits. A regional distributor would supply the dealers, each of whom handled the needs of a major studio. Some of the dealers did not bother selling but left that task to low-level employees seeking to earn extra money. Other dealers took an active role in both providing drugs and encouraging those employees not yet using them to try some. The most outrageous of the latter was the dealer for the Mack Sennett Studio. Known as "The Count," he sold with style. He took bags of peanuts, removed the nuts, and then filled the shells with drugs. Regular customers paid for their bags of "nuts." New customers received their first bag free.

Ironically, as the Hollywood-area film community grew because of the closing of Manhattan saloons, within a few months of Prohibition's becoming law, the number of New York's drinking establishments more than doubled. Studies tallied more than thirty-two thousand locations, many of which offered bands, singers, and other forms of entertainment. The difference was that the speakeasies and nightclubs were mostly owned by organized criminals, the entertainers increasingly having to please the mob in order to work. This led to allegations of mob connections that were rarely a reality, though some singers and comics, most notably Frank Sinatra, worked to parlay their access to organized criminals into the myth that they were gangsters themselves.

The men who had been moving up through the ranks of the Five Pointers were also changing their lives. Charles Luciano, who received the nickname "Lucky," which he never used, after surviving a violent assassination attempt, was becoming a major player in the New York–area rackets. His former friend with the Five Pointers, Al Capone, had become both a rival and the heir apparent of Johnny "Terrible John" Torrio.

' '

I looked on Johnny like my adviser and father and the party who made it possible for me to get my start.

—Al Capone speaking of Johnny Torrio

, ,

By 1910, Johnny Torrio had moved from old-style gang activities to a new business model for crime. From his office in a specially secured room off his James Street saloon in New York, he specialized in gambling and prostitution. He recognized that the police and politicians saw such activities as victimless crimes, and they were happy either not to shut down his enterprises or to conduct raids that never resulted in criminal prosecution, provided they received regular payoffs. Once he had compromised members of law enforcement, Torrio added business extortion to his enterprises. Neighborhood retailers paid him a small fee to avoid broken windows, fires, or worse. The small-business owners were never charged enough to put them out of business, and they quickly learned that complaints to the police never resulted in meaningful investigations of Torrio or his men. A police officer on the payroll dared not act against the man he had let corrupt him.

Torrio also used a business model for his houses of prostitution that allowed white slavery to flourish and was imitated by nightclub entertainers, strippers, and others. Torrio knew that most men who used a brothel returned to the place they felt most comfortable. A welcoming madam, a comfortable room in which to meet the available women, privacy during sex, and a dignified departure which allowed him to feel that he had enjoyed an evening's entertainment rather than that he was such a loser that he could not get a date to bed all resulted in the man's return. Equally importantly, the vast majority of the customers did not form an attachment to any one woman; the typical john was willing to experience the sexual favors of whatever available woman appealed to him, no matter how much he had enjoyed a different woman on a previous visit. He would also eventually want to try someone he had not seen before.

Understanding the john's psychology, Torrio devised a prostitution circuit. The women were regularly moved from one brothel to another. The actually finite stable of women offered what seemed to be an endless variety of choices for the regular customers.

While Torrio was developing his business model in New York, his uncle, Big Jim Colosimo, had achieved great success on Chicago's South Side. Big Jim dominated gambling, prostitution, and nightclubs, his Colosimo Café being one of the most popular spots in the city. He was also flashy, wore expensive jewelry and high-priced suits, and used the sexual services of the women who worked in his clubs. Entertainers, politicians, and business leaders made a point of going to wherever Big Jim might be spending the evening in order to pay homage to the man who provided them with everything from jobs to cash bribes quietly placed in envelopes. His influence was such that if a corpse was found riddled with bullet holes and knife wounds, the autopsy revealing a beating and lethal poison, the coroner would declare death by accident or natural causes if he thought the murder might be linked to Big Jim.

Colosimo had watched his nephew's rise with interest and felt that he should be his heir. He began inviting Torrio to Chicago, and Torrio began spending most of his time in the city. At the same time, Torrio was helping to broaden Capone's experience because he looked upon the young Al as part of his own future.

Johnny Torrio had fellow gang leader Frankie Yale give Capone a job as a bouncer and bartender at Yale's Harvard Inn. As he proved himself, Capone was trained in other rackets, including controlling Yale's prostitution ring. Then, having gotten married and fathered a child, Capone was asked by Torrio to move to Chicago to work as Johnny's chauffeur and bodyguard for $100 per week.

Capone was next given a job at Torrio's Four Deuces at 2222 Wabash Avenue. The ground floor was a saloon with a sliding steel door separating the public business from Torrio's office. The second and third floor contained a gambling operation, and the top floor was for prostitution. Only an unfortunate few ever went to the basement, which was used for the ultimately fatal beating of anyone who cheated or betrayed Torrio. A trapdoor enabled the killer, frequently Capone, to push the corpse into the alley where men would load it in a waiting car and take it to a safe dumping spot.

Having proven his loyalty and ruthlessness, Capone learned that Torrio planned to move against his uncle. Big Jim controlled the South Side and saw no reason to risk a gang war by expanding. Irishman Dion O'Bannion controlled the North Side and likewise was content. Torrio wanted both, and when his uncle refused, Johnny and Capone murdered Colosimo and arranged for the death of O'Bannion. As expected by the older men, a gang war broke out in which Torrio was badly wounded. He decided to retire to New York, becoming the rare mob exception who eventually died of natural causes. Capone was given full control of the South Side.

During these early days of Prohibition, when Capone was becoming a gang leader in his own right, the teenage Johnny Rosselli passed through Chicago on his way to Los Angeles. He was fifteen or sixteen years old, Prohibition had just become law, and Al Capone was recruiting for the gang that would soon be his own. Exactly what Rosselli did in Chicago is not known, but he did prove himself enough to Capone to become a made member of the gang, taking an oath to die before revealing any secrets. Then, he moved on to Los Angeles, determined to see what the movie industry was like and perhaps to become a part of it. Neither he nor the young Capone realized it at the time, but Johnny Rosselli, formerly Filippo Sacco, was about to become the Chicago Outfit's expert on movies, the point man in the assault on the moguls.

Johnny Hollywood: The Early Days

Johnny Rosselli was fascinated by the movie industry, and with his good looks and lean body, he periodically showed up in the casting lines. The work was easy; the pay, adequate to support a family, more than kept him in food, clothing, shelter, and illicit liquor while he explored more lucrative, albeit illegal, activities.

Rosselli lived in the Italian neighborhoods of Los Angeles County when he first arrived in the area. Every generation of immigrants tended to settle in neighborhoods where others spoke their language, shared their culture, and understood their problems of assimilation. In the East, many of the immigrants worked with businesses operated from pushcarts, selling produce, clothing, or whatever else they could offer. Los Angeles's Italian immigrants migrated to the downtown business districts, running small shops. The dream was to move one day to an area such as the San Gabriel Valley, where they could buy land, grow grapes, and manufacture wine.

The lack of language skills and cultural understanding had the same impact on the West Coast as it did in the East. The merchants were targeted for extortion by neighborhood punks. The police would not have helped them in the Old Country, so it was assumed that they would not help them in America. They felt they had to pay what was asked or risk being beaten or having their businesses firebombed or a family member kidnapped.

Many of the punks doing small-business extortion were neighborhood youths everyone knew. Alone, they did not seem important, but they called themselves the Black Hand, as though they were a part of a national organization. This was unlike the Mafia with its established structure, specific positions, and way of learning who had what power. Young men claiming to be part of the Black Hand on one street might not know the youths making the same claim a few streets over. When merchants became both angry and suspicious, banding together to fight back aggressively, the threat usually disappeared.

Rosselli, having been exposed to more professional approaches to crime while with Capone, wanted no part of such petty violence. He worked as a movie extra for immediate cash but would soon be involved with bootlegging Los Angeles style.

CHAPTER Five

Forgive Us Our Press Passes

"

One would think that actors and singers are the only people worth talking about in all this great, busy, active, pushing, enterprising world, and that newspapers are published for the express purpose of perpetuating the doings of actors in private life.

—1888 New York newspaper editorial quoted in
Actors and American Culture, 1880–1920

"

T here has always been a positive side to gossip. The stories we tell each other about people in our community or those in positions of power, influence, or celebrity help establish communal values. We are shocked to hear that a married man or woman has taken a lover only if we value monogamy in marriage. We take pleasure in the breakup of the handsome actor and beautiful actress if we wish to reinforce our long-term relationship with a spouse or lover whose face and figure are far from perfect. Depending on the degree to which we value honesty, we either laud or mock the street person who discovers a large sum of money in a lunch bag that was accidentally tossed into a Dumpster, then turns it over to the police. And we further establish our own perceptions of the incident when we learn whether the person who lost the money has rewarded the finder since we likely would consider the person selfish if he or she did not. Celebrity gossip, politely called entertainment news, transcends the normal cultural reasons for its existence. Beginning in 1880, as touring companies of actors traveled to large and small communities for theatrical performances, the public became interested in many of the stars. Often, the actors were the object of sexual fantasies by young men and women who imagined themselves playing love scenes opposite their favorites. Almost always, the actors were perceived as having the same personality as the characters they portrayed. Thus, an actor working with a company that put on a series of different plays in different cities might be perceived as weak by the audiences in one community, heroic in another, and villainous in a third, depending on the roles performed.

The touring company producers made another discovery about the public interest in actors. Audiences remembered their favorites, and box-office receipts always increased when a beloved actor or actress had a starring role upon the company's return a few weeks or months after a previous visit. An actor who had played the role of a villain, then was suddenly billed as a hero, would likely have a lower turnout than an actor who played the hero each time a new play was presented in the same community.

And then, there was the most important discovery of all, one that would carry over to the movie industry of the 1920s when traveling companies of actors were usually replaced by motion pictures as theatrical entertainment. The offstage behavior of an actor or actress as reported in the local press was the most powerful determinant of box-office success. Gossip, usually in the newspapers and magazines with reporters in the areas where the stars were living, could not go against community values. A development such as the original Hollywood would not tolerate reports of actors drinking or gambling. Sexual promiscuity, homosexuality, abortion, illegitimate birth, spousal abuse, drunkenness, and similar activities would cause the actors to be shunned by community members who deemed such behaviors morally inexcusable.

Reporters assigned to the new motion picture industry quickly learned that their jobs were different from those of newspeople who ferreted out the more important news of the day. Their success required access to the stars that were currently of public interest. They needed to be able to conduct interviews, get inside private homes, and have access to sets during film production.

The studios needed the entertainment industry reporters to provide the type of publicity that would benefit their box-office takes. This meant portraying actors as they appeared on the screen, not as they were in real life. Sometimes this was to protect a "franchise" that would be ruined otherwise; sometimes it was to promote a single movie featuring someone not yet proven with the public.

The portrayal of Rudolph Valentino represented the protection of a franchise. For example, 1923 saw Valentino portrayed by the entertainment writers as the greatest lover in the movies. Two years earlier, he had starred in *The Four Horsemen of the Apocalypse*, followed the next year by *Blood and Sand*. He was filming *Monsieur Beaucaire* with *The Son of the Sheik* to follow.

The actor, whose real name was Rudolpho Alfonzo Raffaelo Pierre Filbert Guglielmi Di Valentina d'Antonguolla, had been discovered by two screenwriters when they visited a New York City dance hall where he was working in 1920. They looked at his face in the changing light, watched how he moved, and realized that on the screen he would photograph as an ideal hero. He was cast opposite Natacha Rambova in one film with a love scene so passionate that women in the audiences were intensely aroused. His sexual magnetism seemed to leap from the screen, and his cameraman, Paul Ivano, reinforced the image by taking favored columnists aside to tell them the "truth" about his overwhelming appeal. Ivano used a camera that required the constant turning of a hand crank. He did his job, watching in shock and awe as Rambova, so beautiful she had obviously enjoyed the pursuit, and perhaps the favors, of many men, fainted in ecstasy as Valentino's lips pressed against her own. Only after the director shouted "cut," when the cameraman was free to leave his post, could Ivano race over to the prostrate Rambova and try to revive her.

The press had the story the public wanted. Valentino was the man every red-blooded American male wanted to emulate in the bedroom, and Rambova, who married her costar because how could she do otherwise, was the woman every fair maiden wanted to be like. Valentino's appeal was such that when the actor was dying of peritonitis in 1924, a half-million female fans spent a nickel each to buy his picture to remember him.

What the public never knew was that if Rambova had fainted in sexual ecstasy, she was fantasizing about her true female lover, Alla Nazimova, one of the screenwriters who had discovered Valentino. As for the actor himself . . .

❝

I am told that the exotic Pola Negri has changed her mind about Valentino. No longer is he her ideal and the one handsome sheik of her life. In short, Pola and Rudy have come to a parting of the ways. Who is next? Well I haven't heard yet but judging from Pola's past record it's a handsome lad, possibly a movie editor.

—Louella Parsons writing in the *Los Angeles Examiner*, April 12, 1926

❞

Valentino was gay and lived with his lover, Paul Ivano, a fact the established members of the motion picture press corps well knew. The lesbian Rambova married Valentino for the publicity each would obtain for their subsequent pictures. The studios knew that if men thought they could be like Valentino, they would come to his movies, study his moves, and try them on their wives and girlfriends. Women would likewise come to see Rambova to learn how she had attracted the greatest lover of the day. And in exchange for printing publicity department–created stories, the columnists gained ever greater access to everyone from studio heads to extras.

The corruption of the reporters who covered Hollywood was not without its perquisites. Their salaries were often as high as $75 a week, 50 percent more than "real" news reporters were making and in line with what better-paid film extras received when they were working. The reporters were invited to parties and screenings. They were allowed on the sets. And the writers became celebrities in their own right, famous for knowing the famous whose images they molded, provided they toed the studio line.

The Hollywood reporters quickly learned what the public wanted to read, as well as what the studios wanted to report. Female actors were sweet, kind, enthusiastic, and virginal when they fell in love with male stars who were strong but gentle, handsome but never self-centered, the relationship being one between two equals who found love in a romantic industry. The 1920s was a time of liberation for women, a period when more and more females were entering the working world, experimenting with going to restaurants alone or with other women, and generally trying on roles previously denied them. Their mothers were either horrified or attempting to adjust, and both generations read about the movie stars to see how they were handling life.

The stories that were written followed a pattern in many instances.

The married actresses loved to be at home with husband and any children. There, they felt happiest and most at peace. At the same time, they enjoyed their work and knew their fans delighted to see them on the screen. That was why they worked hard, supported by their husbands who respected both aspects of their lives.

No one mentioned that marriages were often ordered by the studios for publicity purposes or to hide a star's sexual orientation. No one mentioned the staff of servants employed to raise the children, maintain the home, and otherwise free the actor from ever having to be a parent. No one mentioned the inevitable affairs that occurred when marriage was a business arrangement. And when a divorce could not be avoided, the reason was always acceptable to the values of people in heartland America: "They realized they had simply been too young for such a commitment, and though the best of friends, they sadly realized they had not been ready for marriage." "The schedule had been too intense. Between her active married life and the number of movies her fans insisted she make, she became exhausted and needed to free herself from the pressure that combining marriage and a career on the screen can bring. She is now recovering her health, sadder, wiser, and looking forward to when she will again appear before the camera."

There were only three sexual taboos when it came to covering the movie industry in the 1920s. A star could not be homosexual, a star could not have an illegitimate child, and a star could not have an abortion. Every other transgression could be discussed, so that readers believed they were reading all the secrets of the stars.

The first glimpse of the corruption of the press in Los Angeles came with the deliberate destruction of Roscoe "Fatty" Arbuckle by reporters, ensuring future favors from producers Adolph Zukor and Jesse Lasky of Famous Players–Lasky.

Arbuckle began his film career as an extra who earned the unusually low sum of $3 per week. He was extremely fat, yet a man of great grace, poise, and balance. Instead of the subject of slapstick abuse, Arbuckle came across on the screen as a gentle, loving man, and audiences seemed to root for him to win the heroine despite the often hilarious problems caused by his ungainly size. The public rushed to his films, demanding ever more from him and making the studio millions of dollars. He was also rewarded generously, ultimately earning $3 million for his work in 1921. The pay made him one of the wealthiest actors in film, and though he made far more in profits for the studio,

Zukor and Lasky felt that they were being extorted by a man whose success they had created.

Arbuckle, like so many other stars, had secrets that the public could not know. He was a heroin addict, though the drug use was so widespread and little understood that it alone probably would not have hurt his image. He also was impotent from the drugs, again something never discussed. The damage to his body was so great that he began losing weight and had to be fitted with a fat suit to continue portraying the character he had created in his early days as an actor.

Fatty liked to live as large as his original girth, indulging himself with such toys as a custom-made Pierce-Arrow car that was triple the normal size and featured a built-in toilet. He was always good for copy, and he was considered someone whose acquaintance actors on the rise would want to make. Certainly, that was what brought Virginia Rappe to the private party Arbuckle threw at San Francisco's St. Francis Hotel over Labor Day weekend in 1921.

Rappe was a slut. Sometimes she charged for sex. Sometimes she gave it away. She would bed anyone, from the cinematographers to the actors, and always she left behind one or another sexually transmitted disease. Mack Sennett was so angry that he barred Rappe from his sets after he twice had to have them fumigated because of crab lice infestations.

Rappe may or may not have wanted to attend the Arbuckle party. Not only was she not invited, she was suffering from peritonitis brought on by her sixth, and least-skilled, abortion. That fact was kept secret, not because the studios wanted to cover up her behavior—she had not yet attained a career where anyone would lose money if she stopped appearing on box-office marquees—but because, it is believed, the abortionist was a doctor connected with the same hospital where she would be treated while dying. He was also likely the medical professional who performed an autopsy on her and had to protect his livelihood.

The real story of the Labor Day party was that Bambina Maude Delmont brought Rappe to the party for reasons she never revealed. Delmont was a freelance employee of lawyers who made their money blackmailing prominent men photographed in compromising positions or helping their wives gain high divorce settlements. She would seduce the targeted wealthy man, though exactly how is uncertain since even her supporters admitted she was far from attractive, then pretend shock when a cameraman appeared at the door or she was asked to testify in court.

Her personal history, unrelated to the blackmail and extortion racket, included fifty or more arrests for prostitution and apparently one or more arrests for bigamy. She was also a con artist who participated in scams apart from the sex schemes.

Presumably, Delmont was going to set up Rappe with one of the guests. The party was getting extensive attention in San Francisco because of Arbuckle's notoriety, so there would be high-profile targets. Unfortunately, Rappe became violently ill from the peritonitis and had to be rushed to the hospital where it is believed that the doctor who caused her problem cared for her.

The rumors spread almost immediately that Rappe had been raped by Arbuckle and that this was the reason she was near death. The studio publicity mail quickly turned Rappe into a virgin when executives realized they would benefit more, at least personally, by destroying Fatty's career than by supporting him through a scandal that could still turn the public against him. He may have almost been a countercultural hero, but the mere act of throwing a wild party in San Francisco was questionable for a supposedly happily married man. Lasky and Zukor were about to break his contract using the press they "owned" through favors granted and favors expected.

Several stories circulated, always based on the premise that Rappe had never had sex until that night. It was reported that she had gonorrhea when she died, presumably from Fatty, who also may have crushed the innocent's ribs and otherwise brutalized her with his weight alone. No one mentioned that he was not much heavier than many men by that point due to his heroin addiction, and no one mentioned his impotence, which would have brought the rape issue into question.

A few writers, perhaps aware of aspects of the truth, yet not wishing to offend the studios, claimed that Fatty had not had sex directly with Rappe. Instead, he used an instrument—perhaps a Coke bottle, perhaps a section of a piece of furniture—to penetrate her. The image was one of ripping and tearing tissue, of sexual violence that would have been horrendously painful had she been conscious. The *San Francisco Examiner* went so far as to run the headline "TORTURE OF RAPPE CHARGED."

The truth came out slowly and only after Arbuckle endured three trials, the first two having juries voting 11 to 1 for acquittal. The lone holdout in each case was a plant by the prosecutor.

The peritonitis was noted, but the evidence was destroyed in the hospital's incinerator. Delmont, delighted by Rappe's death and its implications, wired her attorney saying, "We have Roscoe Arbuckle in a hole here. Chance to make money off him." The fact that she was the only one of forty guests at the party testifying against Arbuckle was not stressed in the papers; nor was the fact that one of the prosecution witnesses, Director Henry Lehrmann, was not present.

The public relations staff for Famous Players–Lasky let the bad publicity ride its course. Adela Rogers St. Johns was the only writer who was aware that something was horribly wrong with the case because she was aware of Rappe's major source of income. Lasky and Zukor knew that by not defending Arbuckle, claiming neutrality and a wish not to influence the case, they would strongly hint that whatever bad press Arbuckle received was appropriate. Acquitted, the comic still lost everything. Knowing no one would listen to Arbuckle, the two studio heads refused to distribute his films, including the older ones that made money for everyone, and stopped paying him.

By 1925, it was clear that the press worked for the film studios, even though they were totally independent and free to write what they wished. Many of the movie stars were created heroes, small-town kids suddenly thrust into the spotlight, given massive sums of money, adoration, sensual pleasure, and all the "things" they wanted. Their names were changed. Their histories were altered. They knew that as quickly as they had been created by the studios, they could be made to disappear from the spotlights. And the same was true for the Hollywood press.

Reporters came from big-city papers, but they also came from smaller communities where entertainment news mattered to the readers. It did not really matter how much the reporter made. A hierarchy determined the stories you got and the access you had.

The most important writers, and the ones on the shortest leashes, were those who wrote for publications in the Los Angeles area. Often the studios would assign one public relations employee for each newspaper or magazine. They would assure every whim was met: they might grant access to a star's home (after a crew had cleaned, altered decorations, and done anything else to make it fit the star's image) where reporters could witness a typical day in the star's life (after the makeup

and wardrobe specialists had exited out the back door while the reporter came in the front), or to the set where they might watch a film
being made, or to a wrap party, or to a producer's house. It was not
that the Los Angeles papers had greater influence than those in the
East and Midwest. Actors, producers, and directors simply had egos
that needed to be stroked, and they loved seeing their names in the
papers. Likewise, the writers liked being read by the famous, so each
stroked the other's ego.

Next in the hierarchy came the writers for the major papers, the
syndicated columnists, and those whose work appeared in all the papers in a single ownership chain. They could fill the box office better
than the local papers, but they were still considered secondary.

Finally, there were the lesser publications from around the country.
They were writing for the avid fans, the ones who wanted the stars to
uphold their moral values, even if they stumbled and fell along the way.
They believed in "happily ever after," despite a star's occasional lapses.

But no matter where the paper was located or the impact the reporter might have, the producers and the publicity specialists realized
that they could control stories because they controlled access. So long
as a writer realized that he or she would be banned from a set, from
interviewing the newest star, from going to fabulous parties in seemingly endless mansions, there was a tacit censorship. They would willingly destroy a Fatty Arbuckle either by not asking more questions or
by revealing the truth with the same zeal as they let loose the false-
hoods. They would pretend that no one had same-sex orientation, a
drug habit, a tendency to use abortion as a method of birth control, or
any of the other dirty little secrets to which they were privy.

In Union There Is Trouble

There was one other aspect to the odd relationship between the local
working press and the studios in the Los Angeles area. This had to do
with the unions whose image was changing, whose strength was growing, and whose takeover by the mob would soon become a matter of
concern to the industry. Again, to be a reporter in Los Angeles was not
necessarily to cover the facts as they existed.

The problem for the reporters began in the fall of 1888. Harrison
Gray Otis, the publisher of the *Los Angeles Times*, recognized that the

area was in trouble. It was still an agricultural community, and when the financial panic of 1887 reached the city, real estate values had fallen. Otis thought that if he could organize a chamber of commerce, bringing together business people concerned both about the present and developing the future, the city could grow. When movies began to be made, becoming one of only three industries, with agriculture and oil drilling, that provided the bulk of employment for several years, one of the appeals was cheap labor. Otis was convinced that the community had to maintain that cheap labor in order to survive, and toward that end, he used his editorial voice and the power he wielded in the community to fight all unionization.

San Francisco, well established after the gold rush and a popular destination for ships coming from Asia, was the nearest business competitor for Los Angeles. Each was striving for similar growth. Otis felt that if labor could be kept cheap as new businesses began, Los Angeles would have a competitive edge. He led a group called the Los Angeles Chamber's Merchants and Manufacturers' Association, which worked to sustain low wages as an appeal to retailers and others. He supported film industry executives as they fought trade unions.

The problem for Los Angeles, as far as Otis was concerned, and the reason he insisted that reporters not completely cover the issues resulting in a rising union movement, was growth. The film industry could just as easily relocate to Arizona, which had the same weather conditions, access to railroads, types of scenery, and skilled labor. Films had been made there and would be again. There was no guarantee that the moguls would not move if it was advantageous to do so.

It was 1896, when there was enough theater work in Los Angeles for the National Association of Theatrical and Stage Employees, the predecessor of the International Alliance of Theatrical Stage Employees (IATSE) to charter Stagehands' Local 33 and make it an affiliate of the Central Labor Council, the American Federation of Labor's municipal organization. In 1908, Los Angeles and three others cities were the first to establish a union for the projectionists, and the following year, both of those early unions went on strike with the American Federation of Musicians and the International Brotherhood of Electrical Workers. Their action was against the Regal Theater chain, which had been struck earlier, replacing all union personnel with nonunion personnel, who kept their jobs even after that strike was settled.

The intensity of labor-management hostility that Otis fueled came to a head on the night of October 1, 1910. That night, the *Los Angeles Times* building was dynamited either by newspaper union members or by men working with the unions. The blast killed twenty workers.

Neither side would back down in the midst of the bloodshed, but the *Times* did not let reporters cover the grievances in the growing motion picture unions such as Local 33. Otis did not want the public sympathetic toward the workers being exploited by the early studio heads. There were no stories of workers spending twelve-hour days on the job, including Saturdays and Sundays when shooting schedules so demanded, without breaks and without overtime. There were no stories of skilled workers having to line up at the gates to see if they would be picked in much the same manner as the less skilled extras. There was no mention of arbitrary firing of, or denial of work to, those deemed troublemakers. There were none of the human interest stories that not only sold newspapers but changed living and working conditions in industries in the East and Midwest.

And in 1917, when the Motion Picture Producers' Association was formed, followed five years later by the Motion Picture Producers and Distributors of America and their labor relations arm, the Association of Motion Picture Producers, they were assured of mostly favorable press. Local reporters were encouraged by the area newspaper publishers to be anti-union, and the combination of pressure from the men who paid the writers' salaries and the producers who could deny access to their stars meant that labor issues would be just another of Hollywood's dirty little secrets.

CHAPTER Six

The Last Corruption of Los Angeles (for the Moment)

I   t was Johnny Rosselli who found the aspect of the movie colony that was, it at first seemed to the Chicago mob, most vulnerable to assault—its entertainment, that is, alcohol, gambling, and prostitution, all of which would be protected by corrupt law enforcement and politicians. It was a formula that had worked for Big Jim Colosimo; it was a formula that worked for Johnny Torrio and Al Capone; and it was a formula that Charlie Luciano was using successfully in New York.

Johnny Rosselli was the first mobster to become part of the film industry, but his involvement was initially quite separate from his work in crime. He was a sometime actor by day, then began to involve himself with bootlegging West Coast style in his spare time. And toward that end he began working with a lone entrepreneur named Anthony Cornero Stralla, a.k.a. Tony Cornero, a.k.a. Tony the Hat Cornero.

Tony "the Hat" Cornero, like many mob leaders, was an Italian immigrant, but with a difference. Most of the families coming to the United States just before or after the start of the twentieth century had been so poor that the cost of travel was almost beyond their financial means. The Stralla family had been wealthy and prosperous in northern Italy. They had a large farm of great value and a wheat crop so large and healthy that a high profit was assured the year they planned to leave. However, before their expected departure date, two setbacks occurred.

Tony's father was a high-stakes gambler who got into a card game and became so convinced he had the winning hand that he literally bet the farm. The bet was called, the cards were shown, and his father came in second.

There was still time to sell the grain, the harvest apparently not having been included in the gamble. However, young Tony was playing with matches and accidentally started a blaze that moved to the wooden grain bin. The structure went up in flames, the grain dust exploding and destroying everything that remained. When the Strallas boarded the vessel to take them to New York, they were essentially penniless.

The Strallas lived briefly in New York, and then moved to San Francisco where Tony became a cabdriver. Born in 1895, he turned twenty-five when Prohibition became the law. For two years, his cabdriving enabled him to watch the bootleg industry grow. He drove the various bootleggers and watched as they grew increasingly prosperous. He drove men and women to neighborhood speakeasies that were gradually becoming entertainment centers as well as safe places to go drinking. And he witnessed the distribution of the alcohol, studying the supply and demand, during which time he realized that the bootleggers were serving the low-priced market. No one was meeting the desires of those who were interested in continuing to drink the high-grade liquor they had enjoyed before the passage of the Volstead Act.

Cornero decided to restore his family's fortune by moving to Los Angeles and putting into practice the lessons he had learned from listening to newly wealthy immigrant entrepreneurs. He arranged to obtain the finest bonded liquor, then established a client base among well-to-do families, including the movie industry elite, and the owners of high-ticket nightclubs. Then, he began buying small, rapid boats that he could use to transport the liquor along coastal water routes. There was a risk of arrest, but it was far less than if he used a central warehouse arrangement, as was common in other parts of the country. The roads were vulnerable not only to federal agents but also to every big-city and small-town police and sheriff's department. There was enough patrolling of the water that some of Cornero's liquor was confiscated, and some of his men were caught, but, overall, the idea was sound. Tony the Hat was a multimillionaire within three years of abandoning his "day job."

In 1925, Cornero bought a merchant ship called the SS *Lily* that could hold four thousand cases of liquor and dropped anchor in international waters off the Los Angeles coast. His floating warehouse was technically outside the legal jurisdiction of the feds, and they could not spend their time watching for small-boat traffic. The original distribution system remained viable, and there were even fewer confiscations than before.

The feds were not happy that Tony the Hat had found a way to beat the law. They went to court and managed to convince a judge that Cornero's criminal enterprise was an American one, thus subject to American laws no matter where the *Lily* was anchored. The agents, acting under the jurisdiction they had obtained, boarded the vessel, confiscated the cargo, and issued an arrest warrant for Cornero, who was not on board at the time.

Cornero, learning what had happened, fled the country, traveling extensively before returning to the United States in 1929 at the start of the Great Depression. Tanned and rested, he had money in the bank and was only facing a two-year sentence. He used the time that he was sitting in the McNeil Island Penitentiary in Puget Sound to develop his next big scam. He would move from high-quality liquor sales, certain to be hurt by the stock market crash, to gambling, a business that did well in good times and even better when cash was tight because it offered the hope of a quick, big win. He did not expect, however, that thanks to Johnny Rosselli, who would work closely with him after his release, he would attract funding from the Chicago Outfit, whose previous foray into the entertainment capital had been arranged through a private deal with Joseph P. Kennedy Sr. of Massachusetts.

Act II

In which men of honor, power, and passion descend on Hollywood to steal its money, seduce its women, and take advantage of a business world few understand for its long-term potential.

CHAPTER Seven

The First Star F***ers Probe for Weakness, Then Take the Money and Run

Joe Kennedy went to Hollywood to chase women, pocket $5 million, and keep from getting murdered. Charlie Luciano went to Hollywood to take over the studio-sanctioned drug trade, stayed long enough to get laid by a movie star, then thought it best to kill her before returning to New York. Al Capone couldn't get laid in Hollywood because he was on trial in Chicago for income tax evasion, but he was the first to recognize that the real money was in labor unions if his surrogate, his brother Ralph, could just figure out what to do with them.

Joe Kennedy

Kennedy was first. Joe had dated showgirls in New York before his marriage, a common practice among Harvard College undergraduates who tried to ensure that their classmates' sisters, many of whom they married, stayed virginal.

Broadway showgirls were a part of a married man's past, at least

67

for one whose wife regularly went to Manhattan to shop, see theater, and visit friends and whose fame resulted in his occasionally being recognized and photographed. But Joe's wife, Rose, rarely traveled with him when he was engaged in one or another business pursuits. And because Rose knew that Joe, who had been buying movie theaters since 1923, when he acquired his first in Stoneham, Massachusetts, was interested in getting into production, she thought nothing of his traveling to Los Angeles. She had no idea that he would transgress an unspoken agreement never to embarrass her with another woman, and she had even less of an idea that the consortium he put together for the purchase, one that included money from her father as one of the investors, was meant to remove a contract on his life.

The ordered hit on Kennedy resulted from a rare business miscalculation on his part—in this instance, bootlegging high-end liquor. Joe thought bootlegging was simple. His father had been a tavern owner and liquor distributor, as well as active in politics. Joe had seen how his father's business operated, as well as how politicians bent rules when it was to their benefit. He had not understood, however, that once he acquired both liquor and a customer base, delivering that liquor required more than a boat or a truck and a driver. Organized crime was more cohesive than when gangs ruled individual streets and raided rival territory for the love of the fight rather than for sensible business purposes. But organized criminals still controlled set territories, often an entire city, whereas previously they had ruled but a block or two. And anyone who wanted to pass through their territory in pursuit of his own criminal enterprise needed to seek permission.

There was more to the changes in New York and Chicago than Terrible John Torrio's relocation and the mentoring of Al Capone. For more than half a century, New York had been rife with street gangs. Each group had its own territory, and frequently these groups were formed based on ethnic origins.

The gangs were redefining themselves even before Prohibition. It was one thing to prey on local retailers, perhaps claiming to be part of the Black Hand and extorting from the legitimate business community. It was quite another to be competing for the same dollars when selling women, running gambling operations, and the like. Working together was more cost effective. In the case of prostitution, for example, each gang stopped operating single houses that required a constant turnover of women. Instead, a chain of bordellos used a trusted group of women who were divided among the various houses, then moved to a different location on an every-few-days rotation schedule.

New York, under Charles Luciano, was developing the system considered by most people to be the image of the Mafia. Rivals began specializing in a business model that was the first inclusive means of committing crime. Specialists could work together and spend less time killing each other and more time making profits from the "straight" world. The diversity was especially important to Luciano because he had observed something he felt others overlooked: each ethnic group he encountered seemed to have special skills. Meyer Lansky, a brilliant man with numbers who could not only do elaborate math problems in his head but also understood the business of crime, was still young enough that he wanted to show how tough Jewish kids could be. He and his friend Benny Siegel organized protection for the ships distributing large quantities of bootleg whiskey, as well as quality whiskey illegally imported from Italy, France, and elsewhere.

Frank Costello liked working the gambling clubs, back rooms, and similar locations, as well as handling bribes. He considered "influence payments" an art form and himself the master. Since his clients over the years ranged from businessman Joe Kennedy, who would later become a film studio owner, ambassador to the Court of St. James, and father of President John F. Kennedy, to J. Edgar Hoover after he became director of the Federal Bureau of Investigation, his self-assessment was probably justified.

Joe Adonis was somewhat of a generalist, though he mostly handled prostitution and loan sharking. Louis "Lepke" Buchalter ran protection in the garment district. And Dutch Schultz, the Brooklyn specialist in beer, agreed to join with Frank Costello.

Two non–New Yorkers were also admitted to the elite groups that were forming. One was Abner "Longy" Zwillman, who would have an affair with actress Jean Harlow, perhaps the most mobbed-up female actress in Hollywood because of her family ties, and his enforcer, Willie Moretti. In addition to his affair with Harlow, Zwillman became a backer of Columbia Pictures.

Similar activities were taking place in different states, though often with a mix of ethnic groups. In Cleveland, Ohio, there was the Mayfield Road Gang, almost entirely Italian and the eventual source for some of the early investors in Las Vegas. There was also the Jewish Combination, which combined Jews, Greeks, and Italians and either worked apart from the Mayfield Road Gang or in conjunction with them. And in Detroit, there was the Purple Gang, a mostly Jewish organization.

The various gangs were uniting and morphing into what would become the various "families" of organized crime as we think of them today. The Outfit—the Capone gang that evolved from Torrio's operation and would evolve again when Al was jailed for income-tax evasion—was perhaps the most cohesive in the way it dominated Chicago. Charlie Luciano was also building a stable enterprise for parts of New York, but so were others who had yet to work together—Jack "Legs" Diamond, Dutch Schultz, Waxey Gordon (a.k.a. Irving Wexler), and others. As a result, the lesser-known Frank Costello (né Francesco Castiglia) became a key player, not only in New York but with independents, such as Joe Kennedy and rising figures in other states such as Capone.

Frank Costello was a genuinely nice man, which is why he became that rare gangster who died in bed of natural causes. He had the good sense to see no man as his enemy if he could possibly build a business association with him. That was why, in the years that followed Prohibition, he frequently sat on a park bench in Manhattan with a friend few recognized—FBI director J. Edgar Hoover. The two shared information, and Frank made certain that before Hoover made his famous $2 bets at the horse races (an agent was assigned to place the same bet at the $100 window), he knew which horses would win. Costello was also a resource for columnist Walter Winchell, sometimes meeting him in nightclubs or in the apartment building where they both lived.

Costello also became a liquor distributor, partnering with his brother. They started in the traditional manner, obtaining the liquor through contacts in New York, then using the threat of physical violence to get saloon owners to buy from them "willingly." However, in the early 1920s, the rival bootleggers were attacking one another, and he wanted no part of the violence. He began working with all of them, offering to handle the import and distribution of large quantities of liquor for individual groups. A bootlegger would establish a clientele, and Costello would handle acquisition and delivery. This led to his being respected across the country and the only man able to bring together Capone's people and New York–based men like Luciano.

Joe Kennedy relied on his own resources—his father had been a saloon keeper, politician, and liquor distributor—and the services of Costello, who helped him arranged to have Al Capone deliver some of the orders. Capone was running boats, transporting everywhere from the Louisiana waterfront, where area restaurants used his liquor-delivery service, up the Pacific Coast.

Kennedy, as an independent and not a gang leader, worked with the same handful of trusted associates he used for all his business enterprises. Friends called them the "Four Horsemen." Enemies derided them as the Irish Mafia. The problem was that they had to handle all ventures, and the only ones they truly understood were those related to investments from real estate to the stock market. They looked upon bootlegging as nothing more than a product manufacturing, distribution, and retailing operation, not understanding the nature of the criminals involved.

The problem that brought Kennedy to the Chicago Outfit for help came from his misunderstanding of the way the old street gangs were reconfiguring themselves. It was only the Capone people, initially under Torrio, whose services he needed and utilized. They had set up liquor distribution to several parts of the country, including San Francisco, where Kennedy had Marion Davies, lifelong mistress of media magnate William Randolph Hearst, as his client.

Hearst was a teetotaler, but Davies and their mutual friends were not. She ordered liquor from Joe during his visits, and it would be delivered by Capone's men using high-speed boats that plied the coast. Drinks would be served to guests while Hearst finished dressing in a different part of his castle. There would also be bottles hidden around the house, such as in the guest bathroom, where a guest could sneak another drink during dinner if he or she was so inclined. The only ironclad rule was that Hearst could not see a guest drinking or see or smell the effects of alcohol. If he did, he assumed that the guest had brought a bottle in violation of house rules, and the guest was less welcome in the future. He did not know that Marion, using Joe, would have Capone's men make a beach drop, after which she would have someone seemingly innocuous transport the cases from the beach to San Simeon. One time, for example, Davies gave Patte Barham, the then teenage daughter of Dr. Frank Barham, Hearst's partner in the *Los Angeles Herald Express*, her car to handle the pickup.

The drop, though successful, was not without incident, Barham delightedly related years after the incident. Law-enforcement officers spotted the men and the boat, recognized that they were bootleggers, and though they did not see the liquor, began a pursuit. Bullets flying nearby, Barham loaded the car and quietly drove back to San Simeon.

In 1924, the year before Kennedy made the mistake that would result in a contract on his life, the Chicago mob was undergoing a shake-up that would have long-term implications both inside and outside the city. There were originally five Capone brothers, though only three mattered in Chicago—Al, Frank, and Ralph. The oldest and gentlest, Ralph, preferred helping Al run his business ventures to shooting, stabbing, and dismembering various enemies. He traveled armed and had proven himself deadly when necessary, but his pleasure was in management. Eventually, Ralph's loyalty was rewarded by his being given exclusive control over the bottling and distribution of soda water and ginger ale, both in high demand for mixed drinks when Prohibition ended. Ralph became rich through mostly honest means, acquiring the nickname Bottles.

The deadliest but dumbest Capone brother, Frank, was killed in an April 1924 shoot-out with police as he, Al, and a few other thugs tried to influence voters in Cicero, Illinois, by walking into polling places with guns and showing the voters where to place their x's. Al's survival instincts were better than Frank's. When seventy heavily armed Chicago police officers, deputized to work in the county, rode into Cicero, Al realized he was outgunned and ran, figuring one election did not matter all that much. There would always be power to grab and politicians to control. It was best to live to corrupt another day. Frank, less philosophical, stayed to fight the cops. As his younger brother anticipated, the police won the shoot-out.

A few months after Frank's death, Al again had a shock. Johnny Torrio was ill and planning to retire. He knew Capone's violent side, his vanity, and also his sense of loyalty both to whoever was in power and to the men who worked with or under him. Torrio also felt that there was an innate organizational sophistication to the surviving Capone brothers and that Al would make a capable CEO if given the chance.

Suddenly, all the work that Capone had done, from being employed in the New York bar to overseeing prostitutes and gambling to distributing liquor to bashing heads when necessary, became, in hindsight, a management-training program. Capone was given what would become the "Outfit," taking over the city and working with such stalwart loyalists as Frank "The Enforcer" Nitti, the one man who could override the actions of mob leaders in other states, to killers like "Machine Gun" Jack McGurk, Charlie Fischetti, and William "Three-Fingered" White. The other key leaders were Frank Maritote (a.k.a. Frank Diamond), Mike "de Pike" Heitler, who organized prostitution in much the same manner as Capone had done in earlier days, and Murray "The Camel" Humphreys, normally an expert in planning robberies. Humphreys also understood the importance of maintaining records about those individuals with whom the Chicago organization was involved; thus, he was a source for information about the period.

Johnny Torrio's retirement came in February of 1925 when, after being wounded in mob fighting, he handed Capone a criminal organization more than one thousand men strong with a weekly payroll of $300,000. "Terrible John" realized he no longer wanted to have to keep looking over his shoulder for a rival's threat. He had enough money to return to New York and die of natural causes at an old age.

Overnight, Al Capone became one of the most important business executives, legitimate or criminal, in America. New York's Frank Costello became an even more trusted consultant about East Coast and Midwestern operations and organizations, and Joe Kennedy knew that Chicago's piece of the liquor distribution business would continue as before.

The details of Joe Kennedy's liquor distribution business are sketchy. It is certain that he probably either took on clients in Detroit or tried to establish a delivery system of his own for Detroit-area businesses served by his truckers. In that volatile period, he may also have simply sent trucks through mob territory without politely requesting permission to do so. It is also certain that he in some way violated the bootlegging territory of Detroit's Purple Gang. The Purple Gang, run by the Fleisher and Bernstein brothers, was both important and deadly. Its importance had to do with the physical location of the operation, a short drive to Canada where Prohibition was not the law and liquor was readily available. However, the brothers and their followers were also known for extortion, murder for hire, hijacking, jewel theft, and seemingly any other criminal enterprise. Through the efforts of Frank Costello, there was a relationship between Chicago and Detroit, as there was between Detroit and New York. In fact, Capone had such respect for the controlled violence of Detroit that in 1929, when he planned the famous St. Valentine's Day Massacre of rivals, he hired some of the killers from Detroit because he could trust them.

Livid over Kennedy's transgressions, the Purple Gang ordered him killed and sent a message to warn him of what could be his impending fate. He knew that the warning was part of the punishment, that unless he could find someone to help him, he would be killed.

Joe turned to Frank Costello, who had him contact Chicago, where another mob broker could make a deal on his behalf. This was Giuseppe "Diamond Joe" Esposito, a bombastic character with the flash and attitude of Big Jim Colosimo, but far greater power and influence. Diamond Joe controlled large blocks of immigrant votes, had influence over U.S. Senator Charles S. Deneen (R-IL), and worked among the various bootleggers, gangsters, and other criminal groups to keep the peace. He understood that the flow of money should not be interrupted by petty spats and gang wars. Peace meant "straight" citizens were taking advantage of vice, and the profits from vice were taking care of seemingly everyone, especially Diamond Joe.

A deal was brokered between the Purple Gang, Joe Kennedy, and the Capone mob. Apparently, and here the information is almost nonexistent, the Purple Gang was convinced that Kennedy had not been trying to take over any of Detroit's territory. Any transgression was inadvertent. A mistake had been made. The contract was called off. No hard feelings.

Chicago was a different matter for Kennedy. A favor had been done. A favor needed to be repaid. Joe owed the Capone people, who apparently had spoken on his behalf at the behest of Diamond Joe. Again, the details are unclear, but it is certain that the Capone mob decided to become a silent partner in a major business deal with Kennedy. That business deal would take Joe and the mob on their first trip to Hollywood.

A second contract was put out on Joe Kennedy in 1956. Frank Costello felt that he had spent years doing small favors for Joe Kennedy that had helped the businessman get rich. He also was convinced that Joe did not show respect by returning the favors. Again, Joe had to turn to Chicago, this time to Sam Giancana. He pointed out that Jack Kennedy was a national figure, a man being discussed as a possible presidential candidate. He made it clear that if Sam helped him, he would see that Giancana had Jack's ear after he was in the White House.

Such mob influence in the Oval Office would have been unprecedented. Giancana was pleased to call Costello and have him hold off on the hit.

FBO

Kennedy's move on Hollywood would have happened no matter what his other obligations. He had purchased the Stoneham, Massachusetts, movie theater in 1923, then added to his holdings in the following months. He discovered that the big movie studios and the distributors worked to ensure maximum profits for themselves through their rental fees. They also understood that some movies would play well in one community and not in another, but rather than market according to the type of films an area's audience demanded, films would be packaged together. A theater owner who did well with Westerns and not with costume dramas would have to take both, even though the audience would be sparse for one of the films and large for the other.

Kennedy thought that the theater owners would delight in being able to buy what they wanted at a price that made everyone happy. He could achieve this by owning a production company and making low-budget films for specific regions. However, instead of joining Poverty Row, he would cut costs by using famous personalities with no acting credentials as his stars. Cowboys famous from the vaudeville circuit, football stars, baseball players, and the like had a tremendous draw among the young. He would hire them to play the leads in stories written with their limited talent or experience in mind. His budget would be drastically reduced compared with hiring a Chaplin or a Gloria Swanson or a Fatty Arbuckle prior to his destruction. The box-office sales might not be as high, but the cost-to-income ratio might be better.

The studio that happened to be available at the time Kennedy wanted to make the investment in Hollywood was FBO (Film Booking Office of America), a production company formed by one of the odder partnerships in Hollywood. Rufus Cole had been a wheelwright, and H. F. Robertson had been a blacksmith when they decided that the future was with automobiles, not horses. Sales of cars were increasing, rising production was cutting costs, and there was as yet no dominant brand or brand loyalty. With Americans fascinated by anything new in the field, Cole and Robertson quit their jobs to become the U.S. distributors of the British-made Rohmer automobile. Their company, Robertson-Cole, was an instant success. It was also work they found boring. However, since they were back and forth to Europe, they began importing films from the region that, before the destruction of World War I, had been the largest movie producer in the world.

The importation and distribution of motion pictures made Robertson-Cole far more money than their automobiles. They realized that film was the key to great wealth, and since they were familiar with the existing product and had a distribution company in place, they could become still richer by starting their own production company. The fact that they knew nothing about actors, lighting, production, cinematography, screenwriting, or any other phase of the studio end did not deter them. It should have.

In 1920, using vacant land on Gower near Melrose purchased from the Hollywood Cemetery Association, Robertson-Cole opened a film studio. Then they didn't know what to do next so they hired an executive who shared both their past and their desired future. Patrick A. Powers, a former blacksmith, had previously owned the Universal Film Manufacturing Company, which created the raw stock used in moving-picture cameras.

Two years after Robertson-Cole's studio was constructed, the partners left the business, Powers took over, and the company was renamed FBO. Powers could actually make movies but he had no sense of financing them and went into debt. The British banking firm Graham's of London soon took control of FBO, paying the equivalent of $7 million for the privilege. The firm put Major H. C. S. Thomson in charge, but neither he nor the banking firm seemed to have any greater business sense than Robertson-Cole. By 1925, FBO was quietly being offered for sale. Joe Kennedy was interested.

FBO might be underperforming for the expenses incurred, but it had the same production philosophy as Joe—well-made, low-budget films should be distributed according to community interests as perceived by the theater owners. Joe was aware of such FBO offerings as *Hook and Ladder No. 9*, *Rose of the Tenements*, and *The Bandit Son*, all films that fit the niche-market approach in which he believed.

In order to buy the company, Joe put together a group of investors so that he could offer Graham's of London $1 million for FBO. The front money to which he admitted came from Joe, his father-in-law, John "Honey Fitz" Fitzgerald, Louis Kerstein, who ran Filene's Department Store, and others. Hidden in the pot was the money from the Chicago Outfit—investments by Paul Ricca, Frank Nitti, and Murray "The Camel" Humphreys. The latter was so nicknamed for his penchant for camel-hair coats, but his friends called him Curly. They would take their share of the profits when Joe sold the company after establishing it on a firm financial basis. Neither they nor Joe had any interest in long-term ownership or backroom control. It was a position they would reconsider in the years to come.

Producer Joe Kennedy brought ruthless greed and mob money to Hollywood but not mob influence. The Chicago Outfit saw him place FBO on a budget of $30,000 per week to produce fifty-two films a year in 1926, the same year that he helped to "reform" the quality of films.

Joe was in Hollywood when pressure groups demanded that some form of censorship be applied in the industry. The decision was made to create an office where films and scripts could be reviewed, changes demanded, or stories approved so that outside forces, such as the Catholic Church's Legion of Decency, would stop attacking the industry. To do this, Joe brought in a man as corrupt as the mob, Will H. Hays, who in 1921 helped Warren G. Harding become president of the United States. Hays took a bribe of $75,000 and a loan of $185,000 (which did not have to be repaid) when he was chairman of the Republican National Committee. The money came from oil company interests, and when Harding took office, almost a hundred thousand acres of government oil reserves in Teapot Dome, Wyoming, became open to private interests.

Ironically, Joe was given approval as a Hollywood businessman because of Hays. The December 11, 1926, issue of *Motion Picture World* claimed that "[former Postmaster] General Hays wanted his friend to come into the motion picture industry because he regarded him as . . . a man who, in his business ideals and concepts, as in the fine character of his home life, would bring to the industry much that it has lacked in the past."

At the same time that Joe's FBO production company was earning profits for the Chicago Outfit and the corrupt Will Hays was being introduced as a savior of all that was right and good about America, Joe engaged in a series of affairs with as many actresses as he could seduce, the most famous being Gloria Swanson.

Gloria Swanson, arguably the most beloved actress of her day and thus a sexual trophy for the first of the star f***ers, was not that attractive in person. She wore a child's size 2 1/2 shoe, had shapeless legs and a flat chest, and was only five feet, one inch tall. However, on screen and off she made certain that her image was carefully created. When Joe met her, she was spending more than $11,000 a year on clothing, and $755 on shoes, the latter sum representing almost a year's income for some of her fans. She spent $26,000 on makeup, perfume, and a staff of professionals handling her appearance and chauffeuring her in either her Pierce-Arrow or her Cadillac, two of the day's highest-priced luxury cars. She earned $230,000 a year and was going broke because of her excesses, but Joe helped her increase her studio pay to $7,000 per week.

The story of the affair was legendary because of its crudeness. Both Joe and Gloria were married. Both flaunted their activities, including Joe's bringing Gloria to his Hyannis Port, Massachusetts, home to spend time with his wife and children before the threesome and Gloria's husband spent time in Europe. Eventually, the affair came to an end. Gloria briefly enjoyed a number of lavish gifts Joe had given her before their breakup. It was only after he had returned to the East and her own husband was divorcing her that she learned the truth: Joe had charged most of the thousands of dollars worth of presents to her own account. She had paid for her own seduction.

Joe's attitude toward the women he took to bed in Hollywood was callous. His involvement with the mob was kept to a business arrangement. The real ruthlessness of the man came when he decided to expand his own holdings by buying Greek immigrant Alexander Pantages's chain of seventy-two movie theaters.

At the time Joe decided he wanted to own the Pantages holdings, he had satisfied his lust for Hollywood actresses and netted $5 million for himself and his group of investors. The Chicago mob considered the debt to be paid in full. However, he wanted to make one more investment while the economy was working in his favor. (The year was 1929, and Joe was changing his investments in anticipation of a collapse of the current stock market. The crash occurred in October, the Great Depression followed, and Joe's lifestyle would continue unchanged. But that was several months away.)

Kennedy started openly, making his first offer to Pantages in February 1929. Movie theaters, because of the low price of entertainment, seemed likely to survive good times and bad, much like grocery stores. An additional theater chain seemed a good investment, but Pantages said he would not sell, a statement he reiterated through two more offers. The problem between the two men resulted from their both making the mistake of not fully investigating each other.

Pantages, born Pericles, changed his first name to Alexander after studying the history of Alexander the Great, who conquered most of the known world. It was a sign of the intense competitiveness that would ultimately rule his life.

Pantages was nine when he ran away from the Greek island where he was born, eventually making his way to the United States. In San Francisco, he became a waiter in a German restaurant, fought unsuccessfully as a professional boxer, then made his way to gold-rush Alaska, where he began running a vaudeville theater.

It was as a theatrical producer, theater owner, and booking agent that Pantages found his success and showed his competitiveness. He booked top acts when he could, and when a rival beat him to an act, he either lured it away or arranged for an equally famous act to appear in his theater starting the day before his rival's. This would give him more money and cut the other theater owner's profits.

By 1926, Alexander Pantages owned thirty theaters and had controlling interest in another forty-two. The size of his holdings caused Joe Kennedy to seek to buy them, and when he refused to sell, Kennedy's ruthless side showed itself.

Joe started his assault on the Pantages holdings by going to friends who were involved with the various studio production divisions. He convinced them not to give the downtown Los Angeles Pantages Theater any of their new releases. The other theaters in the city showed the releases as soon as they were being distributed, but Pantages had to wait until the bulk of the Los Angeles audience had seen a new film in some other theater. Only then was he given the movie.

The financial blow was serious, but with only one theater in the chain being targeted at that time, Pantages had the cash to ride out the problem. Joe realized he had to do more than hurt his business. He had to destroy Pantages and perhaps send him to jail. Toward this end, Joe enlisted the aid of Nicholas Dunaev, a writer of limited skill and an agent with a limited client list.

Dunaev had a client named Eunice Pringle whose major talent was one appreciated by directors using casting couches in the privacy of their offices. She was a wannabe actress who would always have a past and never a future.

Pringle claimed to be seventeen when she met her agent, and since she lacked the money to pay Dunaev, she agreed to move in with him, presumably to practice her audition technique regularly. The two lived in the Moonbeam Glen Bungalow Court, a cheap residence motel.

Joe cut a deal with Dunaev for Pringle's services. Instead of being his client, she would declare herself Dunaev's representative for one of the plays he had written. Eunice went to Pantages and told him she hoped that after he read Dunaev's work, he would either wish to produce it for the stage or turn it into a movie. The manuscript has apparently been lost to history, though it is known that Pantages found the work "vulgar."

Pantages did not suspect what was taking place. Playwrights and screenwriters regularly created bad work as they learned their trade, and invariably either the writer or a representative still tried to market it. Pantages had seen his share of inappropriate work, and he knew that it was a common experience for all producers. The difference with Pringle was that she returned to see him. This time, instead of being the dispassionate representative of the writer, she became violently hostile. He later said that she tore his shirt, then grabbed his legs and would not let go.

Pantages finally got rid of Pringle, thinking she was an emotional teenager and the confrontation would be the end of the problem. He did not realize that Joe Kennedy was paying the teenager and her "agent" $10,000 to compromise the producer. Pringle was also assured a part in a film made by Joe's company. For "fame" and wealth, she would not give up. On August 9, 1929, Eunice Pringle hid in the broom closet of the Pantages movie theater at 607 South Hill in Los Angeles to await Alexander's arrival. She wore a revealingly low-cut dress.

Pantages entered the area where the closet was located, having no idea that Eunice was hiding there. As soon as she heard him, she threw open the closet and started screaming to attract the attention of one of the people working there. No one had been in the room when she came out of the closet, so they only heard what Eunice was saying: "There he is, the beast!" She demanded to be protected from the horrible man who had attempted to do unspeakable things to her, including biting her breasts.

The police arrived, and Pantages was arrested for attempted rape. No one took Eunice to the hospital. No one checked to see if there were bite marks, though they would have been obvious based on what she was wearing. And no one seemed to notice that Eunice was young, athletic, and strong, while Pantages was a slight man who could not hold his own in a fight. Pantages proclaimed his innocence. Eunice insisted on his guilt.

At the trial, Eunice said that Pantages was kissing her passionately in the closet, then lowered his head to her breasts and began biting them. Terrified, she managed to escape, saw an employee, and screamed for his help.

Pantages was found guilty because young women were presumed to be honest, virtuous, and innocent. However, Eunice was up against top defense attorney Jerry Giesler. He appealed the fifty-year sentence the judge initially gave his client, then pointed out that Eunice's personal life should have been relevant to the first trial, where such information had not been admissible.

Giesler noted that Eunice might have been underage, but she was living with a man in what presumably were not circumstances of celibacy. The California Supreme Court, while not referring to Eunice as a cheap slut, did note that her personal life with Dunaev was very relevant. She was no innocent, and the existence of a conspiracy to hurt Pantages seemed beyond question.

The reversal was too late to allow Pantages to keep his theaters. He sold to Kennedy, never realizing he was behind the scheme. Pantages made millions on the deal, but it was still roughly half of what he would have made prior to the false accusations or he might have made after his eventual acquittal in 1931.

Two years after the court found Pantages innocent, Eunice Pringle lay dying from what proved to be cyanide poisoning. From her death bed, she confessed to the arrangement with Joe Kennedy. She never suggested that he had arranged what obviously was her murder, but it was likely that either Kennedy or the Chicago Outfit had her killed. Otherwise, her confession might have caused the government to also look into the sale and perhaps cost the Outfit some of the profit Joe had made for them.

Pasquale DiCicco and Charlie Luciano

He was the mob's go-to guy for vegetables—at least, for the money vegetables had made him. Pasquale "Pat" DiCicco's uncle took some rabe and some cauliflower and, with the genius that comes from working the soil and learning to make hybrid plants, created broccoli.

Not that DiCicco liked to play in the soil. He was the nephew, the kid who benefited from family wealth but went to the big city to seek a life of his own. In DiCicco's case, this meant becoming a playboy who went to mob-owned nightclubs and speakeasies to befriend gangsters, whom he treated as equals, not as antiheroes to be worshipped or friends chosen for their image. He genuinely liked mob guys, respected their world, and never crossed over into their territory.

DiCicco first met Charlie Luciano in New York, but it was in Hollywood that they knew they could do business. Luciano was eyeing the drug and gambling businesses, none of which were controlled by outsiders or organizations as in Chicago and New York. DiCicco desired to become a player in the movie business, an effort requiring that he learn as many of the dirty little secrets of actors, actresses, moguls, and drug dealers as Luciano needed to take control. Neither recognized that they would become interdependent when it came to the drug trade or would share the sexual favors of movie star Thelma Todd, whom, in the end, neither wanted. In fact, the entire incident would be just another failed attempt by both men trying to make inroads in a city that had no use for them.

DiCicco moved to Hollywood to become an agent and manager, though he had no clients and no contacts, and no one on the West Coast was likely to have heard of him. To his advantage, he was rich, handsome, and articulate and used his old-world courtliness to impress women. He treated the moguls as equals, making certain to eat and socialize in the same luxury locations they did. And unlike Kennedy, he was not aloof. He was as friendly with the security personnel and the secretaries key to seeing the moguls as he was with the studio heads themselves. No one was more or less important to Pat DiCicco, it seemed to those who met him.

DiCicco had never had to work for a living, even in New York where he first shared his inheritance with everyone from doormen to beautiful women to top mobsters such as Luciano. He was not impressed with anyone, a refreshing change from organized-crime groupies and star f***ers who only wanted access as a way of becoming "someone" by sharing the spotlight with the person they respected, lusted after, or otherwise fantasized about. And because he showed no special deference, organized criminals saw him as a friend, or at least as someone outside their tightly knit group of thugs with whom they could feel safe. He seemed to give without wanting anything in return.

Joe Kennedy privately thought of the moguls as a bunch of pants pressers, glove salesmen, and rag peddlers. Their accents betrayed their Eastern European backgrounds. Their limited education made them semifunctional in two languages. And even the massive sums of money they earned in the entertainment business could not keep them from being mocked. That was why they bought themselves elaborate homes, had chauffeurs driving expensive cars, and ate in restaurants the average American could only fantasize about seeing from the inside.

Many of the actors, especially those working for men like Louis B. Mayer, who preferred creating stars to hiring them, were equally insecure. They were small-town kids who had rarely finished high school, had few, if any, meaningful job skills, and were known only by the names and personal histories the studio heads and their publicity departments created for them. Only in the film industry could they earn more at the bottom than they once aspired to achieve after several years of working blue-collar jobs in their hometowns. The threat that they would be fired, their studio names disgraced, and their futures returned to the bleak sameness that caused them to flee from Dead-at-Night, Iowa, or Dry Gut Gulch, Louisiana, or wherever they came from, was enough to keep them pliant and subservient to people in power.

DiCicco understood all this, understood the inherent insecurity of the immigrant who finds success beyond his or her wildest dreams, whether he or she is from another country or another state. He also knew that when he walked into high-priced restaurants, stayed in ultraluxury hotels, and drove the most expensive luxury sedans, then treated everyone with respect, he was viewed as being the person they were pretending to emulate. His position was presumed before anyone heard his name, received his business card, or was approached for an appointment.

DiCicco used another technique, again with the subtlety of a man who was supposed to be "somebody" in a world almost as foreign to him as it was to the people he was trying to impress. DiCicco let it be known, when appropriate, that he was an acquaintance of Charles Luciano, whose exploits were widely known throughout the country. And when Luciano began making regular trips to Los Angeles, DiCicco made certain that they were seen together, that Luciano was introduced to the right people, and that he never dissuaded anyone from thinking that the Luciano muscle might . . . just might . . . be available to Pat.

DiCicco got help projecting his desired image from Eddie Mannix, the ruthless head of publicity for MGM. Mannix was in the curious position of also being friends with Charlie Luciano from when he had worked with the Schenck brothers, as well as with actress Thelma Todd, who would have an affair with Luciano while married to DiCicco. Mannix was the de facto head of law enforcement in Los Angeles because he had the power to prevent an investigation into crimes committed by the actors, producers, and directors, as well as to guide the "official" results. The ruthlessness of his image was solidified in the minds of those who knew him when his wife, Bernice, was on her way to file for divorce.

Eddie, a notorious womanizer, lived apart from Bernice in their last months as a married couple. The arrangement might have continued had she not accused him of cruelty, of beating her severely enough to break her back, and of committing adultery with a woman named Toni Lanier. She planned to ask for $4,000 a month in alimony, more than a year's salary for most of the nonacting employees at MGM. She also wanted property worth $1 million.

Eddie could afford his wife's alimony but knew Toni, whom he married in name only, not even bothering with a ceremony, was high maintenance. He resented what Bernice was planning to do and knew a judge would agree to her requests. Using his contacts in organized crime, Eddie arranged for a killer to follow Bernice and Palm Springs–area casino owner Al Wertheimer when he started to drive her home the night of November 18, 1937. The killer ran Wertheimer's car off the road, paralyzing him and killing Bernice before she could file. The rest of Mannix's violence related to his work, except when his "wife" had an affair with George Reeves, who then took a different lover, upsetting Toni and interfering with Eddie's womanizing. Reeves, television's Superman, was not faster than the speeding bullet that killed him.

For the first few weeks he was in Hollywood, DiCicco targeted two groups of movie people—the producers, with whom Mannix was also a help, and the rising talent who lacked representation but had the potential to achieve success. He would wear expensive clothing in styles that implied sophistication and custom tailoring. He drove his luxury car to such restaurants as the Montmarte and the Brown Derby. He lunched in Musso and Frank's. And wherever he ate, he made a point of stopping by the tables of the moguls, chatting a few minutes, leaving his card, and telling them he would finish talking with them in their offices, which he would visit the next day.

DiCicco had the look of importance before he was important, and that ensured his access onto otherwise closed production sets, where he liberally passed out cards to the actors. He also generously tipped all those who helped him, from the security guard who had determined who could drive onto the studio lot to the secretaries. He knew he was bribing them. They were certain that he cared about them and respected their jobs instead of focusing solely on the stars like the media and the public. That was why he was always welcome, even in areas supposedly off limits to outsiders.

The approach DiCicco used with the "good guys" of the industry he also used with the studio drug dealers. They told him about their clients, their distribution system, who was an addict, who was a controlled recreational user, and who was a user at the direction of one of the studio bosses. Better lighting equipment and more sensitive photographic film were constantly being developed, but the studio heads still considered full use of daylight to be critical to their production schedules. They also recognized that women needed a certain look on the screen for the audience to find them beautiful. Movie contracts, such as the one the rising star Thelma Todd had signed, allowed the studio to fire an actress whose weight varied by more than five pounds. The extra weight, unnoticeable in real life, allegedly distorted her looks when she was projected larger than life on the screen.

Diet pills were encouraged as necessary. Amphetamines and sleeping pills were available from the studio doctors to help actors, including children, perform at 100 percent, then sleep soundly in the few hours they might have each night. The addictive nature of the drugs and the health risks involved were not understood at the time, except by the men who arranged for their importation and distribution.

Actresses were the most common victims early in their careers. The weight issue was of such concern that many would combine amphetamines and alcohol in order not to overindulge in food. The amphetamines gave them the energy to work despite their not having eaten adequately, and the alcohol helped them wind down and sleep at night. The less emotionally secure the actress, the more likely she was to indulge, and many of the women the moguls developed as stars would do whatever a strong, male authority figure told them to.

DiCicco learned all of this in his first two years in Los Angeles, and as Luciano began coming to the West Coast to see about controlling the drug trade and gambling operations, he shared these details. The two also shared DiCicco's future wife, the actress Thelma Todd.

Charles Luciano/Charles Lucky/Charles Lucifer

You could take the man out of the Five Pointers, but you couldn't take the Five Pointers out of the man. Both Charlie Luciano in New York and Al Capone in Chicago were still looking at Los Angeles through the lens of their street-gang training. They knew how to market women, run gambling joints, and move liquor, though with Prohibition on the wane—the law would end in 1933—the greater concern would be nightclubs and casinos, where people would be happy to spend their money.

For men who had taken control of cities, labor unions, politicians, law enforcement, and almost every aspect of the entertainment industry in the East and Midwest, they were extremely naive about the real potential of the movie business. They also did not understand that the moguls had corrupted the local leadership in Los Angeles to such a degree that the police, prosecutors, and politicians would be foolish to switch loyalties just because they had received yet another envelope filled with cash.

Los Angeles was not the primary concern of Luciano, however. Capone had left for Chicago, eliminating one immediate enemy, but New York was in the midst of what became known as the Castellammarese War.

Luciano was a businessman in the mold of Joe Kennedy. The latter would become famous for his belief that as long as business was being conducted, all other matters were unimportant. Joe felt that even if horrendous governments took control of major parts of the world, such circumstances were the ebb and flow of history and did not matter, provided commerce continued unabated. Luciano had a similar attitude, though on a smaller scale—his concern was the criminal activity within the New York/New Jersey region of the United States. The problem was with the Moustache Petes, the earliest of the immigrant organized crime bosses.

The original Mafia was Italian of sorts. It was true that the leaders, by the late 1920s a group of old male immigrants, felt that not only your country of origin but your city and village were important. Vendettas between the men of two villages in Sicily, for example, required the spillage of no less blood just because the men were living in New York and probably could not remember why they were outraged. They just knew that they were supposed to hate one another, and if that meant wholesale slaughter by rival gangs, so be it. It was the old way, the new way, the forever way.

Except to Luciano. He thought the Moustache Petes were fools, and when the Castellammarese War had gone on for almost three years, he shouted, "Enough!" Then, he brought peace in that most expedient of ways—he murdered almost everyone who disagreed with his thinking.

The focal point of the war was Giuseppe "Joe the Boss" Masseria, a man who had long treated Luciano like a son. Unfortunately, he felt that this "son" had gone astray, keeping company with Frank Costello, who was not Sicilian, and working with Ben Siegel, Meyer Lansky, and other Jews. He wanted everyone to limit themselves to their own neighborhoods, where they could control people like themselves. This was the way it was done in the old country. And this was why the Sicilians fought the Neapolitans, except when the Sicilians from one village were killing the Sicilians from a rival village.

Fighting such vendettas, according to old-timers like Masseria, was the way of men. That was why the old bosses would never work together for the greater good of all and why they would not work with Jews, Irish, or other outsiders from the Italian culture.

The war that began in 1928 pitted Masseria against Salvatore Maranzano of Brooklyn. Maranzano had come to America from Castellammarese del Golfo in Sicily and wanted to take control of New York.

The war initially pitted the young men from each group against one another. Maranzano had such soon-to-be-famous individuals as Joseph Bonanno, Thomas Lucchese, and Josef Profaci. The Masseria men included Luciano, Frank Costello, Vito Genovese, Carlo Gambino, and Albert Anastasia, among others. It was the younger men on both sides who had the most to gain or lose because they were the future of organized crime in New York.

By 1931 it was obvious that the war was an impediment to more important business. Everyone was killing everyone else, and for no good reason. The young turks like Luciano realized that it was better to end the war and the mentality that caused it than to keep fighting one another.

Luciano and Thomas Lucchese plotted to kill Masseria, whose pride and old ways were keeping the violence a problem. By having men from both sides plot the killing and men who worked for Masseria commit the assassination, peace was restored. Maranzano was the new leader, though the young turks instantly recognized that Maranzano, wisely, was insecure. He, too, would have to be eliminated, or he would carry on the violence to protect himself.

The series of assassinations that brought peace to the mob and let them refocus on more serious matters, including what to do about the film industry, began on April 15, 1931. Luciano arranged to meet Masseria at Scarpata's Restaurant, a popular seafood place where men could eat, talk, and relax. The meal, as always, was flawless as it was the last food Masseria would ever eat. It was a sign of respect to wine, dine, and then kill a boss as simply and painlessly as possible.

Lunch was fresh lobster, linguini with clam sauce, and Chianti wine. Afterwards the two men had the waiter bring them cards to play rummy. Finally, in mid-afternoon, Luciano excused himself to go to the bathroom. Four men with pistols then entered the restaurant, fired five rounds each into Masseria's head, and left. Then, Luciano returned to view the corpse. There were no witnesses.

Maranzano rewarded Luciano by giving him full control over Masseria's operations with Vito Genovese assigned to be his underboss. Supposedly, they would be doing business in the newer, more open manner they had killed Masseria to achieve. However, Maranzano was no different from Masseria in his thinking. Giving the organization to Luciano was the same sort of gesture as inviting Masseria to lunch. Once Luciano and Genovese became comfortable in their new positions, Maranzano loyalist Vincent "Mad Dog" Coll was to murder them—along with everyone connected with them, including Ben Siegel, Dutch Schultz, Louis "Lepke" Buchalter, and approximately fifty others, both in New York and Chicago, where Al Capone was also to be eliminated before he could go to prison. The latter move was to ensure that the Chicago mob didn't try to move back into New York, whose ranks of sophisticated thugs would have been thinned.

Vincent Coll was to be assisted in the murder plot by Angie Caruso, a man as heavy a drinker as George Browne. He was in a joint owned by Philadelphia mobster Nig Rosen, talking about Maranzano's plan to solidify control over all organized crime through the mass killings. Rosen listened to the drunken ramblings, knew they were likely to be true, and alerted Luciano. Charlie, in turn, contacted Ben Siegel to work out a way to handle the problem.

The following day, Luciano was scheduled to go to see Maranzano at his 230 Park Avenue office for an important meeting. Charlie knew he was a dead man, so Siegel arranged a preemptive strike. At 2 p.m., enough in advance of Luciano's appointment to allay suspicion, four well-dressed men entered the Park Avenue office. They showed credentials and a badge identifying themselves as federal officers working with the Internal Revenue Service. It was the one government agency the entire mob feared because so many of them, including Al Capone, had learned the hard way that tax evasion meant jail time, even for those who could literally get away with murder.

Maranzano had muscle present—five bodyguards and his secretary—but made certain there was no resistance when the "federal tax men" entered. This was a battle for the lawyers, not the bad guys/good guys having a shoot-out, and everyone surrendered their weapons to the IRS agents.

The agents requested that the books be opened, and Maranzano, suspecting nothing out of the ordinary, led two of the men to a back room where he kept all documents. The other two remained with the six people they had encountered when they arrived. Then, once the inner-office door was closed, Maranzano was stabbed and shot.

The killers burst from the inner office, and the bodyguards and the secretary had the sense to flee the building. The feds, actually Jewish killers who worked for Ben Siegel from time to time, ran after them but did not call attention to themselves by trying to shoot. However, when they saw Vincent Coll arriving to murder Luciano, they stopped and told him to get out of there. Their orders had only been to kill Maranzano.

Over the next twenty-four hours, Luciano and his men conducted what was later called the Night of the Sicilian Vespers. Almost fifty of the old men were slaughtered, and the younger mob figures were contacted to explain the future. Everyone would work together. Luciano was the boss of all bosses, but they would start working in a business-like manner. One group of experts, including Ben Siegel, would carry out murders only after the approval of either Albert Anastasia or Louis Lepke. Others would specialize in narcotics or stolen jewelry, extortion or loan sharking. The ethnic background of the men who participated was never an issue. Only their skill and their loyalty mattered. (Coll was murdered on February 7, 1932, though for reasons other than the consolidation of the mob.)

The war was finally over, and the new crime syndicate, a cooperative effort, was put in place. Now men from different parts of the country, different gangs, and different ethnic backgrounds could sit down in peace to scheme their acts of corruption, murder, and extortion and to devise new ways to separate "straight" citizens from their money.

Not that there wasn't lingering malice. Luciano still hated the Capone brothers, and though Al was going to jail for income tax evasion, Luciano was upset every time he was in the Los Angeles Brown Derby, an upscale establishment he co-owned, and saw his staff politely serving Ralph "Bottles" Capone. And both the Capone and the Luciano people recognized the value of taking control of labor unions, but they did not yet understand the need to cooperate in the entertainment field. However, much of that was coming. The ending of the war was an important first step.

CHAPTER Eight

The Punk Got It Right

ommy Maloy was a punk, a nobody, a loser. He liked labor unions, but that didn't make him bright. The Capone boys liked labor unions, and they were organizing everyone connected with restaurants, speakeasies, service industries, and any other unions with lots of jobs, lots of clout, and lots of money to skim. Luciano was organizing New York in much the same way, and the bosses were eyeing the other's territory, each avoiding an East Coast/Midwest gang war and respecting one another.

Not Tommy Maloy, the loser. He had gone after the business agent's position with Chicago's Motion Picture Projectionists Local 110, and everyone knew the movies were nothing. No money. No future.

Sure, Maloy was inspired. He had been the chauffeur for Maurice "Mossy" Enright, a man who would bash heads and bomb businesses in pursuit of running both garbage haulers and building trades unions. What he perhaps didn't notice was that Mossy was also the first official victim of a drive-by shooting. Then, again, maybe that's why he chose the projectionists since they had no history of problems.

Maloy, himself, had worked as a projectionist, learning the business while running a craps game for extra money. He also acted as an enforcer for the projectionists' union business agent, Jack Miller.

The business agent was the organizer, the guy who was supposed to get more and more members to sweeten the pot of retirement pay, regular dues, special assessments, and anything else worth skimming from blue-collar guys who had nowhere else to turn for jobs. The business agent also hired and fired, giving him a power that would get stronger when the economy tanked.

But the projectionists? The guys who showed the movies in the handful of joints in Chicago in 1920? Nobody but a stupid punk would have thought it necessary to give the former business manager, Jack Miller, an unexpected early retirement and a swell funeral to remind everyone that Tommy was a sensitive guy. The movies were a fad. The big boys gave them a few months, a couple of years at the outside, and it would be over. Why waste your time, energy, and bullets?

Maloy took control using some of the business basics learned from the big guys. You wanted to be a projectionist, you joined the union. Otherwise, no job. Theater owners had to hire union men, or there would be a well-placed fire, movies would be routed to the wrong place so there would be nothing to show for days or weeks or however long it took the owner to see reason, and if all else failed, the owner would disappear. The business agent negotiated with the theater owners equipped with such intimidating weapons as brass knuckles, a club, and the popular Thompson submachine gun, which the Capone mob delighted in carrying for its fire power and concealability.

As for pay, Maloy took a fair salary approved by the men he hired to approve what he did. He also took 5 cents of every dollar given to the union, just because he could. It was all very professional, but in the eyes of the "real" mobsters, the amount of money at stake was too small to pursue.

Nobody thought Maloy had the foresight to see how big movies were becoming. Everyone knew that if nothing else changed, neither would Maloy. He was a kingpin, a big man, the guy you had to see, but on such a small scale that no one outside the business seemed to notice. And if the theater owners hadn't been intense competitors unwilling to pause long enough to work together to squash him, he never would have lasted in the job.

The Outfit watched Maloy like they watched every would-be tough guy. They laughed at his naiveté when he made the even bigger mistake of closing the union to new projectionists. Growth meant a bigger pot of money from which to skim. That was the way the other unions were run, but not the projectionists.

Tommy Maloy watched the growth of movies and the money that was pouring into the theaters. The grosses rose. The net rose. The advent of sound required men of great technical skill. And nitrate film was susceptible to fire and explosion if mishandled. A good man should be paid, and gradually Tommy got the union pay scale to a top of $175 per week, more than most of the younger movie stars and many corporate executives were making. Yet, none of this hurt the theater owners. The projectionists were worth the price because the money was rolling in.

The projectionists were constantly reminded what a great guy Tommy was and how thinking otherwise could cost them the best job they were likely ever to hold. In gratitude, they "voluntarily" kicked back $3 a week to Tommy, a small price to pay. The 5 cents per dollar skimmed didn't count, though no one who knew about it would likely have challenged the practice openly.

The increased number of theaters and the maintenance of union membership at a constant level meant a dramatic shortage of union projectionists. Again Tommy was ready.

A new category of projectionist was created, the permit worker, a man every bit as skilled as a union worker to be paid the same amount of money as a union worker. However, the cost of the permit that allowed a theater owner to hire him was 10 percent of his salary. This still left the permit workers high-income professionals.

Maloy was an equal opportunity extortionist and thief. He approached the largest Chicago theater chain, Balaban and Katz, and told them that the motion picture operators union had some problems with the projection booth employees. The new sound pictures required that a phonograph containing the sound be synchronized with the running film. This would quickly change, but for the moment the combination was needed, and the work was fairly complex. It also could be handled by one man, though Maloy claimed otherwise. He insisted that there needed to be a man handling the recording, called a fader, and a man running the film. This meant double salaries, though if the theater owners were absolutely certain they could get by with one man, a contribution to Maloy's wallet would placate him. And a small increase in pay for the one man left in the booth placated the union members. Neither the theater owners nor the rank and file knew of the scams that were pitting one group against the other.

Eventually, Maloy decided that it was not fair to screw the theater owners without putting it to his members, who were already paying him $25,000 a year (the theater chain owners each kicked back $125 per week to Tommy as well). Special assessments were suddenly needed: strike funds or retirement money or money to help members in trouble or . . . Actually, no one was certain what these funds were for, though they ultimately totaled $500,000. Services rendered for that money included an expensive Caribbean cruise, a first-class European vacation, a major makeover of Maloy's home, and other "necessities."

Tommy Maloy rode his success into the Depression, at which time there were more threats to a theater owner's livelihood than a firebomb or a bullet. The public still clamored for movies as entertainment. People still scraped up the money to go to a show. But the money was harder to come by. The audience was increasingly sparse on any given night. Films shown too closely together could not be attended as they had been in the past. People who had gone to the theater four or five days a week might only be able to afford to go two or three times a month, if that.

The theater owners were at risk of losing their businesses, and the one place they could cut back on expenses was the cost of projectionists. They told Local 110's business agent that union wages were out of line, that they would not pay for union or union permit workers. They would get the cheapest men for the job, and there were plenty of out-of-work men who either had the training or could be trained and who would be delighted to put a roof over their families' heads and food on the table. Even the simplest of luxuries would wait until better times.

Maloy went on the attack. Fire his men, and your theater would be firebombed. Fire his men, and the films shipped for showing would be destroyed. Fire his men, and . . .

The theater owners either rebuilt or opened in another area. The movies weren't going to lose their popularity because of Maloy's antics, and Maloy knew better than to really get the public's attention by attacking a theater when a film was being shown.

The theater owners also went on the attack. They contacted the Illinois attorney general to explain what they had been enduring. They gave enough evidence to put Maloy in the penitentiary. They did not realize that they were also giving Frank Nitti, the man who was running the Outfit while Capone was in jail for income-tax evasion, the information he needed to see why Tommy had done so well.

Curly Humphreys was asked to help Maloy with the state legislators. He was a payoff man for the Outfit, and Nitti wanted to be certain that Tommy got the assistance he needed. Cash bribes led the suddenly safety-conscious state legislature to pass an act requiring all movie houses to maintain two projectionists at the same time. The fact that sound striping of film had been developed and one man could easily handle everything changed nothing. Safety first, unless you negotiated the right deal with Tommy.

Nitti decided that the Outfit would take over the projectionists union, thanking the totally corrupt attorney general's office to stay out of the dispute. Nitti also would handle Maloy. No one gave a damn about the theater owners, who mostly had the bad grace to be honest men.

Frank Nitti had come to know Al Capone when he joined Johnny Torrio's bootlegging operation as a specialist in transporting expensive liquor from Canada to Chicago's South Side. Previously, he had been a barber and a fence, buying and selling stolen merchandise. His skills were such that he acted as a middle manager, capable of getting the men to carry out the organizational wishes of the men at the top. He was a businessman who could resort to violence when necessary, the reason he was called "The Enforcer." Only the mob mythmakers, who had no knowledge of Nitti's real role, believed he was a killer feared by the public and members of the mob who had crossed Torrio and Capone.

Nitti's skills were the reason he worked with men like Joe Kennedy and Tony the Hat. Nitti was also the first to understand what Tommy Maloy was accomplishing with the union no one had respected.

Maloy began to understand the power of the former Capone gang, now run by Nitti, Humphreys, Jake "Greasy Thumb" Guzik, and other close associates of the jailed leader. Members of the Illinois legislature made a partial repayment of the bribes they willingly took by creating legislation to help the projectionists union. Film was dangerous. There had been no problems in the past with one man in the projection booth handling the nitrate film stock, but problems could arise. It was better to have a spare projectionist for safety. Toward this end the legislators passed a bill requiring all theater owners to hire two projectionists per booth and to choose only from qualified applicants—those certified by the union, a requirement that involved the same type of kickbacks as in the past.

Maloy was expected to show his gratitude through a voluntary contribution of $5,000 to Mayor Tony Cermak's Democratic fund, which he did. The problem was that for all his success, Tommy was still a punk. He thought he had gained the respect of the Outfit and the power to become a national player. Instead, he was played for a sucker. He became a front man, the guy with the target on his back so nobody noticed what else was taking place.

Frank Nitti told Maloy that he wanted the business agent to take the projectionists union national. Los Angeles was not a target because there were too many unions; too much power was split among too many people. Worse, many of the craft unions were hostile to outsiders, new membership being given to the family members of current union members.

New York was also ignored, though that was to be a temporary measure. Nitti knew he wanted to go up against Luciano, but he could not do it while Capone had influence on Chicago actions. Capone hated Luciano but he did not want to confront him directly concerning his rackets, at least not until he was sure he could win.

With Tommy as the front man, Frank Nitti arranged to merge the Chicago projectionists union with the International Alliance of Theatrical Stage Employees (IATSE). Rather than diluting his power, he enhanced it by gaining access to the film industry's IATSE membership. He also gained influence over every worker in the film industry. The production people, those who distributed the finished product, and those who showed it on the screen were suddenly all in the same union, all working together, each able to bring filmmaking to a halt at any studio they desired.

Tommy Maloy thought he had it made. He was still a business manager, still skimming the take for himself as well as the Outfit. The only problem, and he believed it was a minor one, was that he wanted to be in full charge of his union. And because Tommy Maloy was a punk, a nobody, and a loser, he went to see Frank Nitti with what he thought was his oh, so simple, so logical request for greater power.

Nitti said he would think over the request, giving Maloy the idea that it was a valid one. Tommy didn't know that Nitti was already talking with another punk, though a more pliable one—George Browne of IATSE.

CHAPTER Nine

Mob? In Hollywood They Do It Bigger and Better, and Everybody Has a Piece of the Action

Al Capone came to Hollywood for Christmas in 1927. He took his wife, his son, a pair of bodyguards, and his secret identity, Al Brown, and fancied himself registering incognito at the luxurious Biltmore Hotel in downtown Los Angeles. The fact that almost no one with a New York accent checked into the city's most expensive location with a pair of bodyguards was an instant tip-off. The fact that Capone was America's most gregarious gangster added to the speed of his "discovery" at the Biltmore.

Capone had originally planned to go to St. Petersburg, Florida, for the holiday, but he was curious about the town Joe Kennedy felt was important and the business of pictures Frank Nitti felt was worth investing in. No one knew who alerted the press, though it was most likely a member of the hotel staff. The hotel was soon mobbed, the reporters hoping for the types of quotes he had given the Chicago reporters earlier in the month. Among other memorable lines, he had foreshadowed what he was unexpectedly about to experience in Los

Angeles when he said on December 5, "There's one thing worse than a crook, and that's a crooked man in a big political job. A man who pretends he's enforcing the law and is really making dough out of somebody breaking it, a self-respecting hoodlum hasn't any use for that kind of fellow—he buys them like he'd buy any other article necessary to his trade, but he hates them in his heart."

Capone's reception should have been a warning to Chicago and New York about taking on a city that was, in essence, a one-industry town. Whatever was good for the moguls was good for Los Angeles, and whatever did not disturb the moguls was allowed to go unregulated.

The reporters assumed that Al was looking at bootlegging. They thought he might be trying to coordinate the alcohol distribution in the city, not knowing that the Chicago mob was already involved with some of the shipping and distribution. They also knew Capone's reputation as a killer and asked him if he might approve the killing of rivals and bootleggers who wouldn't do what he wanted. "I'm a businessman, and getting people murdered is not good business," he explained.

Capone also answered the question of whether or not he was going to be the next big distributor of Los Angeles booze. "Let me tell the good citizens of Los Angeles this. They should get their own booze."

The meeting was friendly, the Hollywood reporters understanding why the Chicago press enjoyed seeking out Capone for his wisdom and wit. However, a second meeting with a different group of citizens followed. These were the detectives sent by the top law-enforcement and business leaders who truly controlled all organized illegal activity that the movie colony either approved or ignored. The leadership, known as the Committee, was already more entrenched in Los Angeles in 1927 than any of the organized-crime leaders in New York or Chicago. They were just more subtle, ruining lives instead of taking them.

The movie colony was coming together both in studio ownership and in the handling of off-hours recreation. The pharmacies sold so many prescription alcoholic beverages—gin, champagne, and anything else desired—that they were little more than legal speakeasies. Film companies provided "starlets" to visiting dignitaries and investors who wanted a "date" for the evening. Other "starlets," some of them actually working in the film industry, albeit as extras or in jobs behind the scenes, were "rentable" by the hour, the day, or the night. Stores and restaurants might have slot machines, high-stakes card games, and other gambling in their back rooms.

The politicians who ran Los Angeles in the mid-1920s were either corrupt or too weak to be effective. Residents of the area joked about such individuals as Mayor George Cryer and police officer Guy "Whistler" McAfee.

McAfee was on the vice squad but earned the bulk of his money from payments provided by the various gambling joints. The officer was so nicknamed because, whenever a raid was planned against a location paying protection, he would call the owner and whistle "Listen to the Mocking Bird." Sometimes all evidence would disappear. Sometimes some of the gambling equipment would be left behind so that no one would know about the tip-off, but any prominent citizen enjoying a dishonest night on the town would be hustled out the back before the police arrived. Those who refused to pay were regularly surprised by raids that either put them out of business or taught them to start giving cash-stuffed envelopes to "Whistler" McAfee.

Mayor Cryer had no interest in power. He took whatever payoffs were offered, letting people run whatever "entertainment services" they desired. The idea that an outsider like Al Capone might be coming to the city to take over the rackets was repugnant to him. Even when he was put out of office by "reformer" Frank Shaw, the new Los Angeles mayor simply wanted to better structure crime and payoffs. But that election would not come until after the wake-up call about outsider intentions had been sounded by the discovery of "Al Brown" at the Biltmore.

There are several stories about what happened when the detectives arrived at the Biltmore. In one, Capone gave them coffee and explained that he knew the concerns of the men they represented and had no intention of staying past the next day. He had heard so much about California, he thought he would see it for himself.

In another, this one witnessed by reporters, Capone was told to move by the Biltmore Hotel manager. "We're tourists. I thought you people liked tourists. We have a lot of money to spend that I made in Chicago. Whoever heard of anybody being run out of Los Angeles that had money."

The police chief came by the hotel and explained that he had twelve hours to leave the city. Capone, his family, and his bodyguards all departed.

The visit by Capone was a wake-up call to the moguls. By the time Capone was in jail for income-tax violation and Prohibition was coming to an end, the film industry was backing Frank L. Shaw as a reform candidate for mayor.

Frank Shaw was shocked by the ubiquitous, disorganized violations of city, state, and federal laws, and he ran for office vowing to reform recreation-related criminal activity. This he did, cracking down on nickel-and-dime, mom-and-pop vice activities. No longer could you find punch boards in small grocery stores, gambling in the back room of a neighborhood restaurant, or young women renting rooms by the hour as they trolled the streets alone. Only more professional activities were to be allowed, and all of them were to be under Mayor Shaw's personal control.

Within months, Mayor Shaw had reformed the vice into a manageable regional business of twenty-three thousand slot machines, six hundred houses of prostitution, eighteen hundred bookie joints, and three hundred casino-type gambling facilities. Joseph Shaw, the mayor's brother and personal secretary, kept track of the locations, visiting most on a regular basis in order to pick up from each the envelope of cash required by the mayor. Those who didn't pay were confronted by Police Chief James E. Davis and his "gang" of uniformed patrol officers. Each was seemingly handpicked for his ability to stand up to bribery efforts by grasping the proffered cash and saying, "Thank you." This meant that any mob effort to move on Hollywood and the environs would meet a better armed, better trained "gang" with the power to arrest.

The studio heads had the power and the influence to combat Frank Shaw if they chose to do so. However, Shaw and Davis, working with the district attorney and the coroner's office, developed an unspoken arrangement to keep the industry as scandal free as possible. The Hollywood studios' publicity departments would put the "spin" on the activities of the stars they were either promoting to the public or trying to maintain as box-office stars, and the coroner and police would create the evidence to support it. No one mentioned that a "virgin" movie star playing virtuous heroines had given venereal disease to every male working on the set of her latest picture. Nonlethal drug overdoses were called illnesses like influenza. Lethal drug overdoses were termed death by natural causes or as the result of an unusually difficult illness. A generation earlier, the flu pandemic had killed millions, so it was not hard for movie fans to accept the idea that even a star could die tragically at a young age from one virus or another.

Even when a scandal occurred that could not be covered up, the story was changed to protect the false image previously created. But Al Capone, curious about the Kennedy deal, was there at the start, and he just didn't get it.

Rosselli Down to the Wire

Johnny Rosselli was making a move that would have important repercussions for the Capone gang, though not until after Al had gone to jail. Moses Annenberg was making a fortune on racing wires and wanted the Outfit to help take control of the Los Angeles area.

Annenberg's history was a colorful one in the style of William Randolph Hearst, had Hearst been an amoral thug. Annenberg first worked in circulation for the *Chicago Tribune* at a time when running circulation meant training young thugs to commit whatever crimes were necessary to take control of lucrative street corners and vendor stands. Beatings, shootings, and arson helped establish new territory for selling newspapers, and so successful was Annenberg as an organizer and leader that Hearst hired him to do the same job for his papers, the *Examiner* and the *American*. Success came by training such youth as Charles Dion O'Bannion and George "Bugs" Moran, whose criminal exploits would dominate newspaper headlines.

Johnny Torrio, the same man who gave Capone his Chicago start, provided Annenberg with the money to buy the *Daily Racing Form*, a newspaper providing tips on forthcoming horse races. Annenberg left Hearst, eventually adding such publications as *Screen Guide*, *Radio Guide*, the *Philadelphia Inquirer*, and the *New York Morning Telegraph* to his growing empire.

Of special interest to Rosselli and the Outfit was the creation of the Nationwide News Service officially in partnership with Frank Erickson, a gambling specialist for organized crime, who was actually a close associate of the New York mob leaders Luciano, Lansky, and Costello. In 1929, Annenberg began working with Al Capone, a longtime friend despite Moses's friendship with Luciano. They established a nationwide racing wire, where fees were paid by bookies to get the results of races.

Annenberg gave Nitti and the other leaders of Capone's gang $100,000 to help him take control of the wire service results for all Los Angeles bookmakers, gambling dens, and other locations that wanted the information. They, in turn, contacted Johnny Rosselli, their man in Hollywood, who bribed city officials and persuaded bookmakers to subscribe.

Rosselli was also given a new man to work with in Los Angeles. Tony the Hat was not going to stay in control for long. He was the flamboyant front man, but Charles Fischetti, Capone's cousin, wanted to move faster than Cornero could handle. He asked Jack Dragna to move from Chicago to Los Angeles to work with Rosselli to take control of offshore gambling.

Dragna, also known as Jack Dragna, Jack Ignatius Dragna, Jack Rizoto, and Jack Dania, was an interesting choice. He was an illegal alien, never having applied for U.S. citizenship after arriving from Corleone, Sicily, with his family in 1898. The family returned to Sicily a decade later when Jack was eighteen, then returned in 1914, at which time Dragna settled in Los Angeles. A year later, he was convicted of extortion in Long Beach, serving a three-year sentence in San Quentin. Although he was wanted as an illegal and for tax evasion and robbery and was convicted of murder in New York, he never served further time in jail.

Jack Dragna had a dual reputation. He was considered a ruthless bungler in his handling of the extortion rackets that interested both Nitti, acting for the Chicago Outfit, and Luciano, acting for the East. He was more likely to murder an uncooperative restaurant owner than to take the time to reduce his business until he yielded to the extortion. He killed drug dealers whose connections he might otherwise have utilized. He killed brothel owners. He created an atmosphere where even the most corrupt government officials might have to break their agreements and start investigating crimes.

At the same time, Dragna was considered an honest man when it came to all the players. He had worked with Luciano and Meyer Lansky. He had worked with Johnny Rosselli and Tony Cornero. He was trusted to act in the interest of all the players and not just the old Capone group or Luciano and his associates.

Dragna and Rosselli were told to focus much of their time on offshore gambling. The mob understood nightclubs. They understood how to get the suckers buying alcohol and women and gambling whatever money they brought with them. And they understood that there were some crimes that, handled correctly, would not result in prosecution.

The exact nature of the money involved was revealed almost twenty years later when the U.S. Senate Special Committee to Investigate Organized Crime (IOC) in Interstate Commerce questioned not only Rosselli but also others involved. In the stories found in volume 5 of the proceedings, such men as California attorney general Warren Olney III explain the huge sums of cash. He mentioned that one bank in Santa Monica had been the depository for funds for one of the gambling-ship operators for several months when the manager could handle no more. As Olney explained, "The bank wrote them a letter and told them that they would close out his account unless they had a truck to handle the money. So he bought a truck."

The money led to conflict in much the way it had during Prohibition. Following Tony the Hat's concept, the schooner *Monfalcone* was targeted by Rosselli and Dragna. It was actually the centerpiece of a quiet war between the local criminal groups known as the syndicate and the Italian mobsters aligned with Chicago. Each wanted to control the money to be made on the gambling ships, and the *Monfalcone*, anchored three miles off Long Beach, was to be the focal point for the initial war for control of such vessels. It was just far enough off the coast that all activities on the boat were legal, even if they were in violation of U.S. law. However, it was not protected from attack.

The *Monfalcone*, a gambling vessel owned by members of the same syndicate that was trying to run local gambling in Los Angeles, was boarded by Rosselli one night in December 1928. It was the same month and year that Charles Luciano was working to organize the drivers of bootleg whiskey during a summit meeting of criminals in Cleveland's Statler Hotel.

The *Monfalcone*, though nondescript on the outside, was 282 feet of nightclub and gambling activity. You could dine and dance to the music of a seven-piece orchestra. The gambling parlor, richly carpeted and furnished like a luxury international casino, had everything from craps, chuck-a-luck, cards, and roulette to a horse book. The latter was of special interest to many in the movie industry who enjoyed horse racing and knew that with the right mob connections, "suggestions" would be made concerning how to bet. Those suggestions were invariably winners.

Rosselli explained that he and Dragna, in effect the Chicago Outfit, were going to be partners in the *Monfalcone*, sharing the profits with syndicate members, including Tutor Sherer, Rasmus "Razz" Pendleton, and "Doc" Dougherty. The "partnership" lasted only a short time before Dragna, Rosselli, and the men they could get to agree to stay with them, such as "Doc" Dougherty, took forcible control in May 1930. Sherer also sided with the Italians but was not involved with the briefly violent shoot-out that led to the takeover of the boat.

The *Monfalcone* caught fire in August 1930 but was soon replaced by the *Rose Isle*, a 336-foot Navy steamer built in 1889, retired from use, and converted in the spring of 1931. The *Rose Isle* was not alone by then, though, for others had entered the business with boats, such as Tony Cornero with the *Monte Carlo*, a boat he obtained after his release from jail, and former police officer Guy McAfee and Farmer Page with *Johanna Smith*. The ships, lined up outside the three-mile limit like a floating version of such future meccas as Monte Carlo and Las Vegas, competed for huge sums of money at a time when Los Angeles was in financial crisis and only the mob and the moguls had serious money.

Hollywood, even during the Great Depression, had an aura of glamour to everyone except the average working man and woman living in Hollywood. Bread lines and soup kitchens could be found in neighborhoods that had once seemed immune to such need. In a city with almost seven hundred thousand men and women capable of working a full day, more than three hundred thousand were unemployed. There was also a lack of industry diversity. Motion pictures, oil, and agriculture were still the primary sources of employment. Manufacturing was a key to survival in other major cities but was almost nonexistent in southern California.

Mayor John Porter, Police Chief Roy "Strongarm Dick" Steckel, and Harry Chandler, publisher of the *Los Angeles Times*, worked together to keep the downtown area looking "nice." Mexicans who had been living and often working in Los Angeles were rounded up throughout the 1930s and taken back across the border, ridding the city of an estimated two hundred thousand or more people. Vagrants were also arrested, with fifteen thousand going to jail in 1932 and similar numbers incarcerated in other years. They were moved through the jails and out of the city. The idea was to ship the problem of unemployment and the negative image of people living on the streets to other regions in California and neighboring Arizona.

Poverty and unemployment intensified the competition for gambling dominance between the New York and Chicago criminals. Games of chance offered some people their only hope for a better tomorrow. So long as the options ranged from games anyone with a few cents could play, such as nickel bingo, to truly high-stakes gambling for the moguls and the handful of wealthy actors, everyone was happy.

The Second Remake of John Rosselli

Just as Filippo Sacco had become Johnny Rosselli, a part-time actor and rising associate of the Chicago Outfit, so Johnny Rosselli remade his image into that of a successful bon vivant. He recognized that he was a stereotype in Hollywood with his Italian accent and background as a street tough. Through observation, practice, and reliance on custom tailors, he learned to speak accentless English and began wearing the highest quality suits popular among top executives in corporations throughout the country. His style was that of someone born to money, education, and the expectation that all doors would always be open to him.

Rosselli's access to the moguls and the stars was critical with the motion picture business in crisis and the theaters showing films to audiences enduring hard times. Two years before the stock market crash, the motion picture business, including all property owned, income from films, distribution companies, production companies, and all related businesses, was the fourth largest industry in the country. It was valued at $1.5 billion before sound was even introduced. "Talkies" brought a million people a week to an estimated twenty thousand U.S. theaters.

Theoretically, everything changed with the Great Depression. Certainly, work hours were reduced, services were consolidated, and other measures affected the lowest-paid studio employees and actors, though rarely anyone at the top. The moguls and the highest paid actors enjoyed drugs, gambling, and women just as they had before the Depression, and the increasingly suave sophisticate acting as their guide was the Chicago Outfit's Johnny Rosselli. His relationships included Joe Kennedy during his time with RKO and FBO and Joe Schenck and Harry Cohn of United Artists and Columbia Pictures, respectively.

Rosselli's service came with a price that none of the studio heads expected. He was quietly gathering information about their habits to use against them. The moguls trusted him with their money, and they trusted him when they talked about their industry. He attended their parties, witnessed their affairs, and came to know many of their dirty little secrets. Information was power, even if it never had to be revealed, and Rosselli acquired whatever he could on behalf of the Outfit.

It was Rosselli who first learned that the studio bosses were working to prevent unions from changing pay scales and work arrangements, information IATSE and the American Federation of Labor valued highly. He also worked to keep studio heads in the dark about his connections with the union activity that was seeking payoffs from many of the same moguls. However, Rosselli first worked to keep the studio heads thinking he was somehow one of them.

One incident occurred on July 24, 1933, a few weeks before the IATSE convention where George Browne would be running for president. The reason for the timing is uncertain, though it is possible that the union wanted to show management its power. The grievances were valid, regardless of the timing.

In the last weeks of 1932, the Depression was severely affecting box-office takes around the country. Production continued, but there was no margin for error when it came to costing and returns, as Fox, Paramount, RKO, and Universal had learned when they all went into receivership after losing millions of dollars in pictures that did not do as well as anticipated. Much of the problem, perhaps all of it, could have been resolved by the studio heads' slashing their own salaries. Instead, they slashed the wages of their support staff—electricians, carpenters, designers, and so forth—by 50 percent. At the same time, a study of the larger industries in the United States found that the twenty-five highest paid executives were all motion picture executives. The statistic shocked President Franklin Roosevelt, who called the maintenance of executive salaries at the expense of the workers "unconscionable." It also motivated the various guilds to start organizing unions aggressively.

Actors, including top stars, and writers had long been a part of the Academy of Motion Picture Arts and Sciences, an organization dominated by the producers. Everyone was getting ready to walk off their jobs, and Nick Schenck asked Pat Casey, the former security head for the Schenck theaters, to handle "negotiations." The workers were in no mood for bargaining, and on July 24, 1933, the union struck. The producers told Casey they had no interest in negotiations. The only answer, in Casey's mind, was to call in Rosselli.

The moguls understood that Rosselli was "connected" in Chicago and were delighted when he brought in outside muscle to act as strikebreakers. Scab workers were hired by the moguls, and Rosselli's strikebreakers smashed the heads of any striker who tried to stop the men from passing through the line. The violence was so brutal—the police looked the other way because they had been bought off far earlier—that IATSE members gave up in a week. The producers declared victory, ended a previous contract arrangement with most of the guilds that provided what amounted to a minimum wage for different positions, and forced an open shop. They would be able to hire anyone they desired as opposed to just union members.

The Association of Motion Picture Producers was so pleased with Rosselli that they placed him on their board. The moguls might have taken a closer look at Rosselli's history first, but the producers had a love/hate relationship with the mob. They were mostly high-stakes gamblers, which was almost the nature of the job since millions would be spent on each film before anyone knew if the public would want to see it. They also were enamored with the glamour of organized crime, even as they were its targets. They had seen the brutality Rosselli could bring to his actions, but since he arranged for thugs to stop the union from shutting down the industry, they felt it was "good" violence. They never thought he might have done the same for the other side had they hired him.

The end result was that Rosselli suddenly had influence on both sides of the labor disputes, as well as inside information about everything that was happening. The Outfit under Nitti was about to take over IATSE, and Rosselli had become a conduit of information for the other side. It was an insider takeover no one had expected.

CHAPTER Ten

Bioff and Browne

Nine-year-old Willie Bioff was living proof that bribery and success in Prohibition-era business did not have to go hand in hand. Sure, law enforcement in Chicago was routinely conducted with a wink, a nod, and an envelope filled with cash. Young men entering business were taught the etiquette of the payoff, learning who mattered, who didn't, and what each individual cost. Profits were figured based on the amount of money set aside for corruption as a known percentage of overhead. But Willie, a kid on the South Side, taught a better way by example.

The truth about street kids like Willie, whether in the 1920s, in contemporary society, or probably back in ancient times, is that they know everybody. A kid is invisible, able to go anywhere, look at anything, and talk to anyone. The kids know the undercover cops, the husbands and wives who are having affairs, the dishonest butchers, the restaurants with back rooms for high-stakes card games, and the activities that fill in each twenty-four-hour day in their neighborhoods. That was why Willie was hired by several South Side Chicago whorehouses whose owners understood that you could run a dishonest business without having to corrupt a cop.

Willie was hired as a commissioned salesman. He knew who was straight, who was a cop, who was a reformer trying to save the neighborhood from itself. He was too young to have reached puberty, too young to appreciate the urges that drove a man to pay for sex, too young to understand what sex might mean. He did know the people of the neighborhood and which young men had the money and the inclination to pursue the pleasures of the flesh. That was why the whorehouse owners had him spend as much daytime as possible approaching men to tell them that his mother was not at home for the afternoon and his sister was awfully cute. The interested ones understood what the kid was saying, and those who weren't interested didn't give a damn that a nine-year-old was pimping a member of his family.

Not that Willie had a sister to pimp. Instead, he would direct the men to one or another whorehouse, each situated down an alley or otherwise out of the mainstream retail district where merchants or their customers might complain. The man would knock, the madam would answer, and a fine array of far-too-experienced women would offer to relieve his sensual tension. He would pay, and Willie would at least get a commission; if the prostitute was unusually good in the customer's eyes, and if Willie was still hanging around, the kid might get a tip as well.*

Willie got older and wiser. He had seen the economics of using kids instead of bribes to keep the brothels both hassle free and bustling with customers. He also began to do the numbers. A man who owned a whorehouse did not have to work as hard as a kid hustling the action. He took a cut from each woman who worked for him. He provided a place for them to work. And he paid a small fee to the cop who had the beat in and around the place. He did not have to stay on the premises. He did not have to see the customers. He made excellent money with very little effort and was free to open other locations or engage in other activities.

Bioff opened his first whorehouse about the same time as he got married, wisely selecting a woman who shared his business sense, his dreams of success, and his amorality. The two of them recognized that most women, given a choice of professions, would not choose to have sex several times a day with a variety of strangers. There was nothing romantic about being a whore. Beatings and participating in what might be deviant behavior were all a part of the job. That was why pros-

---

*There are stories, possibly true, possibly apocryphal, of a ten-year-old Willie convincing little girls to let older boys "play" with them for a dime apiece. According to these stories, girls who agreed, then refused when they realized what the boys wanted, were threatened with acid in the face. It is certain that the acid threat was used on the young women working in houses of prostitution.

titutes grew old before their time and many became alcoholics and drug addicts as they numbed themselves to the horrors of their daily lives.

City girls knew the dangers of prostitution and the men who ran the businesses. They avoided the job offers that came their way. They knew the places where the men came and went on a regular basis, but the women seldom appeared on the streets. The term *white slavery* was not an exaggeration.

Willie and his wife recruited girls who were young, naive, and eager for an adventure. They went to the farm communities and told the girls about the good life in the big city: no chores lasting from early morning until late at night, no isolation from the neighbors, no lack of eligible upper-income men who would be interested in them. Then, they paid all their moving expenses, taking them to the brothel and locking them inside.

The Bioffs were by no means unusual in keeping the girls prisoner. A young woman could be made to cooperate in any number of ways. Sometimes, the brothel owner "seduced," or raped, the women himself, then gave them to favored customers. Sometimes, the owners used sadistic young thugs who enjoyed being given the right to do whatever they wanted with a woman so long as they left no permanent marks or serious injuries. There were also customers who delighted in paying extra to be the first to have one of the new "recruits," and the brothel owner would oblige, even if that meant tying the girl to a bed, then locking the door to her room after the customer was inside.

Bioff would not betray his marriage vows by having sex with the women who worked for him. He only handled discipline, and that could range from deliberately causing a woman excruciating pain to threatening to throw acid on her face. Given his size—approximately 5 feet, 6 inches tall, at least two hundred pounds, with a chest that looked like a commercial freezer on which a head without a neck had been glued—his angry appearance in a girl's room was usually enough to get her to cooperate. However, in one instance, he beat a prostitute who was not cooperating, and she managed to escape and somehow reached police officers who either had not been bribed or felt their share should have been greater than it was. Willie was arrested, convicted of assault and battery, and sentenced to six months in jail. He served twenty-four hours of his sentence, then was released and returned to his business.

It was the stock market crash that finally put Willie and his wife out of the prostitution racket. Sex by the hour was like a contemporary expense-account lunch—a luxury to be enjoyed in good times and one of the first pleasures to be abandoned with a downturn in the economy. Fortunately, Willie had been engaged in other activities.

The teamsters union liked Willie Bioff because he made a good "slugger," or part-time provider of muscle wherever it was needed. During a strike, the sluggers would stand with clubs and slug anyone who tried to cross the picket line to go to work. They would also smash management's cars and trucks. It went unsaid that the sluggers were paid by the hour to work for whichever side hired them. Payoffs by management could result in teamster union leaders' ordering workers back on the job, even when they wanted to strike. The sluggers smashed the heads of workers not willing to go along with what their business agent ordered.

The sluggers also handled men who did not wish to be in the union or who balked at the kickbacks expected of them. After a broken collarbone, shoulder, arm, or leg, the worker was usually more than willing to join.

Willie had a third scam that targeted the Jewish meat-store owners along Fulton Street. Bioff himself was Jewish, or at least he claimed to be. That was why he targeted the Jewish men who sold fish, beef, poultry, and similar foods in bulk. Their customers were mostly restaurants and other commercial buyers, though they sold to anyone who wanted to buy in bulk. They were also more likely to trust others who at least shared their religion, and they were less likely to alert the authorities for the same reason.

Bioff entered the stores impeccably dressed. He was a thug on the picket lines, but he thought extortion was best handled by a man of sartorial elegance, at least to the degree that was possible for someone so obese. Once inside, he told the store owners that the Jews had suffered discrimination in Europe. They had found new freedom in New York, and he, as a streetwise Jewish kid who understood the potential for violence against their shops, was willing to provide protection. For a few dollars a week, no one would firebomb their businesses. No one would attack their employees. Nothing would happen to their families. Such protection was the least a Jewish boy could offer those who had experienced the same anti-Semitism he had.

The truth was quite different. Willie could protect against arson because Willie would be the arsonist if payment wasn't made. Willie could protect the stores from having their windows smashed and their meat tossed where it could not be resold because the only person who would commit such vandalism was Willie. And Willie could assure the store owners that neither employees nor family members would be hurt because the only person contemplating such an assault was Willie.

The extortion scam worked, in large measure because Bioff was not greedy. The police were corrupted, but as he had learned when his prostitute spoke out against his violence, there were always those with a sense of moral outrage, whether or not they had accepted envelopes of cash. He was also a small businessman himself, the brothels requiring sound business judgment in order to be profitable. Thus, he never charged the business owners enough to hurt them financially. They could continue living much as they had been, the weekly payoff never seriously endangering their livelihoods.

Julius Caesar Stein

If Willie Bioff looked like a slab of beef on which two legs, two arms, and a head had been cemented, Julius Caesar Stein looked like he had once been the schoolboy with the perpetually running nose, the over-protective mother, and more books in his arms each day than some of his classmates would read in a year. His father ran a general store, and his mother was an invalid with pretensions, saving what little money was not needed for necessities to buy Julius a mandolin, the possession of which made him even more of an outcast in school.

There was toughness to Stein that belied his physical appearance. He learned to play the mandolin, but more importantly, he studied music so that he was able to pay his way through a prep school he began attending in 1908 when he was twelve years old. He boarded at the school, and two years later, he was leading his own orchestra. In addition to the mandolin, he mastered the violin and the saxophone, then began playing in both dance bands and pit bands for vaudeville, as well as booking bands.

Stein was also a brilliant student who graduated from the University of West Virginia at eighteen, then put himself through the University of Chicago Medical School, where he expected to become an ophthalmologist. He was a medical officer for the Army Reserve during World War I, then went to Vienna to further his studies.

Music had paid for Stein's studies and continued to do so as he added training in business. But he convinced himself he would be a doctor, taking a residency at Cook County Hospital before meeting pianist Billy Goodheart, a friend of one of the hospital staff. Together they formed Kenilworth Music, a booking agency whose primary clients were the Capone clubs.

Dr. Julius Caesar Stein quit his medical practice to go full time with his partner. The year was 1924, and the two men had a total of $1,000 with which to rent a two-room office, put in telephones, and begin booking bands under the name Music Corporation of America (MCA).

Stein, by then calling himself Jules, developed a business plan for the bands that assured him and his partner more money. He demanded an exclusive contract with each of the bands and independent bandleaders he represented, taking 10 percent of the gross paid to them as the agency's share. Then, he told the club owners he did not want to book a single band for weeks or months at a time, the typical arrangement of the day. House bands had their fans, but Stein felt that the clubs would do more business by rotating groups, moving the bands from club to club.

Finally, Stein took the last step in building the strongest booking agency in the city. Dance halls working with an MCA band or bandleader had to sign a contract agreeing to only use MCA bands. Jules wanted exclusive arrangements with everyone in order to maximize his income, and he increased MCA's business by adding such perquisites for clients and club owners as discounts on automobile purchases and insurance.

The one-stop-shop perquisites were meant to defuse some of the hostility being generated by the clubs since they served as bonuses that appealed to some of the people with whom the agency had to negotiate. When they were not enough, MCA hired staff members to look after every aspect of caring for the bands, soloists, and others traveling on the road. Name bands had their own buses. Lesser bands used rentals arranged by MCA. Everyone had lodging and food arranged in advance. All the band members had to do was show up, an arrangement so comfortable (despite the travel, which was a new experience for most of the musicians) that big-name bands began seeking MCA's representation.

In the midst of this success, Jules Stein and Willie Bioff began working together. Club owners recognized a problem with MCA long before the musicians did. MCA was slowly squeezing out all of the competition, so it could name its price, name its services, and deny a club the entertainers that would pack the house. The club owners were increasingly unable to use outside groups, especially the better-drawing "names" represented by other agencies. They would soon face the choice of committing to the MCA roster or watching their income dry up. Before the situation became that critical, a number of clubs in key locations refused to go along.

Jules Stein was furious. He was also connected, a fact that has rarely been discussed.

Stein and the men who worked for him made deals with the Chicago mob. They had to do so. The mob owned the clubs, especially on Chicago's South Side, Capone territory and a major entertainment district.

There are many stories about Stein during this period, some of them true. Allegedly, he decided that if he was already supplying entertainers to a club, there was no reason he shouldn't supply bootleg whisky as well. This scenario has him being threatened with violence and the kidnapping of family members.

It is most likely that if Stein did try a little bootlegging, it was with clubs he thought were not regularly being supplied by the Capone people, perhaps those in territory controlled by Capone rival Roger Touhy, though it makes no sense to think that any major city bootlegger's territory would be seriously targeted by someone who knew the business and wasn't equipped for a war.

Probably Stein simply cut a deal with Capone and possibly a separate deal with Touhy. He knew the booking business. He knew the bands. He knew what the clubs needed and how to plan a rotation for music the way Torrio, Capone, and Luciano learned to rotate the prostitutes among the brothels they controlled. It was more profitable to have Stein give a piece of the action to the Capone people than to force him out of business.

B&B

The Jules Stein/Willie Bioff connection is uncertain. The Great Depression drove Bioff from the business of prostitution. The big spenders no longer had money, and the women, faced with declining business, stopped bothering with pimps and brothels, reducing their prices to whatever the market could bear.

Bioff not only began looking for other scams, but he wanted to keep his employees working. One way seemed to be the hiring out of Fred "Bugs" Blacker, who was a specialist in an unusual form of extortion. He would infest an uncooperative business with bedbugs, and if the bugs didn't disrupt the business quickly enough, he would throw stink bombs.

Jules Stein had Bugs Blacker do his work in the various nightspots that refused to sign an exclusive contract with MCA. Chicago had been a violent town during Prohibition, but everyone knew the violence was among the bootleggers and the feds. The average citizen was never going to see a shooting or feel him- or herself in danger. But if someone knew that a stink bomb had been released in a nightspot that had not signed an agreement with MCA, he or she was not likely to go there for an evening's entertainment. There might be a non MCA act a couple was anxious to see, but stink bombs and bed bugs were far more threatening than bullets. The risk was not worth the effort when there were so many other clubs and so many other acts to see in Chicago.

Willie Bioff and George Browne (B&B) also worked a different show business scam. Strip clubs were becoming extremely popular. Some of the girls were paid. Some of the girls worked for tips. Some were dancers and showgirls; others were prostitutes who took whatever they could while on the stage but made the most money for assignations in the club or their homes.

The strip-club owners cared only that competition was kept down. Men liked coming to a local club, and the fewer clubs there were in a neighborhood, the better their business. The Depression was causing some theaters to look for other sources of revenue, and a strip club was cheap to open.

Browne and Bioff went from club to club, asking the owners to pay for protection against competition. The deal was that whenever a movie house was going to increase its profits by converting to a strip joint or adding a strip show, they would order the stagehands to have nothing to do with the club. No stagehands, no competition.

The scam was effective because none of the club owners knew for certain when competition was coming. They had to take the word of Bioff and Browne since they were connected with the union. Thus, any time the two men wanted more money, they would cry "strip club conversion coming," and the owners of the existing clubs would pay off.

The Outfit paid little attention to Jules Stein's work, whatever it may have been with Bioff, and the protection racket with the strip-club owners. However, when Bioff became part of Browne's union, and the two were able to raise dues 1 percent a week in order to finance their personal activities, some of the Capone people began watching them. The fact that they had run similar extortion rackets when they met, the impeccably dressed Browne shaking down the gentile store owners while Bioff shook down the Jews across the street, was an odd coincidence.

Browne was also the gentler, more scholarly of the two as his thick glasses indicated. Bioff's education had stopped with his learning to read and write. Browne, by contrast, was the intellectual, a man who prided himself on almost completing the fifth grade.

George Browne was likeable; Bioff was not. Browne was a business agent for the Chicago Stagehands Local No. 2. The union was a part of IATSE in its newly expanded domination of most of the cities in the country. He apparently won election to his position legitimately, but he had the good sense not to argue when Frank Nitti recruited him as part of the Capone mob's plan to go after Hollywood.

Browne, like the mob, had watched Tommy Maloy milk the projectionists union and the theater owners. He learned that Balaban and Katz had been paying Maloy and decided to shake down Barney Balaban while he was temporarily in the hospital. He knew that Barney would be tired and would not have his partners around to interfere.

Barney Balaban, his brother, Abe, and his friend, pianist Sam Katz, began buying nickelodeons in 1916. In 1917, they had the first theater chain in the country to offer air conditioning in the summer, adding to the popularity of their growing chain.

Balaban and Katz were ahead of other theater owners in adapting to the film industry. They started when movies were silent and a part of a full vaudeville show, not the sole reason for going to the theater. Talking pictures changed everything. A combination of movie and entertainment was still popular, as New York's Paramount Theater proved when it offered a feature, a comic, a big band singer, and other entertainment on a schedule as often as eight times a day. However, for men who were interested in making the most money possible, eliminating all stage shows was the way to go. People would come for a talking

picture and go home happy after seeing it. Eliminating the live performers meant that stagehands were no longer needed to move the scenery, lighting technicians did not have to place and work the spots, and
orchestras did not have to be hired. The concept wouldn't work everywhere, but certainly the theaters could survive with far fewer employees.

Barney Balaban, who was the primary negotiator with the union,
was concerned about the workers. He wanted to cut their pay by as
much as one-fifth in order to retain as many people as possible. George
Browne, upon coming to see him, told the sad story that with the Depression affecting the rank and file, the 20 percent cut was not acceptable, even though it helped retain employees. He felt that the
stagehands needed an immediate 25 percent raise so they could feed
their families.

Barney Balaban might have been moved had he not recognized an
extortion attempt when he heard one. He admitted that he was paying
Maloy $150 a week to avoid trouble with the projectionists. He would
pay Browne and Bioff the same amount to avoid problems with the
stagehands.

Browne felt certain that the owner of the region's largest theater
chain could easily afford more. The year was 1933. Browne wanted Balaban to pay retroactively for the pay cuts Barney had had to institute
when attendance dropped. The price was $20,000, which was actually
within reason for what Balaban and Katz could afford. Barney agreed
but only on the condition that Browne worked out a payment arrangement that would hide the bribe from the stockholders. It was cheaper
to pay than to have stink bombs go off in every theater he owned, but
his was a public company, and he needed to keep others from knowing
or they would want him to pay out of his own pocket.

Bioff and Browne, having watched the success of Al Capone's soup
kitchens, had opened a soup kitchen for both unemployed stagehands,
who ate for free, and employed ones, who were charged 35 cents a meal.
The food was obtained for free by stealing truckloads as needed. Politicians often donated money as a bribe to ensure that Browne had his
members and their families vote for the men who supported them.
However, when Balaban needed a way to hide his donation, Browne decided to turn the soup kitchen into a laundry for shakedowns.

The soup kitchen arrangement benefited everyone. There were two
rooms carefully separated from one another. One had soup and bread.
The other, in which politicians, judges, high-ranking law-enforcement

officers, and anyone else willing to be corrupted would gather, had a more extravagant menu, from broiled double lamb and pork chops to roast duck with orange glaze, prime roast beef, and other expensive food. No one dared investigate B&B's activities because those who were in a position to conduct such investigations were already corrupted by the men. These same officials also knew that their presence had been witnessed by too many to deny what was taking place if they were ever exposed. More importantly, the politicians were of the "vote early and vote often" persuasion on election day, and it was the multiple voting of the men they met in the soup kitchens, along with their family members, that could keep them in office.

Willie Bioff was crude in his attitude toward what was taking place. He welcomed the dignitaries with smiles and a palm out for checks, but he was later quoted as saying, "I never saw a whore who wasn't hungry, and I never saw a politician who wasn't a whore."

It was also Bioff who, years later, when giving testimony at his criminal trial, would explain the thinking about the Balaban shakedown. He said that with the $20,000, "the restoration of the pay cut was forgotten. We were not interested in that then or at any other time. We didn't care whether wages were reduced or raised. We were only interested in getting the dough, and we didn't care how we got it."

If anyone thought that the union members mattered to either business or labor, that belief was squelched when payment was arranged. Attorney Leo Spitz, who would later become head of Columbia Pictures, the studio owned by Harry Cohn and partially funded with a loan from New York mobster Abner "Longy" Zwillman, handled the transaction. He provided Bioff and Browne with a $20,000 check and told Balaban he was to continue paying the $150 per week. He also explained privately to Bioff and Browne that they needed to pay him "carrying charges" for handling the money. His fee was $1,000 of the $20,000 they had received. They readily agreed to the deal, pocketing all but $5 of the remainder of the money. The $5 paid for two cases of soup.

Bioff and Browne were almost as foolish as Tommy Maloy. Having pulled off the biggest scam of their lives, they made the biggest mistake of their careers. They went to Chicago's Club 100 and got drunk.

Intermission 1 (and a Brief Clarification)

Our story so far . . . The studio system has evolved as an industry into a high-paid, upscale version of coal-mining towns in West Virginia, Kentucky, and similar regions. Jobs exist because of the studios, and to defy the studio bosses is to be exiled in a city where all other work is secondary to the needs of the production companies. There is no company-store equivalent, no place where credit is given so freely and in such excess of earnings that the miners face a lifetime of debt for themselves and their sons. However, in a few years, the three Schwab brothers will open a drugstore where out-of-work actors can get regular meals and access to the telephone, columnist Sid Skolsky has a free office, and the top stars can order a high-priced new car.

The success of Hollywood is determined, in part, by the image the actors and their families maintain in the public eye. Drunkenness, drug addiction, debauchery, and adultery are common, and death by other than natural causes occurs with relative frequency. The actors must be protected from the knowledge of their personal lives becoming public, and toward this end, the working press has been co-opted by the studio system. Reporters are willing to lie and to accept outrageous "family-friendly" explanations for inappropriate and illegal activities if they will be given continued or better access to the stars. Even murder is reported based on the importance of the victim and the killer.

Law enforcement has also been corrupted. The studios have their own law-enforcement personnel whose job it is to make certain that nothing is reported that reflects poorly on the studios or their stars. They also control city and county law enforcement through bribes, celebrity access, and sexual favors so that nothing is a crime until a mogul says it's a crime.

External criminal activity in the movie colony is generally limited to booze and addictive recreational drugs. Prostitution exists, but usually in forms coordinated by the studio heads since beautiful women are perquisites of investing in films, distribution deals, and studios.

Organized crime in Chicago and New York is in relative turmoil. The break between Charlie Luciano and Al Capone leads Capone to follow his mentor, Johnny Torrio, to Chicago, where they work for, then take over, the operation begun by Big Jim Colosimo.

Capone's flamboyance brings him headlines in Los Angeles, which he visits to see what Joe Kennedy, Frank Nitti, and other men he respected were doing. He starts moving into the same style of rackets he had been working in Chicago and is aware that the unions are also ripe for takeover. However, the government wants him for tax evasion, and his time is limited. Instead, he sends his brother Ralph to see what can be put together, leaves Nitti as one of the men in charge of what is becoming known as the Outfit, and begins fighting with lawyers.

Charles Luciano, convinced that he has become the "boss of all bosses" after taking control of the Masseria and Maranzano operations, divides mob activities as he sees fit. Louis "Lepke" Buchalter is given control of the unions in the garment district, as well as any other rackets being run in that business. Dutch Schultz is allowed to continue with bootlegging, avoiding the various taxes through counterfeit labeling of the booze he distributes. Luciano himself keeps the prostitution rackets that he runs from the Waldorf Hotel, where expensive women visit regularly and chauffeurs wait to drive him wherever he wants to go, and he is a regular in nightspots ranging from the Cotton Club to the Paradise and Dave's Blue Room. He is part owner of the Brown Derby in Hollywood as well, ensuring that he will be well treated on both coasts.

As innovative as Luciano may be, as much as he has turned mob activity into carefully planned businesses, he is not as sophisticated as he may think. The Chicago mob is taking control of the entertainment unions on a scale the boss of all bosses had not contemplated. Capone's people are involved with offshore gambling in the Los Angeles/Long Beach area, and Capone's people are going head to head against Luciano's as they all try to take control of the lucrative narcotics trade.

Upset by the lack of control in Los Angeles, Luciano begins making regular trips west. It is because of this that he becomes involved with Thelma Todd, both personally and for business, a situation that will create problems for them both.

And, in other action, the New York hoofer George Raft, friend and associate of Owney Madden, is about to hit the big time with a major supporting actor role in a film that will make Al Capone more famous about the same time that the feds send him to the pen. Johnny Rosselli is hitting his stride as an actor who works in the offshore gambling industry while reporting to the Chicago Outfit. And Bioff and Browne are about to discover that alcohol and secret scams never mix.

Oh, and in Hollywood, Hot Toddy is about to die. Bernice Mannix is about to die. Paul Bern is about to die. And with ever-increasing influence on the part of the studio heads, official reports and clinical reality never quite match up. A movie industry bad guy cannot exist until the moguls say he can, and then only in the ways permitted.

Now, back to our regularly scheduled program . . .

CHAPTER Eleven

The Gangster Played the Actor Playing the Gangster (or Something Like That)

I f there had to be a man who thought he could succeed in two worlds—show business and the mob—it only made sense that he be born and raised in arguably the toughest immigrant neighborhood in the nation. The man was George Raft, and his earliest home was Hell's Kitchen.

The earliest Dutch settlers in New York found an idyllic pastoral area in the location that today covers Eighth Avenue to the Hudson River between Thirty-fourth and Fifty-ninth streets. The freshwater streams, natural vegetation, and colorful flowers led those seventeenth-century immigrants to name the area Bloemendael. By the time of the Civil War, however, the area had radically changed. Tenement houses mingled with slaughterhouses, factories, and warehouses. The stench of blood and smoke was constantly in the air. Disease was rampant, and with three hundred fifty thousand people, mostly from Ireland and Germany, crammed into the small area, the public began calling the location Hell's Kitchen.

Hell's Kitchen was the site of some of the worst antidraft violence of the Civil War, with eight thousand people wounded and as many as twenty thousand slaughtered. Eleventh Avenue became a street of mass graves, the stench of animal death now replaced by the smell of rotting human carcasses. Property losses were estimated at $5 million, and most of the damaged locations had not been fixed when the war ended. Instead, orphaned or abandoned children lived on the streets, forming gangs that often found space in tenements, creating a perverted form of family.

As to the naming of the area, the most enjoyable version, and there are many, goes that Police Officer Dutch Fred and his partner, a rookie being shown the roughest parts of Manhattan, were watching a riot on West Thirty-ninth Street near Tenth Avenue. The rookie allegedly said, "This place is hell itself," and Dutch Fred responded, "Hell's a mild climate. This is Hell's Kitchen."

George Raft was born in a Hell's Kitchen tenement in 1895, and though he had a family, he quickly learned that he either had to fight the kids in the street or be their victim. He proved good enough that he went professional when he turned sixteen, winning his first fight before discovering there were other youths a lot tougher, faster, and more likely to reach the top. He fought seventeen bouts, was knocked out seven times, and never earned more for a fight than the $5 he made after a bout that resulted in a broken nose, black eyes, and an ear torn almost completely off.

Raft switched to pool hustling, a safer sport and one at which he excelled. He went into partnership with Billy Rosenberg, a man who couldn't stop making up songs. Raft admitted he loved to dance, so the two of them broke from their pasts; Rosenberg wrote such hits as "Me and My Shadow" before changing his name to Billy Rose and becoming a noted theatrical producer, and Raft entered—and won—dance contests.

The world of the brilliant male dancer who enters a contest, wows the audience, and wins first prize was not one of instant success. Instead, it made George Raft one of New York's most desirable bachelors—not as a dancer, but as a gigolo who could enthrall on the dance floor, then make more money in a woman's bedroom.

Raft was enjoying himself in one of New York's dance halls when one of the more unusual of the Hell's Kitchen gangsters came into the place. This was Owen "Owney the Killer" Madden, a man who wanted to take control of all U.S. rackets. He was ruthless, having killed at least five men before the age of twenty-three, and an organizer who planned crimes for other gangsters, then took a percentage for his services. The money—$200 a day, seven days a week—enabled Owney, the name by which most people knew him, to live a hedonistic lifestyle of women, dance halls, restaurants, and cabarets. He was also behind every bomb thrown into the stores of uncooperative retailers, every act of reprisal vandalism, and every other crime that kept protection money flowing.

Madden began as a member of Hell's Kitchen's Gopher Gang when he was eleven, and by time he was twenty, he had increased its membership dramatically and started invading other gangs' territories. This led to an assault by the Hudson Dusters, who ambushed him in the Arbor Dance Hall on Fifty-second Street the night of November 6, 1912. There, he was shot multiple times and barely survived.

Owney had several problems, including his ethnic background. As the Mafia took root in New York, he looked to be a part of it but was rejected because he was British, having been born in Liverpool and emigrating to the United States only in 1903 when he was eleven. He had also spent nine years in jail for murder, emerging in 1923 when the New York street gangs, such as the Gophers, were a thing of the past.

Owney adapted to the realities of Prohibition, taking jobs with Dutch Schultz, who ran the numbers racket and was a major bootlegger in New York. He also became a strikebreaker for one of the taxi companies. His violence was of value during Dutch's war against rivals such as Jack "Legs" Diamond, Vincent "Mad Dog" Coll, and others who wanted to control the liquor business.

Not all was violence with Madden. He was a successful ladies man because he was genuinely fun to be around. He opened an office in the Publicity Building on Broadway and Forty-seventh Street, just a ways down from the theater district. Most of the tenants in the building were connected with show business. There were booking agents for vaudeville, entertainment attorneys, actors, dancers, and the like. There were also gangsters working in both worlds, so on any given day, you might encounter a comic, a burlesque star, a serious actress, a songwriter, a dancer, an extortionist, a slugger, a bootlegger, and a columnist, such as Walter Winchell.

Raft was that not unusual street kid from Hell's Kitchen, somebody who had grown up watching the top gangsters become the only men to get ahead in life. They drove big cars. They had expensive clothes. They had good-looking women. Neighbors respected them even if they did not respect their lifestyle. The top street criminals were youths' role models and idols, and Raft, although establishing himself as a dancer, was no different from the other youths who admired the gangsters.

It must also be remembered that at this time Raft was earning more money from prostituting himself (or being prostituted, since club owners liked to be able to assure wealthy female patrons that they could dance with George, then take him home for a few hours of playtime) than from performing on stage. Regardless of his level of self-esteem, being accepted by a guy like Owney Madden felt good.

A professional driver named "Feets" Edson trained George in high-performance driving. He was taught how to outmaneuver anyone trying to attack a car or truck he was driving. He was taught how to use narrow alleys for escape and how to make sudden turns in vans whose tendency to be high profile—to have high sides and a narrow wheel base, thus to go out of control easily—made them difficult to handle. Finally, he was given a gun to carry in case some other gang became violent.

In 1925, when Raft was thirty, Owney bought the Phoenix Brewery on Tenth Avenue. He then began supplying both his own nightclubs, including Harlem's famous Cotton Club, and others on the East Coast. Several thousand gallons of beer were shipped, each container marked "Madden's No. 1." Feets trained Raft to drive one of the trucks, work that would not interfere with his dancing engagements.

One of the last of the big New York clubs in which Raft appeared was the El Fay Club where he worked with a woman dancer, Ruby Keeler, who went on to great success on Broadway. Ruby was fourteen, too young even to be in the club, much less working there, but this was the club owned by Larry Fay, a gangster who worked with Owney Madden, and "Texas" Guinan.

The El Fay Club, like Guinan herself, was flash and fraud mingled with a great show. The truth about Guinan was that she was born Mary Louise Cecilia Guinan in Waco, Texas, attended Catholic schools, and spent World War I in Hollywood, where she appeared in thirty-six movies, most of them two-reeler Westerns. They were all silent, and she received no meaningful acclaim. That was the story of Mary Louise, at least.

Texas Guinan, on the other hand, had a more colorful past of her own creation. No nice Catholic school girl was she. She told reporters that she had lived and worked on a fifty-thousand-acre ranch, breaking wild horses, attended the Hollins Finishing School in Virginia, and then joined a circus. She also said that when war was declared on April 6, 1917, she raced to France to entertain the troops on the stage and in her boudoir so they would have a pleasant diversion before leaving for the battlefield. Since Texas Guinan was not known to be Mary Louise Cecilia Guinan, the fraud was not uncovered.

Guinan's first husband was newspaper cartoonist Jack Moynaham, whom she divorced in 1907 after five years of marriage. She did try her hand at vaudeville, as well as further marriages—to actor David Townsend and journalist Julian Johnson.

Prohibition was the ideal time for Texas. She was in Manhattan, and as the clubs turned into speakeasies, Texas's flamboyant style made her the perfect mistress of ceremonies. Her first job was at the popular Beaux Arts Club; then, she went to the King Cole Room at the Knickerbocker Hotel in the heart of the theater district, a popular place to visit for guests ranging from actors like Rudolph Valentino to the wealthy Vanderbilts.

Larry Fay, another alumnus of Hell's Kitchen, met Texas at the King Cole, and the two liked each other immediately. Fay was a friend and occasional associate of Owney Madden and had grown wealthy from such investments as a cab company. The cab company was also a front for shipping bootleg liquor between Canada and the United States, though Fay was smart enough to make certain the cabs were profitable even when they weren't ferrying booze.

It was Fay who initially opened the El Fay Club, but he quickly brought Texas in for her style and the fact that she could both energize and increase the business. He gave her a cut of the profits and fame, and he let her create a life history that, while outrageous, earned her and the club extensive publicity.

Oddly, the club was not top of the line in many respects. The food and drink were substandard, yet the club's image and the greeting called out by Texas when the floor show started at midnight—"Hello, Suckers"—made it oddly popular. Composer and musician George Gershwin was a regular, as was dancer/actor Fred Astaire. The Vanderbilts went frequently, as did the Astors and other members of the New York elite.

" "

Let's turn this into a whoopee place and have a lot of fun,
And if we sing about you, why, don't get up and run.
We'll sing about the Broadway folks, and anyone you choose.
It'll save you then from buying the Graphic, Mirror and the News.

—Texas Guinan's opening song at the start of her nightly show

, ,

In addition, there were the gangsters who put on their best man-
ners and came from the Lower East Side, Brooklyn, New Jersey, and
elsewhere in the area. Benny Siegel, making a reputation as a fearless
killer, was frequently in the audience.

Guinan recognized that the club's success was its entertainment.
The shows went from midnight to 5 a.m. and were of such a quality
that no one minded the unusually high prices for a speakeasy. It was
true that entertainers—from Raft to some of the chorus girls—could be
rented for after the place closed, but that was for a separate fee.

Fay and Guinan were fair to Raft during this period. He was in
growing demand as a dancer, quite apart from his sexual activities, and
they did not demand that he work with them exclusively. He did what
musicians and others often did when nightclubs flourished in the years
prior to the Great Depression—he worked as many as four clubs a day,
performing in one, leaving after his number was over, and racing to the
next. The result was that George made $5,000 a week "legitimately"
and picked up additional money driving for Owney and Fay and showing wealthy women a good time.

There were numerous arrests—so well known a speakeasy was always targeted—but Fay, Owney, and others around Texas were too well
connected to be troubled by such matters. She was always being bailed
out and going back to work, always delighting reporters with her comments. In reference to the West Thirtieth Street jail were she spent a
night, she commented, "I like your cute little jail, and I don't know
when my jewels have seemed so safe."

And jewels Texas owned. The profits she shared with Fay averaged
$70,000 a month before the club had been open a year. That was also
why every time one of the clubs was padlocked in a show raid, another
club was opened nearby. When Texas and Fay had a falling out over
business in 1925, she opened her own place, the 300 Club. However,
her influence had passed, and though she fought each closure with new

clubs such as the Argonaut, Club Intime, and Salon Royale, the stress of fighting with the authorities took its toll. She was delighted to return to Hollywood for a movie she apparently hoped would reinvigorate her career.

Texas asked George Raft to come to Hollywood to be a part of her perceived comeback. Texas and Larry were shooting their own version of her fabricated life story, *Queen of the Nightclubs*. Raft would play a nightclub dancer—essentially himself—and she would be the star. The movie did poorly, though she was given a second chance, this time playing a nightclub hostess in Walter Winchell's *Through a Keyhole*. It also failed to attract an audience.

The year was 1929, and the nation's life was about to change. Raft's move proved critical for a man on the fringe of criminal life but who wanted a career as a dancer and actor. He decided to stay in Los Angeles, not knowing that he would become the nation's first gangster-actor to play gangsters in the movies. He was about to graduate from small-time hood to big-time star. Ironically, his first major role as the confidant, bodyguard, and ultimate victim in *Scarface* was the last popular entertainment Al Capone would view before going to jail for tax evasion.

CHAPTER Twelve

Lucrezia Borgia Meets Al Capone in a Theater Near You

S*carface* wasn't the first film Hollywood made about Al Capone. *Little Caesar* has that distinction. It was based on the novel by W. R. Burnett written just after the Saint Valentine's Day Massacre in Chicago. That event, on February 14, 1929, was the culmination of a war between Capone and the North Side gang of George "Bugs" Moran. Capone's men disguised themselves as police detectives making a routine raid on Moran's headquarters. Frank Nitti had had Abe Bernstein of Detroit's Purple Gang tell Moran that a quantity of top liquor would be delivered at $57 a case. Moran was assured of having his men ready for the purchase and distribution, but instead of the liquor, they found Capone's hit men dressed like police. Seven of Moran's top mobsters were lined up against the wall and shot to death. The murders were so dramatic and the day so contradictory that the press carried the story throughout the country. *Scarface*, the screenplay co-written by Burnett, was not exactly about Capone in the original planning. Director Howard Hawks and producer Howard Hughes wanted to blend what they knew about the Chicago mob with the history of the Borgia family and to intermingle the storyline with that of *Scarface*, a recent popular novel to which Hughes had bought the film rights. Hughes also wanted his film to be more violent than any previous

129

gangster movie, though in a manner that would sneak past the growing censorship.

To accomplish this, Hughes was introduced by Hawks to the Borgias, a family during the Middle Ages whose members were both more powerful and more brutal than any other criminals in contemporary society and whose lives created the longest-running soap opera in the history of the world—longer than *One Life to Live*, longer than *General Hospital*, longer than *Days of Our Lives*, longer than *As the World Turns*. The family offered a lifestyle that included everything the public wanted for home and office gossip—fathers selling daughters, brothers selling sisters, adultery, incest, and murder. From 1435 through 1520, the men of the family took control of the Catholic Church and committed enough sins to be constantly worthy of forgiveness. And when the family partied, they enjoyed such amusements as bringing fifty of the palace male servants together with fifty Roman prostitutes so they could pair off and have sex in front of Alexander, Cesare, and Lucrezia Borgia; when the show was over, Alexander awarded a prize for "best performance." It was debauchery, though preferable for the participants than some of the other events, such as Cesare's cutting off the hand and tongue of one reveler who became drunk enough to make a joke at a Borgia's expense.

Howard Hughes, who agreed that the Borgias were an outstanding criminal family, perfect for a movie, wanted a more contemporary setting after talking with his director. As Hawks later explained,

> Capone was supposed to have staged a big party for a gangland enemy. First, Capone made a long, polite speech about the man. Toward the end of his speech, he became angry and zeroed in on how the man had deceived him. At that point, filled with rage, Capone was supposed to have beaten the man to death with a baseball bat.
>
> That was to me an act so lunatic and duplicitous that it seemed a modern version of Cesare Borgia and the Borgia family. [Ben] Hecht and I researched the whole Borgia family. Cesare Borgia and his sister Lucrezia were supposed to have been lovers. We copied that.

The only problem with the Borgias was trying to depict their lives as graphically as possible without incurring deletion demands from the

Hays Office censors. For example, when the main character, Tony "Scarface" Comonte finds his sister kissing a man and throws the man out, she yells, "Sometimes you don't act like a brother, you're more of a . . ." He slaps her face, silencing her before she can say the word "lover."

The ending of the film was to have been even more blatant because the sister seduces Frank Rio, the bodyguard for Scarface and his closest friend. She marries Rio within hours of the police arriving to arrest Scarface, but Tony does not realize what has happened. He finds Rio in a dressing gown and his sister wearing a negligee, declares his belief that he has been betrayed, and murders Rio. The sister, rather than being upset, declares her undying love for her brother and prepares to die with him in a shoot-out with the police.

The sexual tension was enhanced by George Raft's tendency to be an observer and imitator of life. He learned to fight by watching street fighters and boxers. He learned the mannerisms of gangsters by observing them. And he was instrumental in creating the relationship between himself and actress Ann Dvorak, the woman who played Scarface's sister, because of an experience at a party in the home of Howard Hawks. As Hawks later explained,

> Ann was attracted to George, who looked magnificent in his evening clothes. George was just sitting there, minding his own business. He doesn't drink, and he didn't look as if he was having too good a time.
>
> Ann asked him to dance with her but he said he'd rather not. She was a little high and right in front of him starts to do this sexy undulating dance, sort of trying to lure him on to dance with her. She was a knockout. She wore a black silk gown almost cut down to her hips. I'm sure that's all she had on. After a while George couldn't resist her suggestive dance and in no time they were doing a sensational number which stopped the party.
>
> I asked Ann, who'd done a few minor parts in films, to be at my office next day. I gave her the Lucrezia Borgia role.

Hawks explained that he had Dvorak and Raft duplicate the dance in a scene in which they meet at a party. It was one of the outstanding scenes in the film, creating the sexual tension Hawks and Hughes had sought.

The Borgia idea was combined with the story line in the novel *Scarface* by Maurice Coons, writing under the pen name Armitage Trail. Coons had been writing short stories and novels based on organized-crime activity he had witnessed in Chicago for a few years. *Scarface*, the novel Hughes discovered, was not the story of Capone, though anyone living and working in Chicago automatically thought of Capone's activities and used aspects of them when writing fiction. The basic plot concept was classic—good versus evil in the same family. In this case, there are two brothers, one of whom becomes a gangster and the other a cop. It was far from an original idea, as in numerous stories and films, the cop and the gangster or the priest and the gangster are either brothers or grew up as best friends from the same neighborhood.

Al Capone himself did not care who the story was really about. He loved the publicity, loved the fact that his life, his exploits, and even a series of myths about his prowess as a murderer had become a cottage industry for publishing. Between 1929 and 1931, starting with Edward Dean Sullivan's *Rattling the Cop on Chicago Crime*, seven books were published either about Capone or containing substantive material about him. Fawcett Publications also created a one-shot magazine devoted totally to Capone's exploits. It was called *Al Capone on the Spot*, cost 50 cents on the newsstands, and resulted in a publicity campaign in which Fawcett leaked the story that the top staff people responsible for the magazine disappeared for several weeks, allegedly held for ransom or punishment. In truth, Capone bought one hundred copies to share with friends.

Capone was also pictured in films and on stage. Edgar Wallace wrote *On the Spot* specifically about Capone with actor Crane Wilbur playing the role of Tony Perelli, or Al Capone. It had a successful British run before it came to Broadway on October 29, 1930, lasting 167 performances.

There were also the better-known *Little Caesar* (Edgar G. Robinson as Capone) and *Public Enemy* (James Cagney as Capone). But Capone as Borgia was a new twist, and the idea of incest should have upset Capone if he thought the film was supposed to be honest. That was apparently why he obtained a copy of the screenplay and sent two of his men to talk to author/playwright/screenwriter Ben Hecht at his Los Angeles hotel.

They showed Hecht the screenplay and asked if he had written it.

When he admitted he had, he later related, they said, "Is this stuff about Al Capone?"

"God, no!" Hecht told them. "I don't even know Al." Then, he explained which gangsters he had known from his work, men who would actually remember his name, unlike Al, whom he had met in packs of reporters seeking quotes for the same story.

The men were not satisfied. "If this stuff isn't about Al Capone, why are you calling it *Scarface*? Everybody will think it's him."

"That's the reason. Al is one of the most famous and fascinating men of our time. If you call the movie *Scarface*, everybody will want to see it, figuring it's about Al. That's part of the racket we call showmanship."

"I'll tell Al. Who's this fella Howard Hughes?"

"He's got nothing to do with it. He's the sucker with the money."

Oddly, the movie proved inspirational to mobsters. Ben "Bugsy" Siegel began wearing the same style suits that George Raft wore in the film, and several gangsters began flipping coins to show that they were cold, ruthless, and unflappable. The latter came from Raft's tossing a nickel throughout the movie. Years after the film was made, it was assumed that Raft invented the bit based on gangsters he had met when working with Owney Madden. It was known that the most successful gangsters were, in effect, actors as well. They created an image for themselves that often belied fear or confusion, giving them an edge. It was assumed that Raft had seen one of the men close to Dutch Schultz using a coin toss to calm himself and distract his enemies. Instead, Raft later explained, "Tossing a nickel was Howard Hawks's idea. Of course, I had to learn how to toss the nickel and practiced for weeks. Finally, I got it so I could almost do it in my sleep."

Hawks had another reason for the bit. Raft was not yet a skilled actor. He had only been in a few minor pictures and had yet to develop the skills he would demonstrate in the years to come. Hawks felt that flipping the coin would give Raft something to do when he had nothing else to do on the set except stand. "Having George flip the coin made him a character. The coin represented a hidden attitude—a kind of defiance, a held-back hostility, a coolness—which hadn't been found in pictures up to that time; and it made George stand out."

The coin toss was especially effective in what is now considered one of the most dramatic killings in film history. Raft later explained,

We start the scene. I'm wearing a silk robe. Muni [Paul Muni played Scarface] knocks on the door, and when I open it, he sees his sister, Ann Dvorak, in a negligee. He turns to me. "You shouldn't have done this to me, Gino. I thought you were my friend!" Then, Muni shoots me. I fell back and my head hit hard on the door—and not intentionally. I had really thrown myself into the scene and banged my head. When I slid down the door, I was slightly unconscious and landed in a small pool of my own blood. My eyes sort of rolled up in my head, like people's do when they are dying. The coin I had been tossing fell out of my hand. I heard Hawks say, "Print." Everyone there said this was the greatest movie death scene they ever saw.

Hawks filmed the coin rolling along the floor until it lost its motion, and fell flat. Hawks told me later, "The roll of the coin and then its falling still told the story of Gino's death."

Gino's death is followed by the one part of the movie that troubled Al Capone. The mobster, who would be in jail for tax evasion shortly after the film was released, did not care about the incest image. He knew that such carryings on had nothing to do with him. It was one of the two endings explored for the film that troubled Capone, according to Raft.

In the first filmed ending, Hawks and Hughes stayed with the Borgia concept as Scarface and his sister, Cesca, are together after the murder of Gino (Raft). Cesca shows no emotion about the death but reminds Scarface how alike they are. She says, "You're me, and I'm you. It's always been that way." Then, she hugs her brother and loads their guns to help him shoot the police. This made the sister too evil, and the censors wanted her passive, staying with her brother out of family loyalty, not out of presumably requited lust for her brother and his lifestyle.

Also in the first ending, Scarface and Cesca embrace, delighted to shoot it out with the police. He starts to close steel shutters, presumably to stop bullets, but is too slow. Cesca is hit and dies, the bullets followed by an exploding tear gas round.

Tony "Scarface" Camonte, almost overwhelmed by the gas, races downstairs toward police officers. "Don't shoot," he yells. "I don't got nobody. . . . I'm all alone!" and with that he is felled by dozens of bullets.

In the ending eventually used to mollify the censors, Cesca dies, but Scarface is captured by the police. Then, there is a close-up of a judge presumably in a courtroom talking directly to Scarface. "There is no place in this country for your type," he says, after which a gallows is tested, followed by what is obviously Scarface's death.

It was the first ending, with Scarface dying in a hail of bullets, that upset Capone. Shortly before he went to prison for tax evasion, Capone had Raft come to his office where Raft remembered him saying, "Georgie, so you been playin' my bodyguard, Frank Rio, in this *Scarface* pitcher."

"Yes, I did, Al," Raft said. "But it's nothing personal. Actors do what they're told."

Capone rubbed the long scar on his face. Then, kidding on the square, said, "Well, you tell them guys in Hollywood that they don't know Al Capone. They bumped me off in the end, and nobody's bumpin' Al off while he's running Chicago. Yeah, you tell 'em that."

Capone, before admitting that he liked the film, also mentioned the coin tossing. "Just a little theatrical touch," Raft said he told him.

"A four-bit [50 cents] piece, yeah?"

" 'No, it was a nickel."

" 'That's worse. You tell 'em that if any of my boys are tossin' coins, they'll be twenty-dollar gold pieces."

"I wasn't sure if he was kidding or meant it, but I promised to convey the message to Hollywood."

CHAPTER Thirteen

Hello, George, Goodbye, Tommy

The joint was called Club 100, and it was owned by Al Capone's cousin Nicky Dean (a.k.a. Nick Circella). Like every other Chicago nightclub owner, he had the good sense to know that providing information to the Outfit was a way not only to stay healthy but also to benefit in unexpected ways from time to time. Capone was in jail, so it seemed to make sense to go to Frank Nitti, the front man for the Outfit. The Capone gang was actually headed by Paul Ricca and assisted by Curly Humphreys. But Nitti was the front man, the go-to-see-guy to get anything done.

Dean listened to the bragging Bioff and Browne the night they came into the club to celebrate the shakedown of Balaban and Katz. He watched the money they flashed, buying food and drinks and gambling. His brother, August Circella, ran burlesque houses that employed stagehands, so he had an understanding of the union and what they could do. He knew something important was happening, something that the Outfit would want to hear about. That was why Dean provided Bioff and Browne with his finest liquor, as well as two of his women to keep them occupied in the upstairs rooms. Then, he called Frank Nitti to tell him about the bragging scam artists who were dropping serious money in the club.

Nitti was intrigued. He knew another side of Browne. The man was often drunk, and when he'd had too much, he would pull out a pistol and start waving it around like a tough guy. Dean had deliberately gotten him drunk that night so that the two men would brag about what they were doing. They might be fools and thugs, but it seemed they had come upon a scam that might have greater potential than they could achieve on their own.

What happened next has become the subject of mob history and mob myth. Frankie Rio made the first contact with Browne; some stories report that he waited a couple of days and some say it happened the next day, with George getting the call while he was in bed, trying to sleep off the drunk.

In the second scenario, Rio ordered Browne to meet him at a nearby street intersection where he picked him up in his car. Then, again according to the story, Browne was driven around like a man who had offended the mob and was going to be punished. Browne was supposedly pleading for his life, yet not certain exactly why he was in such terror.

Whatever the case, all stories agree that the first sit-down meeting took place a few days later. Again, there are two versions. In one, Bioff and Browne were told to come to the Lexington Hotel where Nitti maintained an office. In the other, they went to the home of Nitti's next-door neighbor, Harry Hochstein, a man who served Rio in much the manner that Rio had formerly served Capone.

The attendees at the meeting told more about what could be expected in the immediate future than Bioff and Browne might have understood. Charles "Cherry Nose" Gioe was present, along with Phil D'Andrea, Louis Campagna, and Paul "The Waiter" DeLucia, sitting alongside Frank Nitti and Frank Rio. Also present was Louis "Lepke" Buchalter, who was head of Murder, Inc., and represented Charles Luciano's New York interests. This meant that a national operation was being planned, one possible reason the meeting was not held earlier, since Lepke needed time to get to Chicago.

Bioff and Browne were told that they were not going to be playing with just the Chicago union and theater chains. More was about to take place, and everyone who mattered in organized crime was either represented or directly present. In addition, it was assumed that Curly Humphreys had previously been consulted since his expertise was in union and labor corruption.

Neither Nitti nor Luciano was a novice in the use of labor unions for skimming and extortion. Nitti, with the advice of Humphreys, had been working on taking over the trade unions related to the restaurant and nightclub business at the same time that he, like Luciano, was trying to get a handle on the movie industry narcotics trade. Both understood the same businesses, the same potential, but neither had extortion and skimming on the scale that Bioff and Browne seemed to have discovered.

Nitti, knowing that George Browne had narrowly lost the 1932 presidency of IATSE, asked him if he wanted to be president after the next election, a year from the time of their meeting. Browne said that he would and explained which regional locals had failed to vote for him. Nitti said that such matters would be handled in exchange for Browne and Bioff's benefiting the mob. Browne and Bioff would be free to steal or skim whatever money they could get from the union dues, pension fund, theater owners, film distributors, and anyone else they thought would pay. All they had to do was provide an accurate accounting, then pay the mob's share to Nitti, who would handle any laundering through the Capone-originated soup kitchens. Essentially, Nitti wanted to own the Stagehands' Local 33, while Bioff and Browne acted as collectors for all the money they could get.

George Browne realized he was facing wealth and power beyond imagination. He also understood, based on the ranks of the men present, that to refuse this opportunity would likely mean his death.

There were two meetings with Bioff and Browne, followed by a meeting among just the leaders of organized crime. Luciano attended the latter, although it was called by Nitti and scheduled in Chicago. He deliberately arrived ten minutes late as a sign of disrespect and an assertion of his own power, but he was interested to hear what was possible with the control of unions in the motion picture business. He, like everyone else, had been looking at the money being made and spent in Hollywood, yet did not fully understand how to take advantage of it all. This meeting would hopefully clarify that question because, among others, Johnny Rosselli was going to speak about how the film industry worked. He was making large sums of money for the Outfit through the gambling industry, but his grasp of the studios, the unions, and the power positions in Hollywood was probably greater than that of Pat DiCicco, Luciano's man in the industry.

Luciano realized one fact when the meeting was over, and to him it was an important one. Nitti was more powerful in the entertainment unions than Charles had imagined. However, Nitti needed Luciano and his closest associates to truly make the shakedowns work.

Rosselli explained the structure of the movie industry unions. He discussed how the industry workers were frequently not unionized. The stagehands had been organized because of their long history with theaters. The projectionists were also well organized. But much of the industry was disgruntled but hadn't come together for formal negotiations.

The moguls had created a system they controlled far better than the mob. Many followed Louis B. Mayer's lead in developing talent from small towns. Names were changed. Personal histories were created. High salaries were paid for hours worked. And fame was assured through the studio publicists. However, if someone was creating a problem, the studio system could work against that person in the manner it had done with the destruction of Roscoe Arbuckle. The hours worked would be cut and the shooting schedules increased so that an actor, in order to be a star, might have to put in sixteen-hour days, six or seven days a week, on a very tight shooting schedule. The actual time in front of a camera might only amount to a few weeks a year. And the actor did not exist until the studio created his or her persona, a prime example being the Ohio dentist's daughter, Theodosia Goodman, who was unknown before, but after four years of stardom during which Hollywood publicists named her Theda Bara, she was well-known as "The Vamp."

There was money to be made in two ways. There was the usual union skimming—levying special assessments on the members, taking a percentage of the dues, and skimming from the pension funds. There was also the use of the unions to shut down businesses that were not cooperating.

Bioff, Browne, Tommy Maloy, and others who had been in the trenches of the union leadership understood the attitude of the rank and file toward their employers. They believed that the moguls were trying to keep costs and benefits down and that strikes might be necessary. The union would be willing to create a strike fund, the employers would be willing to pay fees separately for labor peace, and the mob could take portions of both without challenge from either side.

Nitti said that he wanted all the bosses to work together to take national control of IATSE and the other unions connected with Hollywood. It was a business decision that made sense, even to Luciano, who was still livid with Nitti for moving in on the drug, nightclub, and restaurant businesses he was trying to control in Los Angeles. He worked a private deal with Nitti to take a cut of the Chicago Outfit's earnings from the restaurants and clubs and obtained Nitti's promise to stop trying to increase his control. However, Nitti refused to commit to stopping his efforts to control narcotics. It was the best arrangement Luciano could make, and though he willingly worked with Chicago to gain a foothold in the film industry, each man quietly resolved to destroy the other's efforts in the drug trade if possible.

There was one other meeting of the mob bosses on Al Capone's Palm Island estate in March 1934. This was the last planning meeting for the takeover, and it is interesting to see who was not present. Ralph Capone, who had been in training with Johnny Rosselli during several trips to Hollywood, was at the gathering, along with Rosselli. Nicky Dean was there. Paul Ricca and Frank Nitti attended, as did Ralph Pierce, whose labor knowledge came from assisting Curly Humphreys. Not present was Luciano. Not present was Lepke. Not present was Ben Siegel. Not present was Meyer Lansky. The Chicago Outfit was making a power bid, and New York be damned.

It was at this final meeting before the elections that all the facts about the business of Hollywood and the unions were discussed. Rosselli explained that 40 percent of the overhead of any film came from the cost of the craft unions. Nitti showed that the theater chains essentially ran the motion picture studios as subsidiaries of their operations. If you hurt the theater owners and their wholly owned subsidiaries, major studios such as Metro-Goldwyn-Mayer would not be able to operate effectively, if at all.

The friendship with the moguls that Rosselli had cultivated became an obvious ploy when the plans were laid out. The theater chain owners would be expected to pay to prevent strikes, damage to their films, and disruption of theater operations. If anyone tried to get tough, blackmail would be used. All of the men had skeletons in their closets, even if they were only hiding lives far less moral than they wanted both the public and their wives to know about. They would all pay.

Tommy Maloy knew nothing about the meeting of national mob bosses where it was decided to put George Browne into the presidency of IATSE. Not knowing that everything was already rigged, he was hoping to run for first vice president. He figured that between his existing reputation and the help of the Outfit, he could win and, from that national base, eventually gain full control. With that thought in mind, he went to see Nitti for help.

Tommy actually brought two issues to the Outfit. Maloy had been cheating on his income taxes, and though that was not an unusual activity, the federal government was building a case against him as solid as the one against Capone. Maloy knew he was going to the federal penitentiary, only not for how long.

Nitti said that he could rig the sentencing so that Maloy only spent six months in jail. He would also back him for the union position, but he needed a full understanding of the racket Maloy had been running.

Maloy, still not realizing that he was of no value to the Outfit other than for the information he held, quickly agreed. He provided the names and addresses of everyone on the projectionists union payroll. He wrote down who was being bribed and for how much money. He noted how skimming took place and where it was active. Then, assured that he still had Nitti's support, Tommy went off to jail. He was told that George Browne would act as caretaker of his position with the projectionists while he was in jail but that he would have everything back when he left prison.

The international convention of IATSE was held in the Brown Hotel on Broadway in Louisville, Kentucky, in June 1934. The election was fair and open, or so the newspeople were told when they were barred from attending. To keep it that way, men who were formerly outsiders were present. The New York delegates were personally greeted by Luciano, Lepke, Lansky, and Siegel. The Cleveland delegates were warmly welcomed by Big Al Polizzi. Longy Zwillman of New Jersey, a man who would later back films by Jean Harlow and the studio of Harry Cohn, greeted the men from his area. Johnny Dougherty handled the reception for St. Louis. And Chicago, long the production capital, had Nitti, Humphreys, and all the other top men from the Outfit.

The meeting, closed to the press and the public, also had security in the form of men lining the walls holding machine guns. There were three candidates for president—Browne and two others—when the delegates arrived. Once the two rivals saw how the room was stacked in favor of mob members, who explained that George Browne was going to win, they agreed to drop out of the race.

B&B finally achieved a score they both could enjoy. George Browne, who would continue to draw $250 a week as business agent for Chicago

Stagehands Local No. 2, was given $25,000 a year as the new president of IATSE. Willie Bioff was appointed his friend's "personal representative" for $22,000 a year. They suddenly had so much money that the mob did not worry about their going for more. They readily agreed to turn over two-thirds of whatever they could skim or steal to the Chicago Outfit. It was presumed that everyone else would get his proper share, though Nitti had no intention of sending money to Luciano. In addition, Browne authorized the use of IATSE funds to pay all traveling expenses for the men who had so graciously talked to the delegates before the voting and provided security while they cast their ballots.

The Outfit did have one unexpected surprise, however. George Browne suddenly had a chance to be a national figure advising the president of the United States.

Franklin D. Roosevelt had entered office in 1932 using what was called a brain trust—several university professors who met with him to help shape his ideas for taking the country out of the Depression and restoring as many jobs as possible. The concepts and speeches that evolved were credited with helping Roosevelt win the popular election and regain both houses of Congress for the Democrats.

The Depression worsened between the election and the inauguration, and by early 1933, there had been a series of bank failures. Efforts to combat the problem included the passage of the National Industrial Recovery Act and the establishment of the National Recovery Administration. It was toward this end that the government agencies set codes for employers, including a minimum wage of 30 to 40 cents an hour and a maximum workweek of thirty-five to forty hours, that he created another panel of advisers. Unlike the brain trust, this panel included men from organized labor. George Browne was among those asked to participate in his new position as president of IATSE, which would have elevated him to a degree of influence that might have undercut the Outfit. Nitti told him he could not participate.

Whether or not Browne wanted to rebel, he recognized his position with the mob at the end of 1934. Tommy Maloy still held his post as head of the projectionists union, but he was having great difficulty shaking down the theater owners. The cost of doing business with the union was too great, and neither firebombings nor beatings nor general vandalism had much influence with the theater owners whose businesses were already in crisis.

The post-IATSE election activity was meant to establish the power of Browne, who would be "assisted" in Los Angeles by Johnny Rosselli, the one man the mob could completely trust, and Bioff, whose handler would be Nick Circella. They first went to New York to meet with the heads of the Producers' Association. Then, they returned to Chicago to bring the unions together and approach the theater chain owners whom they had yet to extort.

The standard ploy in Chicago was to order the theater owners to have two projectionists in the booth at all time. It was explained that the annual cost of such an action would be as much as $500,000. However, for just $60,000, the pressure would be off, and there would be no further demand for extra employees.

In the case of at least one small theater owner, the money came in a "partnership" arrangement in which Browne got a little over $300 a week, every week, for several years in exchange for causing no problems. The money was originally based on the success of the theater. But this was the Depression, and when business was bad, the payoff remained unchanged.

Nathaniel Barger owned different businesses to try and get through the hard economic times. The extortion from the movie theater, his oldest holding and one that had long been a family business, killed the profit and endangered the operation. Barger chose to sell a burlesque house he owned in order to pay off on the movie theater. To his shock, Willie Bioff, who was doing the collecting, took half the money from the sale of the burlesque house and personally pocketed it.

On Christmas Eve of 1934, the Chicago mob leaders connected with IATSE met with Browne and Bioff at a party ostensibly held to celebrate the holiday. Browne and Bioff were told that Maloy had no intention of giving up his position, yet he was no longer able to control the theater owners. That night, Maloy's fate was sealed.

Slightly more than five weeks later, at noon on February 4, 1935, Tommy Maloy was driving his Cadillac along Chicago's Lake Shore Drive. A second car pulled alongside, the passenger window open. As the car paced Maloy, the passenger poked a shotgun out the window and blasted Maloy. The shattered car, Maloy slumped over the steering wheel, was found some time later. No one was ever charged. Most likely, no one was ever investigated. IATSE, with both the stagehands and projectionists as members, now belonged to Nitti. Years later, though, investigators were certain that the hit men were Joe Accardo, later a key figure in Chicago nightclubs who hired such big-name entertainers as Frank Sinatra, and Gus Alex, a younger man learning the business.

Maloy was quickly replaced—by Nicky Dean. Shortly afterwards, all the theater-related trade unions in Chicago were a part of Browne's IATSE except the theater janitors union. Gaining the extra place required the murder of its leader "Three Gun" Louis Alterie. No one else in the Chicago union movement challenged the authority of Browne and Bioff.

CHAPTER Fourteen

"Hot Toddy"

Thelma Todd was the ideal Hollywood star for rich and powerful men looking to have a beautiful, successful woman they could dominate personally and in business. She was the daughter of a domineering mother and a Lawrence, Massachusetts, police lieutenant who moved into politics and was known to be involved with influence peddling and rewarding contracts in return for bribes. Alice Todd delighted in the power her husband wielded and the image it gave her and their daughter, but the marriage was over for all purposes by the time Thelma was nine.

Thelma was desperate for attention, wearing what, in the day, would be considered erotically inappropriate clothing. She was a tomboy and preoccupied with sexual fantasies. She was also interested in becoming a teacher, enrolling in the Lowell State Normal School in 1923. Her summers, however, were spent as a fashion show model for events held at the Empire Theater, the local movie house. The manager, Napoleon DeMara, was in love with the young woman and arranged for men connected with the New York movie industry to see her and try to get her jobs. However, she felt that the serious movie people were with production companies too small to matter, and the rest of the men were sexually interested in her.

The only other job Thelma held lasted but a day. She was hired by a department store to sell cosmetics. She wore a low-cut outfit that showed her figure to advantage, then began flirting with the men until they crowded around the counter. None bought cosmetics. That was left to their wives. They just stood around with Thelma, flirting.

Thelma continued with her plans to be a teacher, but her flirting paid off in unexpected ways. A former high school classmate who was a member of Lawrence Elks Lodge 65 nominated her for the Miss Massachusetts Beauty Contest, and in August 1925, she learned not only that she had been entered but that she was a finalist. The preliminary judging had been handled with photographs, and the youth had used one clipped from their yearbook.

Thelma won the contest, and this time the movie industry interest in the young woman was more serious. A genuine talent scout working for Famous Players–Lasky wanted to make Thelma a contract offer if she would come to Boston for a screen test. She was beautiful in person, but the studio wanted to be certain she would look good on the large screen. Then, if all went well, she would be trained at Paramount Pictures, the parent company owned by Adolph Zukor. The school would last six months, and when the screen test was a success, both her parents decided she should attend.

As a student in the first class of the Paramount Players School—Stars of Tomorrow, Thelma was informed of a problem that ensured her becoming one of the clients for Luciano's drugs in the years to come. She was barely within her proper weight limit. Both Adolph Zukor and, later, Hal Roach, both of whose studios she would work for, were clear that she could not gain weight. Diet pills coupled with alcohol became her method for avoiding additional pounds.

Todd's success was almost immediate because she had the good fortune to be teamed with the comedy team of Laurel and Hardy, and it was with them that she showed a talent for slapstick and more sophisticated types of screen humor. She acted with her best friend, comedienne Zasu Pitts, and was chosen to work with the Marx brothers. She also became both the lover and eventually the business partner of director Roland West.

The relationship among Todd, DiCicco, and Luciano was one that could only have happened in that transition period. DiCicco was fascinated by Thelma Todd. She was beautiful, educated, outgoing, and sensually exciting. She was also so insecure that she thought a man who was at once handsome and hard, professionally successful after signing ever more important talent to represent, and dangerous because of his relationship with Luciano was the perfect person to take care of her. She did not expect, however, that he expected her not to question his activities, either with Charles Luciano in New York or with other women. Todd also discovered that DiCicco had a violent temper and would beat her if she pushed too hard.

Their marriage was emotionally over almost from the moment they eloped on July 18, 1932. Todd would not get the wedding annulled, but she began drinking more heavily and taking more diet pills.

The DiCiccos had been married for several weeks before Thelma was able to meet Luciano. She was thinking of going into business with Roland West, and by chance, the two of them stopped in a restaurant where her husband was meeting with Charlie Luciano. The two were introduced, and it was obvious that DiCicco was not happy about sharing this aspect of his life. It was not because of the criminal element. He was afraid that Luciano would become sexually interested in Todd. It was a valid concern.

Charles Luciano was fascinated with Thelma Todd. She was beautiful, intelligent, and increasingly addicted to both amphetamines, which he readily provided, and alcohol as a way of getting through the day and night. She understood the danger of being with him, which made him more exciting. Whether she also thought of him as a buffer with DiCicco is not known because the two had stopped living together most of the time. They were finally divorced in March 1934 as the mob was finishing its takeover of IATSE.

Todd's relationship with Luciano was as much about business as it was about his pleasure in a woman he kept on the amphetamines to which her ex-husband had first introduced her. He had been increasingly uncomfortable with the way men loyal to Capone were taking control of Los Angeles and felt the need to have an increasingly personal presence.

Todd, by contrast, was getting herself involved in worlds she did not know existed. Luciano was a man of at times barely controlled violence. She seemed to like the danger he represented, though the truth may simply have been that she could not face withdrawal from the drugs to which she was addicted. It was convenient that her lover also supplied her with whatever she desired to get high enough to work all day and calm enough to sleep all night.

Luciano was actually following a pattern he began in New York with the prostitutes who worked for him. He liked controlling women, and he found that when he ran prostitution and narcotics, he could dramatically increase his income by getting the prostitutes addicted to drugs. The women would work in his brothels, earn enough money to lead a straight life, then spend it immediately on the drugs that he sold. They were desperate to please Luciano as their supplier, a subtle form of domination and violence that is rarely discussed.

Thelma Todd was bright and beautiful, like many of the young women who came to work for Luciano. He needed to break her quickly, and "helping" her by giving her drugs was a trick he had used many times. It was also one that DiCicco knew about, adding to his anger. The problem, one that DiCicco could not overcome, was that any arguments on his part would get him beaten or killed. He had to watch not only as Thelma was taken from him but as she became totally controlled either by Luciano when he was in town or by one of his men when he returned to New York.

Todd was unaware of what was happening. Like other wealthy Hollywood movie people, she decided to diversify her financial interests shortly after her divorce. This was also the time of the seemingly unrelated election of George Browne as national president of IATSE.

A longtime friend, Roland West, wanted to open a restaurant. He had the expertise for day-to-day operations, and his ex-wife, Jewel Carmen, had the money and desire to pay for all start-up costs. Carmen was unable to stay married to West, but she understood that he had the skill to run a successful business venture. She also made clear that the money provided to open the restaurant was all that would be available. The cost of operation would have to be earned through the customer base.

Thelma Todd was asked only to put her name on what became known as Thelma Todd's Sidewalk Café, a restaurant specializing in seafood. They obtained a building on the Pacific Highway, convenient for highly paid movie stars who became regulars at the café after it opened in August 1934. The restaurant took up most of the space on the first floor, and a drugstore rented a smaller portion of the building. The second floor had a bar and also the offices from which West and an accountant worked, as well as two separate apartments, one used by West and the other by Todd. The top floor was allegedly unused. However, there was private gambling—card games, dice, and betting on horse races and other sports—for a few friends.

There was other housing on the grounds. The business treasurer, Charles Smith, and his wife lived in what amounted to an efficiency apartment above the garage and below the main house that served as

housing for Jewel Carmen's brother Rudy Schafer [frequently miss-
pelled as Schaefer], the café's business manager, and his wife.

Thelma was to have nothing to do with the daily operations,
though she spent her free time in the café because her filming schedule
involved two weeks of shooting and two weeks of downtime. She also
was spending time with Luciano, though not in the restaurant or her
apartment. Neither the mobster nor the actress wanted the public to
know about their affair.

Luciano was incapable of separating business from pleasure. He
wanted to turn Thelma Todd's top floor into a full-scale casino-gam-
bling operation. He was going to have his men put pressure on West to
allow the mob full control.

The shakedown began slowly and became obvious to Todd only
when she realized that, despite the fact that the restaurant was usually
packed and a favorite hangout for many movie stars, the café was losing
money to the degree where Thelma was paying up to $2,000 a month
out of her own pocket. This was not what she expected, and when she
confronted West, he tried to avoid the truth. He explained that many
of the customers put their meals and drinks on a tab to be paid later,
a not uncommon practice in Hollywood and one that would be repli-
cated in such locations as Schwab's Drug Store. He also talked about
the little things, such as the purchase of linens, the purchase of tables,
and the replacement of various items.

The needs were all well and good, but Todd reminded her partner
that the original idea was that she would provide her name and her
physical presence, Jewel would put up the capital, and Roland would
run daily operations.

The problem was with Charles Smith, who was being pressed by
Luciano's men at the same time that Luciano was bedding Todd. He
had been pressured in ways that West would soon understand. Luciano's men came to him as they had to Smith and explained that the café
was changing suppliers.

Restaurants establish buying arrangements with those suppliers
who offer the type of food they wish to serve at a specific, consistent
quality and price. Other suppliers offer durable goods such as linens
that require periodic replacement. West had established the connections that made the restaurant succeed, but suddenly he was being told
that these arrangements would change. He was told he would be provided with the meat and liquor he would serve at a new price. He would

be hiring union bartenders and using a different laundry for linen. The price would be fixed, the quantity would be fixed, and if he didn't need everything he was to order, he could refuse whatever he did not need. However, he would pay the same price, no matter what. And the quality would be whatever he was provided.

West assumed that Smith was also involved in the shakedown, either because he was forced or because he was also dishonest. He confronted Smith, who then blamed Schafer. Both accusations were too uncomfortable on a personal basis to explore further since Schafer was West's brother-in-law and Smith had been a trusted friend for years. West also did not know whether the shakedown was being directed by Chicago or New York, though he realized if it was the latter, it was being done under Luciano's orders. Since Luciano was supplying Thelma with drugs and sex, he knew better than to discuss the problem with her.

Todd had other problems at the time. Like a number of popular entertainers, she was being victimized by men who tried to take advantage of her fame and hated her for reasons that made sense only in their fantasies, criminals who wanted to see how far they could go before she called their bluff. She regularly received death threats and extortion notes. One man went so far as to demand that she pay money to men she had known in the past, then contacted those men and ordered them to have her pay. It was all seemingly irrational and extremely frightening. Todd routinely had her maid take the notes to the police, and she bought a small handgun, which she carried with her everywhere. She also bought a white bull terrier to protect her apartment.

Ultimately, a series of extortion notes mailed from San Francisco, then New York, led Todd to contact the FBI. She also wrote notes to the man, telling him she wanted to meet him face to face, then left them where his latest extortion letter told her to leave money. This he did, but each time he was scared off before Todd could identify him. Ultimately, he was traced by the FBI and found to be the most feared of all dangers in Hollywood, an obsessed fan who was also a stalker. His name was Harry Schimanski; he was thirty-four years old and an apartment-house manager in Astoria, Long Island. He was jailed on August 19, pleaded not guilty on October 31, and was held over for trial.

On November 8, after tracking a new series of extortion notes threatening to burn Todd's café if she did not pay, another New Yorker was arrested. This was Edward Schieffert, a twenty-eight-year-old drugstore employee who proudly confessed what he had done. He was madly in love with Todd and thought that if the public believed her to be in danger, the publicity would help her career. That was all he wanted to accomplish by scaring her. He didn't want her money. He thought the extortion showed his love.

Schieffert was tested by the court and found to be mentally ill. He was committed to Bellevue State Hospital that year, where authorities suspected he may have been responsible for the letters they originally thought Schimanski had sent. All that mattered for Todd was that the stalking had ended.

Frustrated by all that was taking place in Hollywood and with the Sidewalk Café, Luciano personally met with Roland West to tell him that it was his men who had been putting pressure on him when it came to the suppliers. West had seen how a popular restaurant could lose money or be put out of business as costs rose and quality deteriorated. Matters were going to get worse unless West allowed Luciano to offer full-scale gambling on the top floor.

It was one of the rare signs of respect for Thelma Todd that Luciano did not know that gambling had been taking place on the top floor almost from the time the café opened. The operation was not a big one. There may have been no police payoffs. But the money was substantial because the clientele was wealthy. Luciano had never had his men look too closely at the hidden side of the café, though what he had in mind was more involved than what was taking place.

Luciano wanted to run a straight operation. He was going to establish a leasing company that would use the top floor for a gambling casino. The leasing company would be unconnected with Todd or the current operations. It would handle getting all the permits necessary for the addition. Everything would be honest, and if there were any problems, they would be the concern of the leasing agency.

Roland West only wanted his own restaurant. Thelma Todd's Sidewalk Café had been the culmination of a long-held dream, and he was potentially good enough as a restaurateur to carry it off. Certainly his ex-wife believed in him when she put up the money.

West had done well. The restaurant was popular and seemed to be heading toward long-term success, rather than being just one of the locations that was popular one day and then empty as another restaurant became the newest "in" place among Hollywood's top stars. Even the little gaming that was taking place did not bother West because this was Hollywood in the 1930s. Seemingly everyone gambled, and if customers wanted to adjourn to another floor for high-stakes cards, he saw no reason not to make that possible.

West did not, however, expect Luciano's pressure or to be in the middle of a quiet mob war between Chicago and New York with Los Angeles as the battleground. He wanted out.

Thelma Todd was livid. She had no intention of ending her affair with Luciano. She felt that the books were being juggled by one of the three men she had so long trusted. She had no intention of selling to a gangster, even if she was bedding him, and she had no interest in buying out West.

Todd was a drug addict and heavy drinker, but she was not a fool. She was in a glamour industry, but she had come to the industry after getting an education and becoming a school teacher. She knew how to research. She knew how to learn exactly what was going on, including the relationship between Bioff, Browne, Luciano, the studios, and places like her restaurant.

It was October 1935 when Todd first began to answer some of her own questions. She attended a party given by Joe Schenck, which was attended by Willie Bioff, a man she had also seen at the studios. Some of the guests were industry professionals like herself. Some of the guests were connected with IATSE, though in ways that represented the new Hollywood labor movement, not the old. The people in leadership, men who hung about the studios intimidating the administration, looked like thugs. There was a tension that had not existed in the past. It was obvious that a violent criminal element was moving in on the city and the industry. It was also obvious that Luciano was in some way connected with Nitti, Bioff, and Browne.

Todd took a week's vacation, then returned to work. Through much of November, the problems seemed to be over. Business increased with the approaching holiday season. Smith, who had been warned of an impending audit of the books, either had not been stealing or had the sense to stop. Bills were being paid from the receipts, not from Thelma's earnings. And requests to use the top floor for gambling had stopped. Luciano was spending most of his time back east, and Thelma felt more comfortable than she had in the past.

Luciano returned to Los Angeles shortly before Thanksgiving, taking Thelma for a ride as he always did when he wanted to talk. This time he demanded the use of the third floor, and she adamantly refused. He apparently threatened her with violence, but she was used to her lovers getting physical. Instead, she began asking Luciano about what was going on between the unions and the studios. Once again, he talked more freely than he should have, and when he returned to the issue that mattered to him, taking the top floor for gambling, Thelma threatened to go to the district attorney.

The pressure on Luciano by Nitti was growing. The Chicago Outfit was moving in on the restaurants and the gambling joints, the drugs and the unions. Luciano fought back, but the stress was showing. He alternated between talking with Todd about his problems, something he would frequently do with the prostitutes who worked for him (and later testified against him during the trial that resulted in his deportation from the United States), and becoming physically violent when she argued. He told her about Bioff and Browne. He told her about the theater shakedowns. He told her about Nitti and how they were operating. And in those rare moments when he reflected on what he was doing, he realized he was telling her too much.

Todd, naive about the import of what might be considered a civil war between two syndicate divisions being fought just outside public awareness, figured that she could always go to the district attorney. She did not consider that the legal system might be corrupt. She had no idea that at least two of Luciano's men worked in the district attorney's office to learn both how far Nitti had gone in dominating the rackets, as well as who might actually have the nerve to want to reform the system.

District Attorney Buron Fitts himself had long been mob connected, as was his brother, who was involved in the construction business and had been charged, then acquitted, of murdering a rival cement contractor. Fitts had been the lieutenant governor of California in the 1920s, when he watched the direction power was drifting. Businessmen were getting rich by buying critical land, gradually crippling public transportation to profit from the growing auto industry, and obtaining water rights so they would literally profit from the lifeblood of the community. He realized that there was more power and money in being district attorney, controlling access to evidence in criminal cases, determining who would be prosecuted, and otherwise being a key to all corruption. He could be honest and upright when it benefited him, for instance, convicting his predecessor, Asa Keyes, of bribery, and quietly quash complaints when that was in his interest. He may or may not have known that Luciano's men were in his office, but the various mob factions knew Los Angeles justice could be bought by the highest bidder.

Luciano began putting more pressure on Todd, though exactly why has never been determined. Perhaps he did it to "prove" to those who knew he was dating the actress that he was not involved with the shakedown of her club. Such convoluted reasoning made sense because it could be assumed that he would not try to hurt someone he was bedding with her encouragement. Perhaps Luciano just did not care and liked the money potential of the third-floor casino.

Whatever the situation, Luciano made certain that both Thelma and Roland West were aware of his organization's presence. His men would come to the café, buying little and just looking around. His men would follow Thelma, pulling alongside her car on the street or brushing past her on the sidewalk when she was shopping. They did nothing hostile, nothing that would concern bodyguards she had begun to use when she was nervous. It was clear, however, that these were not local residents.

The pressure on Todd was too great. Luciano seemed to want West to give up the restaurant so his people could run it as usual, with the addition of the gambling operation. Todd, on the other hand, decided to fight back by telling all she knew to that heroic, crusading district attorney, Buron Fitts, who was in his own way as dangerous as Luciano. She called him for an appointment on December 11.

Fitts was not in the office when Todd called, but a "representative" got back to her at the café an hour or so later. He wanted to know why she wanted to talk with the district attorney. She said it was personal and that she needed an appointment.

The representative, presumably either one of Luciano's employees or someone beholden to Luciano, eventually set an appointment between Todd and Fitts for 11:30 a.m. on December 17, 1935. She was exhausted, scared, drinking too much, and taking drugs, but somehow she felt she had triumphed just by setting up the meeting. Emboldened, she explained to Roland that she was going to convert the third floor into a steakhouse, ending both the existing gambling and the opportunity for it to be a full casino. She explained her plans to both West and Schafer, noting that she would pay for the steakhouse creation in the same way that Jewel Carmen had paid for the initial seafood concept. Eventually, all the money would be pooled, and the operation would be handled as a single venture, but she recognized that while the seafood location was popular, the steak restaurant on the top floor would have to build its clientele. However, since they were in a beach area where most of the restaurants featured seafood, the addition of a steak-specialty dining area should have strong appeal.

Later, when friends and acquaintances of Thelma Todd were interviewed about this period at the end of her life, the belief was that she thought she had found a way to get out from under the pressures of the mob wars. She was thwarting Luciano's ambitions for her place as well as preventing anyone else from moving in. Her appointment with the district attorney would be insurance, as was her posting a sign visible to all her customers: *"Thelma Todd Announces the Opening Upstairs January One . . . The Finest Restaurant in California . . . Serving and Specializing in Steaks of Joya's . . . Unequalled $2.00 . . . Private Dining Room Available."*

The publicity for the new restaurant was all favorable, of course. She spread word among the actors about the quality of the food she would be serving. She also focused completely on the project, leaving West not only to handle the management of the main facility but also to greet and work the customers as Thelma had previously done during every other two-week period when she was not shooting a film. The fact that holiday parties were being booked and had to be specially handled solely by West during this period added to the tension. However, Todd seemed to be more stable than ever, relieved that she had found a way to deal with Luciano that she felt would not result in reprisals or other problems. Luciano, in her mind, was a man of action. If the third-floor gambling operation had been so important to him, he would have sabotaged her plans for the steakhouse as soon as she made the announcement. He hadn't. Remodeling had started. All was well. At least in her mind.

CHAPTER Fifteen

How Do You Corrupt Them Down in L.A. When Their Hands Are in Your Pockets?

Charles Luciano was concerned with the Los Angeles rackets and the Thelma Todd Sidewalk Café, but Bioff, Browne, Joe and Nick Schenck, and other movie industry people were working on a way to extort money from one another, while all of them put the screws to the federal government.

The basics were simple. Theater owners had always been looking for ways to save money on labor costs. The fewer people they could hire as stagehands, lighting technicians, and the like, the more money they could make from the box office.

The onset of motion pictures was exciting for the practical-minded owners because they understood the potential. A company hired a group of stagehands and other specialists, paying them to do what they always did for any production. Everything was filmed, the set was struck, the stagehands went home, and for days, weeks, months, or years afterwards, the theater owners could make money from the movie being shown over and over again throughout the country. Not one cent beyond the base wage for hours worked was paid to any of the people who had created the motion picture. It was an ideal arrangement and one reason that theatrical unions started in 1890, about the time that the motion picture was created.

Franklin Roosevelt felt strongly about allowing labor unions to have more power in the nation. He recognized that the working man was the last to benefit as the nation slowly moved out of the Great Depression. He began promoting what became the National Labor Relations Act, a concept that went against the interests of the film producers, who knew that their corporate financial success would be determined by keeping wages low and employees on the job. The new legislation, which went into effect on July 5, 1935, made certain that the workers had a right to collective bargaining. This meant that organized labor, if it included enough of the crafts people in Hollywood, could hold the production companies and their parent theater chains hostage to their demands.

Bioff and Browne knew what the producers feared, and they saw that a new union, the Congress of Industrial Organizations (CIO), which would later merge with the American Federation of Labor (AFL), of which IATSE was a part, was looking to challenge industries that were mostly not yet unionized. It was time to work out an extortion plan with the studios.

Joe and Nick Schenck worked out the extortion agreement with Bioff and Browne. They would recognize the union as the sole bargaining arm of the stagehands and others in IATSE. Then, they would sit down and iron out a contract, approved in advance, that would last seven years, the longest time allowed under California law. Under the deal, wages might be increased slightly each year, but they would be kept lower than the producers could afford. In exchange for this generosity, the rank and file would not be allowed to strike the studios. And for creating this pro-production company package, Bioff and Browne would receive $150,000.

The deal was a better version of an arrangement made with RKO on July 15. That deal required General Leslie Thompson, who ran RKO, to pay a total of $87,000 for strike insurance. This was presumably a somewhat open-ended payment, and the agreement was not for at all as long as the seven years granted the Schenck brothers. The savings to the motion picture theater chains was an estimated $1 million.

Years later, Local 306, the union involved with the initial Loew's and RKO shakedown, had its officers admit what they had done. Their out-of-court settlement was for just $100,000. Even with the ultimate penalties, everyone prospered.

But the Local 306 shakedown was a warm-up for the next show of strength, one meant literally for show. Saturday, November 30, 1935, was the date of the dramatic "strike" that had been carefully coordinated months earlier. Paramount Pictures sent a film crew to take aerial shots of the city for use in a movie called *Thirteen Hours by Air*. Neither the film nor the studio was important. What mattered was the non-IATSE crew—the cinematographers were members of the International Brotherhood of Electrical Workers (IBEW), which was on the losing end of a war with IATSE for control of all the guilds related to the movie industry.

The plane handling the aerial work landed at Newark Airport, a location within the union jurisdiction of IATSE. The IBEW camera crew was told to present their IATSE membership cards, which they did not have. Then, the "outraged" George Browne was alerted and immediately placed the calls that triggered a walk-off of all projectionists working for Paramount theaters in New York, Chicago, St. Louis, and smaller cities.

The strike was handled in two parts. On Saturday night, November 30, films were shown as usual in Paramount theaters. Then, in the middle of the film, the projectionists walked out for a preplanned fifteen to thirty minutes. No picket lines went up. The theaters were not emptied. It is possible that dating couples in the balcony never noticed since their interest was often not on the screen. Eventually, the projectionists returned, the movies were resumed, and a message had been sent. Or, so the public was to believe.

The next morning, on a slower day so that the box-office take would not be damaged too badly, IATSE pickets were stationed outside every Paramount theater. The projectionists would not cross the picket line.

"Panicked" by this "unexpected" turn of events and "shocked" by the anger of the union leaders since Paramount did have a union crew—just the wrong international—the theater chain owners arranged a hasty private meeting to "save" their industry. Bioff, Browne, Barney Balaban, and others gathered at the Union League Club, where they met in a private room. Food was ordered. Presumably, cigars were smoked. Perhaps cards were played. No one present ever talked about exactly how the "meeting" was handled. The end result was preplanned, and though the men may have been at odds with one another, they were all essentially hustlers and con artists, each trying to assure that he benefited from some aspect of the scam.

Finally, the men emerged. The theater chain owners agreed to a closed-shop arrangement in which IATSE would be the labor union of the movie industry and the negotiating arm of labor. IBEW had lost to IATSE, and the IATSE leadership would determine the role of the IBEW in the IATSE-dominated movement. Ultimately, this meant that the producers gave permission for IATSE to represent all the technicians except the sound technicians and the maintenance workers. The maintenance workers were allowed to stay with the IBEW, and the membership of the sound technicians was tabled for further discussion.

No one mentioned the fact that the producers had no authority in any of this. *Variety*, the industry trade journal, did suggest that one of the reasons for the deal was the creation of the new CIO, a rival to the AFL prior to their merger many years later. Browne and Bioff could have left the AFL to join the CIO, taking millions of dollars in union money to the new upstart.

The producers never said how delighted they were with the deal. They were paying for labor peace, and IATSE could be the justification for all manner of excesses, including cutting wages and personnel. The producers would be able to blame the labor agreement at the same time that the IATSE officials were taking special assessments to fight for their members. Ultimately, despite the payments and kickbacks, the no-strike clause and the union leadership's decision to keep wages low put the producers an estimated $15 million ahead of where they would have been without IATSE or with an honest deal.

The union sold out its members, embezzling funds and hurting their financial future. The theater chain owners got into bed with the devil because they saved a fortune in costs. And every industry observer thought the Paramount-triggered strike had been genuine instead of street theater planned by both sides.

CHAPTER **Sixteen**

Kiss the Girl and Make Her Die

T helma Todd had to die before Tuesday, December 17, 1935. That was the day she was scheduled to talk with District Attorney Buron Fitts about all she knew concerning Luciano, Bioff, Browne, the union/production company problems, and other criminal matters.

Todd had long known she was in danger from the men she played with, from her ex-husband, and from her lover, Charles Luciano. She was also naive enough to think that if she went public, very public, no one would touch her. After all, she was a successful movie actress, an important box-office draw, and, in the Hollywood area itself, a respected businesswoman. Sure, her operation seemed to rest on the narrow line between legitimate business and, with the use of the third floor for modest gambling, illegal activity, but that was a minor concern in Los Angeles. Prohibition was over. The Great Depression was easing a bit. Gambling as it was done in her extra room was more along the lines of the private high-stakes card games the moguls held in one another's homes. She was respected. People cared about her. Thelma Todd was certain that going public would keep her safe.

The problem was that Todd did not realize that the district attorney's office was corrupt. Luciano "owned" Buron Fitts. If she kept her appointment, Fitts would not dare tell her to go home and forget about what she had discovered for the same reason she thought she would be safe. She was too well known, and he would become suspect. On the other hand, if he opened an investigation into the people from whom he had taken payoffs, he would be killed. The only way to save everyone from embarrassment was to kill Thelma Todd before her appointment.

The hours leading up to the murder were relatively pleasant. She had been making movies for Hal Roach and earning less money than her popularity warranted. The films were distributed by Nick Schenck at Loew's. He had observed her work, liked it, and just offered her a contract, which she accepted, to go to MGM, the Loew's production company subsidiary, for considerably more money. Actress Ida Lupino, one of Thelma's friends, threw a party in the Trocadero nightclub in honor of Todd's success.

Almost everyone currently in Thelma's life was invited to the party with the exception of Charles Luciano, who was too private a man to come even if he had been asked, and Pat DiCicco, her ex-husband. Pat heard about it and wanted to come. He told Ida Lupino he would bring a date if she would allow him to stop by, and the actress saw no reason to refuse.

Thelma was not pleased when DiCicco and his date, actress Margaret Lindsay, arrived around midnight. DiCicco spoke briefly to Thelma, both of them becoming agitated according to the other guests, and then he adjourned to a table well away from Todd but where he could see everything. Approximately an hour after they arrived, Pat and Margaret left the nightclub.

Todd, seemingly relaxed and enjoying herself again, began talking with Sidney Grauman, the owner of the Chinese Theater on Hollywood Boulevard, where his walk of stars had become a major tourist attraction. Grauman, like many theater owners, was familiar with Luciano and the men who worked for him in Los Angeles. Later, Grauman would mention that he and a few others thought that three of those men had been sitting with Todd before she left the club. One man was noted with some certainty, and it was presumed they were all together.

It was close to 2 a.m. when Thelma asked Grauman to call the Sidewalk Café and let Roland West know she would not make it back in time to help him. She knew he expected her at 2 a.m. and that the drive took a half-hour under the best of circumstances. She wanted Roland to close on his own but to be available for when she arrived. She was too drunk to operate a car, but her driver, Ernie Peters, would get her there. She wanted West to help her to her apartment if she could no longer handle the steps on her own.

West was annoyed. He closed the café, then took Thelma's white pit bull for a walk. Then, he took the dog into his own apartment so they could both settle down and get some rest.

The dog awakened at 3:30 a.m., its whining rousing West. He heard water running and called out to see if Thelma was home. There was no answer, the dog quieted down, and he assumed that she had made it home and was safely in her adjoining apartment.

Ernie Peters was the driver who picked Thelma up at the Trocadero. She was agitated and talked about needing him to get her to her place in Santa Monica as quickly as possible; otherwise, she was likely to be kidnapped or killed by gangsters. She was also drunk.

Peters wasn't certain what to believe. Thelma Todd was famous, the times were rough, and the general public knew that in Los Angeles there were criminals operating so openly that they had to have some sort of immunity. He had to believe that perhaps both she and he could be killed. He took off, driving as quickly as seventy miles an hour before pulling up to the steps that led from the street by the Sidewalk Café to Thelma's apartment. Then, he started to get out to see her to her door, but she told him not to bother. He could go. She would be fine. And Thelma certainly seemed calmer. Ernie drove off, glancing in his mirror long enough to see that Todd was lingering in front of her restaurant.

What happened next was pieced together from the accounts of various witnesses. Presumably, while Todd was still outside her restaurant, Charles Luciano drove up and told her to get in the car so they could take a drive along the coast. He had been called when she left, either by Grauman or one of the three men who had been sitting with her. He had undoubtedly been waiting for her return, though with a fog that early Sunday morning, it was unlikely that Ernie Peters would have noticed Luciano's vehicle unless the lights had been on.

Todd and Luciano argued as they drove, Luciano still trying to get her to take his offer concerning the third floor, which Thelma was turning into a steak place. The business was not that important to Luciano's gambling operations. The club might generate substantial revenue, though no more than similar locations throughout the region. It seems most likely that Luciano realized that he had told Thelma too much, that perhaps his man DiCicco had said too much, and that Thelma had guessed whatever she had not been told; she was

Gloria Swanson in 1950. She began an affair with Joe Kennedy in 1928, during which he lavished her with gifts—all paid for from her own bank account. *Cleveland State University Library, Special Collections.*

Joe and Rose Kennedy.
Cleveland State University Library, Special Collections.

In addition to being known as a song-and-dance man, James Cagney was famous for playing gangsters in the movies. *Cleveland State University Library, Special Collections.*

Fatty Arbuckle before the scandal that nearly ruined his career. *Cleveland State University Library, Special Collections.*

A gangster and a gangster-turned-actor playing a gangster: Bugsey Siegel and George Raft.
Cleveland State University Library, Special Collections.

Jack Warner.
*Cleveland State University
Library, Special Collections.*

Louis B. Mayer.
*Cleveland State University
Library, Special Collections.*

The elder Jean Harlow,
mother to the talentless
and promiscuous actress.
*Cleveland State University Library,
Special Collections.*

Jean Harlow in all her
abundant radiance.
*Cleveland State University
Library, Special Collections.*

Marino Bello, lover to both Harlow women, at the time of the younger Jean's mysterious death. *Cleveland State University Library, Special Collections.*

Lucky Luciano.
Cleveland State University Library, Special Collections.

Pasquale DiCicco, Jean Malin, Thelma Todd, and Lois Wilson. Todd may have been the target of the mob's most infamous hit ever. *Cleveland State University Library, Special Collections.*

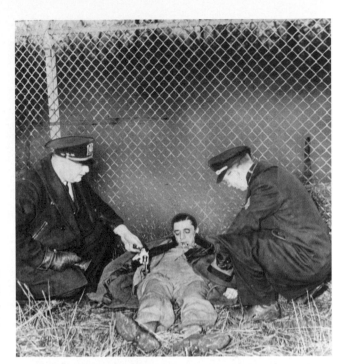

Police examine the corpse of the gunned-down Frank Nitti. *Cleveland State University Library, Special Collections.*

Ever the subject of gangster involvement, Frank Sinatra ironically depended on the police to protect him from his adoring fans. *Cleveland State University Library, Special Collections.*

A reporter interviews Lana Turner as Johnny Stompanato and Cheryl Crane exchange words. *Cleveland State University Library, Special Collections.*

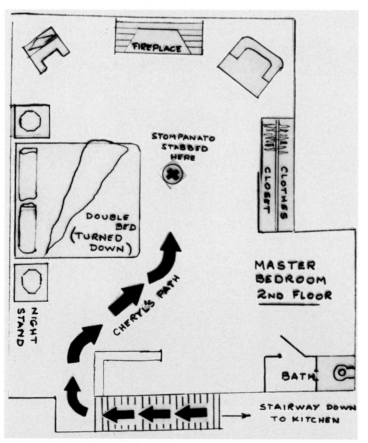

Artist's rendering of the crime scene where Cheryl Crane allegedly stabbed Johnny Stompanato to death. *Cleveland State University Library, Special Collections.*

Mickey Cohen surveys the damage following the bombing of his home on February 6, 1950. *Cleveland State University Library, Special Collections.*

Meyer Lansky (right). *Cleveland State University Library, Special Collections.*

Marilyn Monroe shortly before her death. Her drug overdose was, in all likelihood, neither a mob hit nor suicide but an accident. *Cleveland State University Library, Special Collections.*

too high profile to be allowed to have that type of knowledge. He either had to kill her before she reached the district attorney or he had to corrupt her, something he seemed to prefer.

If the top floor of Thelma Todd's Sidewalk Café had a full gambling casino she would no longer be treated with a wink and a nod. She would be liable for criminal prosecution. The proper authorities would, of course, be paid off so long as she cooperated, and if she began to make noise about what she knew, Luciano would make certain that her place was raided, she was arrested, and her career was ruined. Todd, too drunk to understand that she did not have the upper hand over Luciano just because she had an appointment with the district attorney on Tuesday, again refused the casino.

Finally, around 9 a.m. on Sunday, Luciano and Todd were in downtown Los Angeles in the vicinity of Eighth and Figueroa. She told him to stop the car so that she could get a taxi to take her home.

Thelma raced into the nearest open business, a cigar store owned by W. F. Persson. She never identified herself to either the owner or Robert E. Fisher, a customer. She was still drunk, feeling the effects of too much alcohol and too little sleep. However, Persson was an avid fan and later claimed that he recognized the crying actress.

Todd told Persson that she needed to make a telephone call. There was a pay phone in the middle of the store. He held the receiver and dialed the number she gave him.

According to Persson, Todd looked out the door as he dialed. Then, as he listened for someone to answer, Todd apparently raced outside again. He did not see her after that, no one answered the ringing telephone, and he could only remember that the last four digits of the number were 7771. The police never checked to see if they could determine whom she had called, and neither Todd's mother nor the friends questioned could think of a telephone number ending in 7771.

According to Fisher, there was a man waiting outside with a fur coat on his arm. He met the woman both Fisher and Persson were certain was the actress, then walked with her to Eighth and Hope streets, where the First Methodist Church was having services. However, they apparently did not go inside because Fisher remembered the two of them returning to a car about ten minutes later. Whoever the woman was, she was apparently calm and relaxed, no longer frantic as she had been roughly ten minutes before.

Roland West awakened at 10 a.m. and again could not find

Thelma. However, at that hour, he was not surprised. He figured she was either in the café or had gone out somewhere. He also checked the ladies' lounge in the restaurant because a couch was kept there. He had not locked all of the entrance doors the previous night to make certain she could get inside. However, if she was drunk enough to think she could not get inside, she would sleep on the couch. It was a habit she had gotten into when she had locked herself out in the past. This time Thelma was not there, so once again he went to work alone. It was 11 a.m. and he started to get the café ready for Sunday business.

Bartender Bob Anderson, a man who doubled as Todd's auto mechanic for such cars as her Phaeton convertible, was able to take a break from the Sidewalk Café around 2 p.m.. He walked to the main house where Thelma parked her car. He found it empty and backed into the garage. By then it had been approximately twelve hours since Sid Grauman had telephoned West on Todd's behalf.

The next Thelma Todd sighting was two hours later, at 4 p.m., in a Beverly Hills drugstore at the corner of Sunset and Crescent Heights boulevards. Sara Kane Carter was the witness this time. She was a customer who was surprised to see an attractive blond in an evening dress and fur inside the store on a Sunday afternoon. The woman she was convinced was the actress was using the telephone.

The timing of the witnessed telephone call was the same approximate time given by Martha Ford, a friend of Thelma's, who was planning a party for the actress in much the manner that Ida Lupino had done the night before. She said that she recognized the voice and that Thelma identified herself. Apparently, Todd thought that she was running a little late for a four o'clock party, but the event was actually scheduled for three hours later.

There was discussion about what each woman would be wearing, and Thelma said she would be bringing a man along. She did not identify him, though it was presumed from the conversation that it might be Luciano. Certainly, he was the only man she was seeing at the time who could surprise her hostess. However, she never showed.

There were discrepancies in the story about the planned party, including issues of time. There was also another sighting of Thelma in a chocolate brown Phaeton, the same color as her car. Sometimes she was the driver. Sometimes she was the passenger. However, the man who made the sighting and kept changing his story was alone in his memory. Neither his wife nor son noticed what he claimed to have seen.

Another confirmed incident occurred around 7:30 p.m., when George Baker of the Roach Studios called the Sidewalk Café looking for Thelma. He apparently was at the Martha Ford party, and Thelma had not shown up. Roland West took the call and explained that he did not know where Thelma might be. However, he promised to have her call Martha when she arrived.

Later, it would be learned that Todd and Luciano had dinner at the Beverly Hills home of one of his associates and the associate's wife. The meal—roast beef, potatoes, peas, and carrots—mattered because an autopsy would show that this was her last meal. Attempts would be made to say that she had died following the Ida Lupino gathering, but even if witnesses had not seen her alive after that, analysis of the food established a later time of death. None of what remained in her stomach had been served at the Trocadero.

It was also learned that Luciano wanted to know what Thelma planned to tell Buron Fitts. His curiosity likely stemmed from more than a fear of what she would say about his activities because he knew that the district attorney dared not investigate. It was probably a check on himself, to find out how much he had said, since he was known to try and impress women by revealing his activities. Usually, they had the sense to remain silent. Thelma was better educated, better known, and wealthier than the prostitutes and madams who were his usual recipients of pillow talk.

Thelma claimed that she was going to tell Fitts that Luciano was putting the squeeze on her restaurant, making her pay far more for what she bought than it should have cost. She knew that he was doing the same thing to others, and she claimed she had a list of restaurant owners and other victims. She also claimed to have photographs of the men who kept showing up at her place. It was all hidden away. It was all safe from anything he might try to do to have it destroyed before she could take it to Fitts.

To further claim power, Thelma said that she had turned over information related to Bioff, Browne, Luciano, the unions, and the film industry to the FBI. There had been a time when she was receiving threatening letters from out of state that the FBI had assigned men to guard her. She said she told them what she knew, and what she knew could bring down Bioff, Browne, Luciano, and the others working the rackets.

It was mostly a bluff. If her knowledge about Bioff, Browne, IATSE, and the film industry shakedown were more than hearsay, someone from law enforcement would have contacted Luciano already. Many of the federal agents were honest and did not like the Hollywood corruption. The men who worked for Luciano and Nitti were well known. Todd would have provided names and dates if she really had them.

The restaurant shakedown was worse in that Todd's knowledge might be enough to warrant an investigation. There was no telling what she would do if Fitts either did nothing or went through the motions of whitewashing the whole matter. Thelma Todd was going to die, not necessarily for what she knew but because she could not be counted upon to keep her mouth shut when she did learn something. It was also feared that even if she did not know as much as she implied, she might lie, creating a furor based on nothing but that would still shine too much light on projects best left in the dark.

Luciano and Todd left the friend's home and were again seen. Jewel Carmen, Roland West's ex-wife, was certain she noticed the Phaeton in the Sunset and Vine area of Hollywood. Carmen was certain it was Thelma. She was less certain about the man. It could have been Luciano. It could have been DiCicco. It could have been someone else from the same ethnic background. She just knew that he was dark and foreign looking, which was no longer unusual for the area.

The one definite stop on the way back to the Sidewalk Café was at the Christmas tree lot of the S. J. Cummings family. Todd was out of the car, had obviously been drinking, and was readily recognized. Neither Cummings, his wife, nor their daughter recognized the man. What mattered to all of them was that she selected a tree, paid for it, and said she wanted it silvered. She said she would return to pick it up. The time was 11:45 p.m. on Sunday night.

Luciano took Todd back to her property, letting her off at the garage on Posetano Road where she kept her car. As she walked toward the structure, she was grabbed from behind and choked. She struggled violently, but the assailant had the better angle. He was able to hold her so her air was limited while pounding at her face with his fist. Her nose was broken. Two of her ribs on the right side of her body were cracked. A front tooth was chipped. She also had a blood-alcohol level of 0.13, high enough that she was legally drunk, which perhaps helps explain the lack of evidence that she defended herself.

The assailant took Todd and shoved her into her car inside the garage. She was propped a little to the right of where she would have sat had she been driving, but it was obvious that he wanted her to look as though she was sitting behind the wheel. Then, because the keys were in the ignition, he started the car, left the car door partially open, and left the garage, closing the door. The garage quickly filled with carbon monoxide fumes, killing the battered actress.

Exactly who killed Thelma Todd has never been determined with certainty. The man who seems the most likely killer, or perhaps the person who arranged for the death on behalf of Luciano, was Albert (Allie) "Tick-Tock" Tannenbaum, a member of Murder, Inc., who was regularly dispatched to the West by Lepke. Murder, Inc., often did business by sending hit men to work in regions where they were not known. Tannenbaum was based in the East, which meant that most of the hits he was assigned were west of the Mississippi. He would not be known to law-enforcement officers or to anyone connected with his victims. The Murder, Inc., reasoning was that even if the criminal was seen, no one would be able to identify the man. That was why Tannenbaum regularly made trips to Los Angeles and some of the mobsters based in Los Angeles were periodically called to New York. And train service was such that if Tick-Tock was in New York when he got the call, he would have had time to get to Los Angeles well in advance of Todd's appointment with the district attorney.

Luciano was innocent of committing the murder himself and knew that he would be covered by the authorities, but he took no chances. At 7:45 a.m. on Monday, he was on a flight to New York City. He would never again return to Los Angeles. One hour and fifteen minutes later, Pat DiCicco, the one Hollywood semi-insider connected to Luciano in everyone's mind, boarded a plane to Long Island. He claimed he had to visit his mother. Neither man was ever questioned about the murder.

There were three other possible motives for Todd's murder in the minds of various reporters who looked into the affair many years after the fact. The first was that Frank Nitti had had Todd killed as a warning to Luciano. He wanted exclusive rights to the majority of the rackets in the movie industry, and this was his way of telling Charles that he would die if he kept fighting for territory. The fact that Luciano drastically reduced the presence of his organization in Hollywood after the death shows that there could be some validity to the story. However, he was also facing another problem from the business of which he was least proud, New York prostitution. He would soon go on trial and was in as much danger of going to jail as Capone had been.

As for others named as possible murderers, Pat DiCicco has frequently been mentioned, even though the reasons for this thinking are unclear. Luciano would not have asked him to handle the murder, and he had been divorced from Todd long enough that there was no passion fueling a desire for violence. At the same time, he probably did know that she would not live to see Buron Fitts. He may have attended the Ida Lupino party to watch Thelma and report when she left, an idea that evolved from one witness to DiCicco's making a telephone call before he left the party that Saturday night.

And then there was Roland West. He was intensely passionate about Todd. He loved her, though their relationship was neither sexual nor emotionally intimate after his divorce from Jewel Carmen. He was also the person primarily involved with the members of the mob sent to shake down the Sidewalk Café. In later years, he confessed to feeling that if he had handled the thugs differently, perhaps being more forceful or giving in to their demands, Thelma would not have been murdered. That was probably why, years later when he was dying, he confessed to Hal Roach that he "killed Toddy." It was not the guilt of direct involvement. It was the perceived guilt of past inaction.

The facts seem to indicate that it was Luciano who ordered Todd's death because of what she was threatening to expose. She was a danger if she had the facts. She was a danger if she implied facts she could not prove but that might be investigated by outsiders who could not ignore the statements of a prominent actress.

Todd's death was a major turning point for the mob assault on Hollywood. No one seemed to notice the corruption evident in what took place after the corpse was discovered. Captain Bert Wallis of the Homicide Division of the Los Angeles Police Department (LAPD) was the first officer of rank to arrive at the scene of the murder, but when he realized that the victim was Thelma Todd, he ordered his investigators from the garage. Only he and Los Angeles County's medical examiner A. F. Wagner would handle the preliminary investigation.

That is not to say that the crime scene was protected. In addition to their own careful work to make the scene fit the ideas they would be promoting, Wallis and Wagner invited reporters and photographers into the garage to see what had happened. Any trace evidence was destroyed.

Some experts felt that the two men were initially preserving the evidence, but their egos got in the way of their common sense. Most observers felt that they were checking on the death and planning to make the evidence fit the crime as others would want it reported. The latter was probably the case since opening the area to reporters assuredly limited what could be found.

Wagner, well aware of the power of the studio personnel and that Thelma Todd was involved with a less than reputable element in Los Angeles, wrote that the crime scene indicated she had died of carbon-monoxide poisoning. Coroner Frank Nance did a full autopsy, ignoring the strangulation marks around her neck, and claimed that in the few seconds before her death, her body convulsed involuntarily and her neck jerked, slamming into the steering wheel. That was why her nose was broken and her ribs were cracked.

The bruises and swelling were noted. They were clear indicators of a beating, but in Wagner's deft spin, they became reactions to ingesting the carbon monoxide.

There were curiosities never investigated by law enforcement. The garage was at the base of approximately 270 steps leading to the apartments in which West and Todd lived, and it served both Jewel Carmen's mansion and accountant Charles Smith's small living space. The Phaeton that Thelma drove was a twelve-cylinder car known for its great physical size and less-than-quiet motor. The car, with the engine running, could certainly have been heard inside Smith's apartment. Smith claimed to have heard nothing.

No one suspected Smith of the murder, but no one would have been surprised if he was mob connected in some way. Todd did not trust his accounting. At best, he seemed careless. At worst, he was embezzling for himself or Luciano's people. She was planning to have the books audited. He was not someone who would commit murder, but he would make certain he saw and heard nothing if the wrong people were involved.

The investigators tried to convince the public that West, angry with Todd for being out so late when they needed to share the work that weekend, allegedly locked some of the entry doors Todd would have used. She then was supposed to have climbed the stairs and passed out in her running car, dying from carbon-monoxide poison and sustaining injuries related to the trauma of death. The problem was that her blood-alcohol level was not high enough to cause such full impairment. Equally important, she did not like the steps and never tackled them alone late at night, especially when the evening had been damp and cold.

Buron Fitts briefly investigated the death, primarily because

Thelma Todd's mother was outraged over what she rightfully felt was the murder of her daughter and the seeming lack of interest in the killer. However, he never sought a suspect because it wasn't in the studio's best interest to dig too far into the private life of an actress who let men beat her and bedded a mobster, while acting in wholesome comedies on the screen. He also had more pressing concerns at the end of the year, including the vehicular homicide case of Busby Berkeley in September 1935.

Berkeley was a choreographer who delighted in creating elaborate production numbers with hundreds of singers and dancers. He had worked on Broadway with Flo Ziegfeld. He had worked in Los Angeles at MGM and Warner Brothers. He was also a drunk.

On September 8, 1935, when Thelma Todd had not yet signed her own death warrant, he left a party and began driving on the Pacific Coast Highway. Maybe he lost control. Probably he fell asleep. Whatever the case, he crossed the median just north of Sunset Boulevard and slammed into two cars. Three people died. Two were seriously injured. He was relatively unhurt.

Berkeley knew what mattered. You could only get away with murder—in this case vehicular homicide—if the studio said you could. He called Whitey Hendry, the chief of police both for MGM, where he made his serious money and to which he felt the greatest loyalty, and for Culver City. He was a skilled investigator who made certain that the outcomes of his cases matched the best interests of the studio. Felony murder or jaywalking were all the same to him. That was why Berkeley called Whitey, and Whitey, in turn, called attorney Jerry Giesler, the finest representation that money could buy. He made guilty men innocent and innocent men guilty and generally assured his clients that it didn't matter what they did if they had adequate funds and were on the right side of the moguls.

Buron Fitts was aware of what was taking place and eventually had to be certain that Berkeley went to court. However, before there was a serious risk of jail, seemingly inevitable because of non-studio-employee eyewitnesses, Giesler created a parallel life for a trial that opened the same day that Thelma Todd's body was found wedged in her car.

Berkeley was a victim, Giesler declared with Whitey cheering him on. The poor man was driving a car with defective tires that caused the accident, seriously injuring the choreographer. For added emphasis,

Berkeley made his appearance with his head and leg wrapped in bandages, his body covered by a sheet, an orderly wheeling him into the courtroom.

There was no denying that some people said Berkeley was drunk. However, actors like to work, and stars needed to stay in favor with the studios. Actor Pat O'Brien, Director Mervyn LeRoy, and around a dozen other Hollywood legends who had attended the same party as Berkeley said that he had not been drinking. By the time the early testimony was complete, no one at the party had had any alcohol whatsoever, even though Prohibition was over and the people attending were known for their fondness for liquor and fine wine.

The jury was not as stupid as Giesler hoped. They split, and a second trial had to be held. Again they split. Finally, apparently abandoning all common sense since the idea of a nondrinking party involving two hundred show business professionals was not believable in Hollywood, the third jury acquitted Berkeley, who returned to work—and drinking. MGM paid $100,000 in civil damages to the families of those killed and injured.

It was strange to have the first Berkeley trial start the day Thelma was found. It was even odder when Pat DiCicco was involved in a similar death on July 11, 1936, though he was an innocent bystander rather than the person responsible.

DiCicco was at the restaurant Trader Vic's with an unnamed woman and the maverick producer Howard Hughes. They drove in Hughes' Duesenberg, a high-speed, high-performance car that Hughes drove too quickly to be in control.

Hughes approached the corner of Third and Lorraine as Gabe Meyer, a furniture salesman for May Company, was legally in the crosswalk. Hughes slammed on his brakes, leaving fifty feet of skid marks and sending Meyer one hundred feet down the road.

Once again, the studio had to intervene. A call went to Los Angeles County coroner Frank Nance, who proved his worth as he had in the Thelma Todd murder. Thelma Todd committed suicide, according to Nance, her death from carbon monoxide poisoning, her broken ribs, bruises, and so on, all caused by her death throes. In Hughes's case, the accident had been unavoidable and was certainly not anyone's fault, except maybe Gabe Meyer's as he had had the bad grace to be going home from work.

And again, Pat DiCicco quietly slipped away.

Intermission 2

I n which Charles Luciano is permanently taken out of the Hollywood game and the relationship between producers and union leaders becomes less and less comfortable.

There was a quirk in the way the U.S. tax laws were enforced. No one collecting the money cared how someone earned his or her living. You could be a member of Murder, Inc., or you could be a waitress in a small-town coffee shop. It was all the same. You were to report what you made honestly. You were to determine your gross and the percentage you owed the government and to send that portion to the IRS. The legality of what you did to get the money did not matter. The information would not be turned over to the police. That reality, coupled with the fact that a number of gangsters, such as Al Capone, went to jail for the least important criminal charge of which they were guilty, income tax evasion, led to unexpected prosecutions. Men who were invulnerable because of bribes, intimidation, or some other factor when it came to city or state prosecution were suddenly being charged with the one crime for which they could not claim innocence.

Charles Luciano was fortunate to observe this new reality before it hurt him. He watched as Al Capone was convicted of tax evasion. He watched Frank Costello go to jail. He watched as Dutch Schultz was targeted for prosecution. And he listened to the man who had first brought Capone to Chicago. He later explained,

> Johnny Torrio told every one of us that we better start fixin' up our income tax returns. A lot of us did that, startin' with 1928, to show legitimate business. In any case, I declared an income of sixteen thousand bucks and through the next four, five years, that figure went up to about twenty-five grand a year, from "gamblin' enterprises," and I listed myself as a "professional gambler." Y'know, I always thought it was funny that the United States government would let anybody declare taxes on any illegal business

and then keep the money without prosecutin' the guy for breakin' the law.

The problem for Luciano came not with tax filing but with Thomas E. Dewey. The future governor was acting as assistant to George Medalie, the U.S. attorney for the Southern District of New York, and later as both an investigative prosecutor and the district attorney.

Dewey was especially interested in Charles Luciano because he felt that Luciano dominated the mob in New York. The mobster agreed. Later he reminisced,

> Even after Prohibition was dumped, I was runnin' one of the biggest businesses in the world. We was in a hundred different things, legit and illegit. If you add it all up, we—I mean, the guys all over the country—we was doin' a business that was grossin' maybe a couple billion dollars a year. I was like the head of that big company, not as Boss of Bosses, but as a guy a lot of people came to for advice, a guy everybody expected to be in on the big decisions. But there was no way I could know what was goin' on everywhere all the time.

In a statement reminiscent of corporate CEOs invoking C.Y.A. (cover your ass) reasoning, Luciano said that many criminal operations were handled by underlings. They often spoke as though Luciano not only knew, but approved, of their methods, such as with the business of prostitution. That was why it seemed he might be guilty of crimes he knew nothing about.

The prostitution issue was an emotional one for Luciano and a number of other mobsters who also shared his love/hate relationship with the business. Most of the women who worked in the brothels were undereducated, often from poor, rural families who needed one less mouth to feed, and they had often been deliberately hooked on drugs like so many in the film industry.

There were several levels of prostitution, starting with women who worked for $2 on an assembly line basis; the person who ran the brothel would knock on the door after ten minutes and demand that the prostitute finish the customer so the next one could be serviced. Usually, the $2 prostitutes were worn, haggard, sickly has-beens whose bodies and minds could take no more violence.

The somewhat more attractive women cost more. Some houses had a flat rate of $10, though a rapid turnover of customers was still expected. There were also women who worked outcall, going to homes, apartments, and hotels for fees as high as $100 or more. The split was such that the prostitute, who worked from ten to fourteen hours a day, made too little to escape the life.

The arrangements varied with the price of the woman and the services she performed, but there was a consistency to the lifestyle. Many of the girls had pimps, and those who didn't worked in brothels where others took care of them and arranged for the men.

Half the money—usually a sum that ranged from $1 to $50, depending upon the price—went to the madam of the whorehouse. She then had to pay off the higher-level mob personnel and top law enforcement, including Dewey, a man who was later revealed to have worked on both sides of the law when it suited his wallet.

The other half of the money also paid expenses, though these were the expenses of the prostitute. All the girls put between 5 and 10 percent into a fund that would pay for bail and legal services if they got arrested. Another $5 per week was charged for medical services. The man who arranged for the girl to work a particular brothel or to change locations to assure variety received 10 percent. Finally, since the girls were expected to live in the brothel, there was another fee for room and board. And they also paid for the drugs to which they were addicted in much the manner as Thelma Todd had been

During the trial, Dewey explained that "the vice industry since Luciano took over is highly organized and operates with businesslike precision." He added, "Lucky was way up at the top in this city." He did not "actually see or collect from the women." However, Luciano was "always in touch with the general details of the business."

According to Florence Brown, a drug-addicted, shabbily dressed young woman in her early twenties also known as "Cokey Flo" and a former prostitute who worked as a madam for Luciano's men, he had said, "I'm gonna organize the cathouses like the A&P."

The case was a strange one. Dewey used seemingly false testimony. Prostitutes who claimed to have visited Luciano in his luxurious hotel suite could not identify the details encountered when walking through the entrance to the elevators. Staff members were familiar with Luciano but not some of the associates with whom he supposedly was meeting on business in the hotel. It seemed that Dewey had worked with the witnesses to "remember" what they had never seen, though Luciano had also lied, especially about his connection to Al Capone.

Later, Luciano explained what troubled him about the trial, besides the fact that he was convicted. Dewey met with reporters after getting a conviction and said, "This, of course, was not a vice trial. It was a racket prosecution. The control of all organized prostitution in New York by the convicted defendants in this case, together with other criminals under Lucania [when Luciano was tried, the prosecutor listed him under his real last name], have gradually absorbed control of the narcotics, policy, loan-shark and Italian lottery syndicates, the receipt of stolen goods and certain industrial rackets." Dewey explained that since he couldn't get Luciano where it mattered, he got him on a minor charge just to put him away. It was a statement that outraged Luciano.

> After sittin' in court and listenin' to myself bein' plastered to the wall and tarred and feathered by a bunch of whores who sold themselves for a quarter, and hearin' that no-good [Judge] Mc-Cook hand me what added up to a life term, I still got madder at Dewey's crap than anythin' else. That little shit with the mustache comes right out in the open and admits he got me for everythin' else but what he charged me with. I knew he knew I didn't have a fuckin' thing to do with prostitution, not with none of them broads. But Dewey was such a goddamn racketeer himself, in a legal way, that he crawled up my back with a frame and stabbed me. If he'd hauled me into court to stand trial for anythin' I done, includin' conspiracy to commit murder, I'd've taken it like a man.

Dewey never intended to do more than put Luciano in jail and, hopefully, gain the attention to run eventually for higher office. He did not realize he had changed the dynamics in Hollywood. From that period forward, the assault on the moguls would be coordinated from Chicago, and the one law-enforcement agency that repeatedly emerged victorious was that connected to the Internal Revenue Service.

Still, there would be East Coast mobsters playing on the West Coast, as Jean Harlow would discover to her delight. The fact that her most notorious relationship could have topped a tabloid magazine's list of America's sleaziest undoubtedly would never have deterred her.

CHAPTER Seventeen

Longy Had a Little Locket

His name was Abner Zwillman; he was one of seven poor Jewish kids raised in Newark, New Jersey, by an immigrant father who sold live chickens until his death when Zwillman was ten. Abner quit elementary school, selling fruit to support his family, then turning to crime. He grew tall and strong, acquiring the nickname "Der Langer"—the tall one—which eventually became just "Longy."

In 1925, when Longy Zwillman was twenty-six years old, he moved into the liquor business. He worked hard, delivering bootleg hootch by the truckload, moving fifty such loads each night. He organized a large group of rumrunners and began taking both liquor and other contraband over the Canadian border. He came to dominate Newark's Third Ward, making an estimated $40 million a year and becoming a partner in what some called the Big Six, criminals who agreed to work together instead of challenging one another. These included Ben Siegel, Lepke Buchalter, Meyer Lansky, Charles Luciano, and Jake Shapiro, along with Zwillman.

Zwillman, like Rosselli, was never flamboyant, though he could be violent in ways that got him in trouble. He did time in the state prison for the savage beating of Preston Buzzard, a black pimp whose life has otherwise been forgotten. However, the greatest respect Longy received was for a present encased in a gold locket that one of his girlfriends gave him to wear around his neck. She also gave him some duplicates to give to his special friends to prove both that her unusual hair color, platinum blond, was natural and that, in her bedroom, he had gone where others never would. Such were the romantic notions of Harlean "Baby Jean" Harlow, the sentimental sleaze. And encouraging Harlean every step of the way was her stepfather, Marino Bello, who was delighted to pimp his wife's daughter if it made a member of the mob happy enough to remember his name.

It is easy to forget one reality about Hollywood starlets. The glamorous "women" who appeared on the screen as extras, in small roles, and in their first starring appearances were usually kids. Many would not be old enough to get a driver's license today. Most would be too young to get a drink or vote in an election. In industrial cities in the Midwest, where jobs in the steel mills, on automobile assembly lines, and in similar physically difficult manufacturing plants were available to strong teenage boys willing to work, marriages frequently involved barely pubescent girls. Some of these marriages were arranged, the result of the culture from which the parents came. Some were simply expected because the families had known each other for many years. Harlow was no different, a girl/woman ripe for molding by the moguls. The studios emphasized her beauty and a raw sexuality through makeup and costuming (assisted by Harlean's reluctance to wear undergarments) so that she seemed an experienced woman of the world—at seventeen.

Harlean "Baby Jean" never fancied herself a Hollywood star. Such ambitions only existed in the heart of her mother, Jean Harlow, who was first married to a Kansas City dentist named Dr. Montclair Carpentier.

Had Jean Harlow Carpentier had a different father than Sam "Skip" Harlow, matters might have been different. He approved her first husband because he had a good profession, was a quiet man, and was willing to let Sam dominate the marriage. The couple gave birth to Harlean, a girl her mother would forever call "Baby," and Sam decided he had to oversee the raising of his granddaughter. Jean had to go to the school with the right social status. She was better than most other children and could not be corrupted by those with less money, a different religion, or other undesirable qualities. That was how she ended up at the Barstow School for Girls, a place so proper that just mentioning a child was in attendance instantly established one's social standing.

The problem for Mama Jean was that she was bored. Her husband was boring. Her beloved daughter was in a snooty private school with little time for her mother. And her father's ultraconservative demands were stultifying. The only answer was an uncontested divorce from Montclair on September 19, 1922, when Harlean was nine years old. Alimony was set at $200 per month, and Mama Jean was given sole custody of "the Baby."

Jean and "the Baby" traveled to Hollywood in 1923 so that Jean could break into the movies. She was a beautiful woman, young, sexy, and seemingly willing to do anything to become a star. The only problem was that she was "elderly" by Hollywood standards at thirty-four years old. Studios wanted teenagers who, with skilled makeup, could look exactly like Jean Harlow Carpentier. They did not want the real thing.

Mother and daughter rented a room in an old mansion that had been divided for the rental income, and "the Baby" was enrolled in the Hollywood School for Girls, the same school used by parents such as the Louis B. Mayers and the Cecil B. DeMilles. Harlean isolated herself from the other students, uninterested in the movies, delighting in reading, and developing a sexuality that made the others feel awkward. She gave the impression of being a sexual sophisticate in the way she walked, talked, and dressed. However, she was mostly trying to please her flamboyant, overprotective mother, who was living with both dreams and disappointment.

Mama Jean had little time to find a career. Her father told her that he wanted Harlean in Kansas City. She could return the child and live in Hollywood, or they could both return home. Any other choice would result in her being disinherited.

The $200 a month was good money in those days, but Skip Harlow was wealthy, and Jean was no fool. Mother and daughter returned home in the spring of 1925.

Jean Harlow was frustrated with life. She was young, beautiful, and divorced and felt thwarted by an industry that announced that any woman over the age of thirty had no present and no future. Harlean was enrolled in a convent boarding school, Notre Dame de Sion, because Skip wanted her to have a conservative education. The family was not Catholic, and both Jean and Harlean chafed at the isolation and strictness of the convent school. That summer, when Skip sent Harlean to Michigamme, Michigan's Camp Cha-ton-ka, where she developed a serious case of poison oak, Jean went to nurse her, then took her home by way of Chicago. There, she met Marino Bello.

Marino Bello was yet another punk, though he had more class than most of the young men who thought they would like to be gangsters. He worked where he could get a job, and he hustled whatever would bring him extra money—an occasional prostitute, a load of food stolen from a truck. He was in his early forties when he stopped by the table where Jean and Harlean were having lunch in the College Inn dining area of the Sherman Hotel.

Today, Bello seems a quaint caricature of a man from another time, but in the 1920s, he was continental and exciting. Tall and handsome, he walked with a cane which hid a sword that could be brandished whenever he felt slighted and wished to duel with the offender. His hair was dyed and his mustache waxed. He approached women by taking their hand, turning the wrist so the palm faced up, and kissing it. Perhaps most important to his success was the fact that he seemed to come by his actions naturally, and his clothing was always in the latest style. He appeared to be someone with a past of both danger and sophistication, though he actually survived by feeding off wealthy women and their families.

Bello's first wife was Mildred Maas. She was an American; he was Italian. The marriage was his ticket to Chicago and a job with her cousin, Ernest Byfield, who owned the Sherman Hotel. His actions with other women are not known for he was extremely discrete during the seven years following World War I when he lived in Chicago, worked at the hotel's Colony Inn, and became a naturalized citizen. Then, he began looking for his next score, finding her in Jean Harlow Carpentier, who was wealthy, beautiful, and as hungry for sex as he was.

Ultimately, Mama Jean and Marino Bello were much alike. They each wanted someone exciting, both in bed and in life, even though neither had much to offer other than, it turned out, Harlean.

Harlean originally had a mind of her own. In the summer of 1927, a few months after her mother's marriage to Bello on January 18 (his wife had divorced him in December of the previous year, claiming physical abuse), Harlean had a blind date with Charles McGrew II, an orphan raised by his grandparents and heir to a small fortune. They fell in love and married on September 21, 1927, when she was sixteen. He was four years older and received his first inheritance payment of $200,000 on his twenty-first birthday. The problem was that he was an alcoholic, and she had no idea what that meant. She felt that if drinking brought him pleasure, there was nothing wrong with his having fun.

The change from married woman to actress came when Harlean visited Hollywood to see her mother's aunt Jetta Belle Chadsey, a woman who had lived a countercultural life from the time she married, also at sixteen. She gave birth the following year, divorced her husband at eighteen, and moved in with an Osage Indian lover. She became pregnant with twins by the lover, married him, gave birth, was widowed, married once again, and moved to Hollywood, where she became friends with some of the young girls seeking stardom. One of these, seventeen-year-old Rosalie Roy, became friendly with Harlean, who, in the spring of 1928, drove her from a luncheon engagement to Fox Studios, where the aspiring actress had an appointment. It was there Harlean was spotted and asked to go to central casting. Though she had no interest and did not do what was asked, her new friend and her mother's aunt both encouraged her to go back. She did, not taking matters seriously, instead using her mother's first name and maiden name, Jean Harlow, when she got hired.

❝ ❝

Jean Harlow, playing a customer in a dress shop, asks the clerk if the dress she is holding is see-through. The clerk, certain she has lost the sale, honestly answers that she is afraid so. Harlow's character happily answers, "Perfect, I'll wear it."

—A scene added to the movie *Red-Headed Woman,* which featured Harlow, who had white blond hair and was known as "the Platinum Blond"

❞ ❞

The Longy and Jean Harlow love story was one of those odd experiences that could only happen in the early years of Hollywood, when literally anyone could become a star. The studios had yet to establish their training schools. Some colleges and universities might offer theatrical training, but most of the wannabe actors were kids with a dream and little education, whose names were changed, whose clothing and makeup were made proper, and whose lives were fantasies promoted by the studio publicists who dreamed them up.

Jean Harlow had married young, but her mother was determined that she would have a career in the movies once she got the chance, and Marino Bello began helping.

Bello's nature was becoming increasingly obvious; he was a man who wanted others to support him. He stopped working after Harlean married, counting on her wealthy husband to give him money. He felt that his wife's son-in-law should be generous. Chuck felt Harlean's stepfather should get a job.

The marriage was doomed from the start because of Mama Jean's interference. She was so controlling of her daughter that when Harlean got pregnant and told her mother, Mama Jean convinced her to get an abortion and not tell her husband. Twenty months after the marriage, the couple divorced, and because Harlean was beginning to work in the movies, Bello decided to act as her manager. He also allegedly tried to get her into bed, but when she refused, he did not push the situation. He and Mama were doing too well living off the Baby's new success, which included a costarring role with Jimmy Cagney in the movie *Public Enemy*.

 ❛ ❛

Jean Harlow has a voice like a Missouri barmaid screaming for a keg.

—Independent producer Howard Hughes, before he hired her for
$1,500 to be in his movie *Hell's Angels*

 ❜ ❜

Marino Bello was thrilled. He and Mama Jean could live with the Baby in the manner to which he hoped to become accustomed. Bello also accompanied his stepdaughter on a personal appearance tour, the type of event used to make a minor player into a star. She had no talent for a one-person show, though her physical appearance in tight gowns that revealed the absence of undergarments delighted crowds. It was suggested that, for her act, she simply bend over. The tour was humiliating, but it delighted Bello, who decided he could use her to better his own circumstances.

Marino Bello was always a few steps behind everyone else. The mob was looking to the unions, Hollywood, and other enterprises to earn the money that would be lost when Prohibition was repealed. Bello paid no attention to the news of the day and its implications, deciding that he if could use Jean's money and whatever mob connections he could nurture, he might be able to buy a speakeasy or otherwise involve himself in bootlegging. However, as nice as Chicago might have been, he failed to make connections with the Outfit. He also failed to understand that the Outfit would not back a business that was passé.

Bello next turned to the promise of the New York tour and what it might mean for him when he accompanied Harlean.

New York proved the turning point for Bello's career. It is not certain how Bello knew Abner Zwillman or even if he did. Zwillman might have been fascinated by the actress and contacted Bello. Whatever the case, Longy, well known as a rising star in the gangster world of New Jersey and part of Meyer Lansky's operation, was emotionally taken by Harlean. She likewise lusted for him. He was tall, handsome, and tough in the way of a man who has proven himself so decisively that he will never again have to resort to violence to prove his toughness. He wanted Harlean. Harlean wanted him. And Bello wanted Zwillman to help him work for Lansky in New York.

Longy Zwillman was not a novice in Hollywood, though his interest was strictly financial. He saw the film industry in much the same manner as some wealthy New Yorkers viewed Broadway. There was a constant need for preproduction money to launch major shows and to film movies. Longy, like the men known as "angels" for backing Broadway plays, was willing to put some of his wealth in businesses that would yield a solid return in the short term.

The story of Longy's involvement with Columbia Studios has been debated by various film historians, though the mob statements have been consistent with what is provable and thus appear, in the case of Zwillman, to be accurate. It is their version of Zwillman's relationship with Harry Cohn that follows.

Harry Cohn, like the moguls and the mob, was raised on New York's Upper East Side. Born in 1891, his parents were immigrants, his father working as a tailor. Education was important, which is why he stayed until he was fourteen, and he had unusual skills, including playing the piano in the new movie houses. He also worked the streets, his most unusual activity done with his brother Jack. The two were highly skilled bowlers, the type of kids who, a century later, would go professional. At the time, though, professionals were hustlers, and they were among the best. They would travel to areas where they were not known, enter the alleys, and pretend to be either beginners to the game or drunk. Either way, they were soon challenged by bowlers who thought they could take the youths' money. The embarrassed brothers would lose the first few games, the stakes would be raised, and suddenly their skill would become evident. They beat every opponent and earned enough to meet their living needs.

Cohn was a tough guy who liked using whatever power he had over others. He was vulgar and profane, and toward the end of his career, he had a pair of identically designed and furnished offices connected by a passageway, the entrance to which blended into the wall. He had couches in each and is said to have kept scripts he was reading open to the identical page in each office. He could "audition" talent on one couch in one of the offices, while an actress waited in the other, his alibi if someone said he demanded sex in exchange for a movie role, an action that, by then, was illegal.

Screenwriter Ben Hecht called Cohn "White Fang," but even more telling was his adoration for the Italian dictator Benito Mussolini. He went to Italy in 1933 to see the man who was becoming a dominant power in that country. Upon his return, he stole a trick from the dictator that J. Edgar Hoover also used. He had his desk raised up on a platform so that he would always be looking down on anyone who sat in his office. Hoover did not use a platform for his desk but stepped onto a box behind his desk so he would seem taller when greeting visitors.

Johnny Rosselli enjoyed a close relationship with Harry Cohn, probably because they had similar backgrounds and contrasting styles. Each was everything the other was not. Rosselli could stop by Columbia Pictures any time he desired over the years. He visited Cohn's home when the producer was married, and when Harry got a divorce from his first wife, Johnny found him a suite in the apartment building where he lived. But it was Cohn's financial concerns that led to his meeting Longy Zwillman.

Harry Cohn was a gambler in the worst sense of the word. All producers were gamblers of a sort because each film was created based on hope and luck. However, Cohn seemed willing to bet large sums on almost anything, and Rosselli arranged for a racing wire to come directly into Cohn's office. Cohn also regularly accompanied Rosselli to the race tracks where Johnny would make betting suggestions, sometimes because he knew the horses running and sometimes because he knew the races were rigged. Eventually, the two men created their own gambling pool of $15,000 to use in whatever proportion seemed appropriate for the betting they were doing. They also became financially involved in a racetrack, with Johnny taking ownership and Harry loaning him $20,000, repaid in three months, for the investment. However, in 1932 Zwillman came into Cohn's life through Rosselli.

There were three partners in Columbia Studios—brothers Harry and Jack Cohn, and Joe Brandt, who had previously worked in the advertising business with Jack. In 1932, the relationship that had created the studio was not working. Harry was a skilled producer who understood how to put together movies on a tight budget, much like Joe Kennedy had done. Filming had to be done on time and at the preplanned cost; as a result, even a picture that was relatively unsuccessful with the public made at least a modest profit. The studio was a success because of Harry's business ways, but his relationship with Jack turned hostile. The two men constantly fought, and Joe Brandt decided that he did not want to be in the midst of the battles. He said that either brother could buy out his one-third share for $500,000.

Jack, hoping to wrest control from Harry, began seeking the funds. His contacts were primarily in New York, however, and the gradual relocation of the film industry to California reduced New York banks' interest in movie companies. The Depression also made the investment questionable if there was no way to carefully study the studio's operation on site. In the end, none of the New York banks would make the loan.

Harry Cohn, determined to beat his brother and knowing he would fail if he went the same route, turned to Johnny Rosselli. Prohibition was still in place. The mob was still making millions from bootlegging and illicit clubs, and Johnny knew that Longy Zwillman, perhaps using the business knowledge of his mentor, Meyer Lansky, would be interested in making the loan.

Zwillman was not seeking to hurt Cohn. He had no interest in using loan-sharking tactics to take control of Columbia or to become a hidden partner. Harry needed $500,000. Zwillman had $500,000 to spare. Johnny undoubtedly received a small piece of the action from Cohn for the arrangement, but the loan plus interest was as fair as if it had come from a bank.

The action meant several things, none of which were particularly obvious at the time. First, the film industry moguls saw that Harry Cohn had gotten his money without a hassle. It was a sign that members of organized crime, always cash flush in their minds, would be willing to do straight business deals in Hollywood and perhaps even finance individual pictures. It also made Longy an instant man of importance and acceptance among the moguls, an important situation when Marino Bello introduced Longy to his stepdaughter.

The Zwillman relationship within organized crime was critical for Bello's hoped-for future. Bello could theoretically begin using some of his stepdaughter's income for his business. However, running a speakeasy meant more than creating a nice joint where people wanted to come. It meant understanding whom to pay off, how much, and when. Politicians, police officers, and federal agents had to be bribed. Make a mistake, and Bello would go to jail where all his pseudosophistication would do him no good. That was why he told Harlean to go to bed with Zwillman. He had not counted on Zwillman's using Johnny Rosselli to begin watching out for her in Los Angeles. Nor had he suspected the crudeness of Harlow's sexual relationship or that word would get back to both Mama Jean and Eddie Mannix, a longtime friend of Zwillman's who was working for Louis B. Mayer as MGM's publicist and fixer.

Howard Hughes allegedly slept with Jean during the time she worked for him, the one perk for using an actress who all agreed was terrible. He also helped her career by boosting interest in *Hell's Angels* with a dramatic premier at Grauman's Chinese Theater, where two hundred searchlights illuminated bomber squadrons flying overhead. The country was between major wars, and the military was rentable for special events. Hughes was thus able to use the Army Air Corps. Self-deprecating Jean told friends that the planes probably got better reviews than she did, and she was undoubtedly right. She had no future with the Hughes organization.

The one person who believed in the Baby more than Mama Jean was Paul Bern, who had become enamored with Harlow simply because she was both beautiful and disreputable. She was the type best able to play sexually aggressive women who had no shame and were quite comfortable in embarrassing moments.

Longy Zwillman was drawn to Jean's eroticism. Paul Bern was drawn to the woman he thought he could help Jean become.

Bern was born Paul Levy in Germany, one of seventeen children, nine of whom died before their first birthdays. The family emigrated to the United States, where he took the name Paul Bern. His mother felt overwhelmed by the stress of the new land, the large family, and the seemingly endless tragedies. She eventually committed suicide.

Paul was twenty-two in 1911 when he first fell in love with a woman named Dorothy Millette. Stories of the family dynamics are far-fetched, though the results of their problems were horribly real.

Paul was Jewish. Dorothy was not. Henrietta Levy, Bern's mother, thought that her son should marry within his faith, so Paul and Dorothy lived as common-law husband and wife for a decade before Henrietta, supposedly as overwhelmed by having a sort-of daughter-in-law who was gentile as by the trauma of raising her children, jumped into a New Jersey canal. The drowning death so upset Dorothy that she became a recluse, living in New York's Algonquin Hotel, while Paul moved to Hollywood to work in the film industry as a producer, director, and writer. He sent checks to cover Dorothy's expenses, but he apparently did not see her again. All that is certain is that she became severely mentally ill and was hospitalized in a Connecticut sanitarium for what was expected to be the rest of her life.

Hollywood was good to Bern's romantic fantasies but not to his real life. He fell in love with actress Barbara LaMarr, a promiscuous drug addict who worked her way through five husbands before her health failed. Supposedly, Bern was so distraught that he did not get to be either husband five or six—he proposed before she married her fifth, and she died before she could wed again—he allegedly tried to commit suicide by drowning himself in the toilet. Most likely, the story was made up to discredit him after his own death.

Paul Bern spent a portion of his time in Hollywood trying to nurture actresses, frequently falling in love as he succeeded. Jean Harlow was no exception, and Paul took her to the Hughes premiere, then fought to get the producer to loan her to other studios. Hughes had no interest in using her, and Jean's career would develop as she worked. Besides, the other studio, in this case MGM, would pay to have the actress when she was working in one of their films.

The arrangement with Bern, Zwillman, and Harlow became rather complicated. Zwillman delighted in the actress and she in him. They slept together whenever possible. He bought her expensive gifts ranging from jewelry to cars and more. However, he also seemed quite comfortable that Paul Bern was not only helping, but was falling in love with her. Bern, by contrast, despised Zwillman for wearing Harlow's pubic hair in the locket. Bern could not bring himself to admit that it was Jean who had provided the hairs as a gift. It was easier to blame the recipient of her supposedly erotic largesse.

Hughes agreed with Bern about loaning out Harlow, and she went to work for other studios, including Warner Brothers for *Public Enemy* and Bern's MGM where she did *The Secret Six*.

It was while working for MGM that Eddie Mannix, the publicity director for MGM, learned of the infamous Zwillman gold locket. He passed the information to Louis B. Mayer, confirming in Mayer's mind that she was a slut. She was also a woman in whom Mayer had no sexual interest.

Longy Zwillman agreed with Paul Bern's strategy but knew he could do better for her because of his influence with Harry Cohn at Columbia Studios. There had been no interest on the original loan; apparently, hiring Harlow for two films was to be the payback. Not that Longy wanted to hurt Harry. He also paid her $750 a week of his own money.

The investment paid off. With Frank Capra directing and Lincoln Quarberg handling publicity (and inventing the name "the Platinum Blond"), the movie *Gallagher* was a box-office success, though not with its original title. The film, too, was called *The Platinum Blond*, a change meant to help generate intense publicity for Harlow. Her acting ability had improved little since she came in second to squadrons of bombers, but Quarberg was relentless. He invented the Platinum Blond Club, one of the early fan groups coordinated by studio personnel, and three thousand chapters were started throughout the country. The members tried to look like Jean, dressed like Jean, dyed their hair to match Jean's, and performed whatever other fan silliness he or they might invent. It went without saying that the members had to watch all her movies more than once.

Mama Jean was thrilled with what was happening with the Baby, though she hated Zwillman's locket of pubic hair. She threatened to divorce Bello for introducing Zwillman to her daughter. Bello backed off, recognizing that the money he enjoyed came from living with Jean, not owning a speakeasy.

Mama Jean was a pragmatist about using her daughter's sexuality and promiscuity to get ahead in the film industry. In order to make Jean's breasts look aggressively "perky" under her tight clothing, she rubbed her daughter's nipples with ice to keep them hard just before she went on the set to film. Apparently, Mama Jean never had any doubts about whether or not her daughter should be pimped on her way to stardom. It was simply a question of by whom and to whom.

Longy Zwillman gave Harlow the boost she needed, but he stepped out of the way when Paul Bern helped negotiate a deal among Nick Schenck and Irving Thalberg of MGM and Howard Hughes. The contract was purchased for $30,000. Harlow's salary was $1,250 a week with MGM, and her first film was the oddly named *Red-Headed Woman*. The contract, for just under seven years to avoid the "indentured servant" clause in California's work contract law, would rise to $5,000 a week in the years ahead.

In May 1932, Paul Bern solved the problem of the leaching Marino Bello and Mama Jean. He married the Baby.

Later, when talking with friends, Jean explained the attraction to Bern, a short, balding man far from the image of a Longy Zwillman. He loved her for herself. He liked to talk with her. He thought she had a brain and helped her learn the business she was in. He was the only man she had known intimately who did not want to jump into bed first and then, after sex, learn who she was. Or, as she was alleged to have explained, "He doesn't want to talk fuck, fuck, fuck all the time."

In what might be considered a minor event in the life of Hollywood during the mob era, though a significant turning point for Harlow, she discovered the power of both the mob and the moguls. The date was September 5, 1932, Labor Day, and a naked Paul Bern was found face down in front of a mirror, a revolver on the floor.

Dorothy Millette had spent years in a sanitarium, either unaware of the passage of time or not tracking the events of her life. The story of her life with Paul was first explained a week before Bern's death to MGM writer/producer/story editor Sam Marx, who detailed what happened both during interviews with this author and in a book written with Joyce Vanderveen.

Bern explained that he had fallen in love with an actress, who was the most beautiful girl he had ever seen. They moved into the Algonquin Hotel together, living as common-law husband and wife. Some people called her Dorothy by name. Others, especially the staff of the hotel, knew her as Mrs. Bern. Whatever the case, the couple never felt the need to marry and lived happily for five years.

No one ever clearly defined what had happened to Dorothy. Paul told Sam that he had awakened one morning to find his lover in bed, unmoving. He tried and failed to wake her, realized something was horribly wrong, and called for a doctor. She was alive but in a coma, and none of the medical techniques of the day could bring her out of it.

The doctor said that she would never recover, though she might live for years.

Paul had work opportunities in the film industry and decided to leave Dorothy in a sanitarium where they could keep her comfortable and attend to her needs. They were apart for ten years, Paul paying the bills and receiving unchanging reports. There was no need to divorce, though it is possible that their holding themselves out to be Mr. and Mrs. Paul Bern may have created a de facto legal marriage that required a genuine divorce. Paul never checked. There was never any reason. He simply continued his life, dating, falling in love, and eventually marrying Harlow.

The awakening was also never explained. One minute, Dorothy Millette was in a coma; the next, she was fully awake and aware of the events of ten years before as though they had happened that day. She knew she was living with Paul in the Algonquin, though she didn't understand why he wasn't in New York with her. She was able to learn where he was from the hospital staff, contacted him, and said she wanted him to come immediately to New York.

Paul was emotionally overwhelmed. He was living and working in California, married to the most exciting actress of the moment. Dorothy was a stranger to him now, just as he would be to her. He explained that his work schedule did not allow him to come east at the moment, and he did not offer to arrange for her to come see him. Finally, she took matters into her own hands, found the money to come west, and traveled to San Francisco, staying at the Plaza Hotel. She explained that he could at least come north, and that if he didn't, she was going to come down to see him.

The story that Sam Marx kept quiet for a week following Paul's revelation broke on Wednesday, September 7. That was when Paul's brother, Henry Bern, denied that Paul had ever married Dorothy Millette. The denial caused the press to start pressing for details because they had never heard of Dorothy Millette, and no one had ever discussed a previous wife. The comment was made when Henry was in the terminal of the Kansas City Airport on a refueling stop during his flight to California to see about his brother's inquest. The press knew more than Paul would have liked, but they didn't know how Paul really died. That knowledge took more than a half-century to come to light and revealed the power of the moguls.

There were two stories about the discovery of Paul Bern's "suicide."

In one, John and Winifred Carmichael arrived at the house at 11:30 a.m. She was the cook and set to work making coffee. He was the butler and went back to the dressing room, where he discovered Bern's naked corpse on the floor. In both stories, a gunshot wound to the head had left a pool of matted hair and blood. In both stories, the butler fainted, though in the one story he awoke and ran to get the gardener, Clifton Davis, who was already at work. Winifred Carmichael, alerted by her husband, called Mother Jean at the older woman's home, where Harlean was visiting.

In the second story, Clifton Davis arrived for work without seeing the Carmichaels. He walked by the swimming pool and saw a broken champagne glass. He picked it up, accidentally cutting himself, and realized that the glass was so delicate because it was expensive. Whoever had used it must have been important to the Berns.

Davis thought there might be a way to repair the glass, the shards being fairly large. He took them into the house and gently washed them in the kitchen.

After he finished with the champagne glass, Davis looked down the hall and noticed Paul Bern. Before he could move closer, he saw a second body, which slowly stirred. It was John Carmichael regaining consciousness.

In both versions, Harlow is at her mother's home, and it is her mother who is called. And in both versions, Mama Jean does what she knows is right in such a crisis. She calls a mogul.

Louis B. Mayer was always prepared for a crisis. He contacted MGM's security chief Whitey Hendry and Howard Strickling of the publicity department. Strickling then called Virgil Apger, a trusted still photographer who worked for the studio. Harold "Slickem" Garrison, bootblack and chauffeur, picked up both Hendry and Apger at the MGM studio and drove them to Paul and Jean Harlow Bern's home.

Mayer next left for the house, calling Irving Thalberg, his partner in the studio, and actress Norma Shearer, Thalberg's wife, along the way. Thalberg, in turn, alerted Mayer's daughter and son-in-law, David O. and Irene Mayer Selznick. Irene remained at home, still recovering from recent childbirth. David raced to the Bern/Harlow residence.

In case you've noticed that at no time were the local police or an ambulance summoned to the home and at no time was anyone outside the MGM "family" made aware that a death had taken place, you're not the first. While others were en route to the house, Whitey Hendry and

Virgil Apger arrived at 12:15 p.m. They expected to see patrol cars, an ambulance, perhaps someone from the coroner's office. They expected to see a thorough police investigation in progress. Instead, they were alone, except for their driver and the staff.

Apger was especially shaken by what was taking place. He was ordered to take photographs of the interior of the house, of Bern's corpse, of everything. He was to do the work normally done by a police photographer. He was also to leave all the images with Howard Strickling, who arrived fifteen minutes later. Apger never again saw his film or the processed pictures. He knew better than to ask questions. As Fatty Arbuckle and others had learned many years earlier, the studios were an island unto themselves, and however they wanted life to be, that was the way it was.

Louis B. Mayer and Howard Strickling had several concerns. The most immediate was the logical one. How do you justify the suicide of a happy man with a successful career, a beautiful wife, and everything to live for? Yet, Paul had to have committed suicide because that was the only story that would protect their investment in Harlow.

Jean Harlow was a kid from a tough background, promiscuous, with a wannabe mob figure for a stepfather and a real mobster for a lover. She was playing the role of tart on the screen, but there was something so over the top about her sexuality, along with a seeming unawareness of what she was doing, that her future as a star seemed assured. It also helped that she was in a happy marriage, "proof" that the screen roles were not related to her "proper" personal life.

Truth was uncertain. Harlow easily could have murdered her husband. She was young and strong and everyone knew that occasional violent arguments were not uncommon in their marriage. And when the fights got especially rough, it was likely to be Harlow who was on the attack.

The Platinum Blond had an alibi for the time of the murder, but the alibi was Mama Jean. She had been at her mother's home when Paul was killed, though her mother would have no way of knowing if she was there during the "suicide" or if her daughter arrived after murdering Paul. Both scenarios were possible, and Mayer and Strickling suspected that Jean was the murderer. When they learned that the couple had been overheard arguing the night before, the issue of guilt seemed to be resolved.

Paul Bern's death could only hurt Jean's career, a growing source of studio revenue, if she had killed him. Fortunately, Howard Strickling realized that the box-office take need not stop when he noticed a guest book on a table near the corpse. He knew how to save the studio's investment.

Guest books were popular with the wealthy and prominent. They were books much like those found at weddings and funerals—leather bound and filled with blank pages in which visitors write their names and any comments they might wish to make. Paul and Jean's book had names ranging from actor Gary Cooper to producer Ben Fineman. It also held what was later shown to be a partial note unrelated to the death. Although never fully explained, the few words on the paper were enough for Strickling to create an acceptable death scenario:

> Dearest dear,
>   Unfortunately this is the only way to make good the frightful wrong I have done you and to wipe out any abject humiliation. I love you.
>   Paul
>   You understand last night was only a comedy.

When Mayer arrived at 12:45 p.m., he wanted to destroy the guest book in case it connected Harlow with the death. However, when he was shown the note, he decided, along with Strickling, that it could be used out of context.

At 1 p.m. the rest of the men and women involved with planning the cover-up—the Irving Thalbergs and David O. Selznick—arrived. A few reporters were outside the house, though they were neither told of the death nor taken near the crime scene. How they learned about the trouble remains a mystery, though someone's assistant was probably paid to tip them off. No one alerted the police.

Finally, at 2:15 p.m., with a cover-up story planned to protect the property known as Jean Harlow, the detectives were summoned to view the "suicide" scene. They found a .38 caliber revolver in Bern's right hand with his forefinger still on the trigger. The gun was loaded with six rounds, one of which had been fired and passed through his head, ending in the wall. A second .38 caliber revolver was next to the guest book. It was not fired. The guest book was opened to the page on which Bern had written the partial note. The page had of course not been open when Strickling first found it because it had nothing to do with the death.

The coroner was called, along with a police photographer. No one mentioned Virgil Apger's pictures.

The Los Angeles County coroner's inquest on Thursday, September 8, was interesting for who was not present—Paul's brother, Henry Bern, and his widow, Jean Harlow. Everyone in attendance had their stories straight. In the three days following the death, information came to Mayer about a trip Paul Bern had taken to the Ambassador Hotel on Saturday night. There was mention of a woman in a limousine. The guest book was no longer called a guest book but became a "diary" in future references, adding to the image of personal plans to commit suicide. Harold Garrison also dishonestly stressed that Paul Bern frequently talked of suicide when he was driving him one place or another.*

Much of the testimony at the inquest consisted of lies and half-truths. For example, the coroner noted that Irving Thalberg called for help almost immediately. Some of those present, especially the police, changed what had taken hours into an almost immediate notification.

Detective Lieutenant Joseph Whitehead of homicide, who had been called to the Bern house, also stated that the death was suicide. The coroner asked about the fact that Paul was gripping the revolver when suicides drop the weapon at death. Whitehead answered that this was not always the case. There were no challenges.

Ultimately, some truth came out. The woman in the limousine was actually the lover of a married man. The hotel incident was more unset-

---

*The language of the day and into the 1960s would impact on a number of controversial death cases, most notably those of Bern and Marilyn Monroe (discussed later). The term *diary* generally referred to a book of private writings—a record of daily life and feelings, musings about others, and so forth. Certainly, that was the meaning of the term when Bern died, while a guest book would have the date of a visit, the visitor's signature, and maybe a line or two about how much the person enjoyed the evening, the food, the company, or whatever. *Diary* also referred to an appointment book, a common reference when Monroe maintained a "diary." Her "diary," and she used that word, was a date book that told what appointments she had, with whom, on what day, and at what hour. Nothing more. Language, used differently by different people and at different times, can fuel conspiracy theorists' thinking or make a key source of information seem less relevant than it really is.

tling and not made public. The woman was Paul Bern's wife, or had lived with him as such.

Years later, the full story would be disclosed. Dorothy Roddy, an orphan born in Columbus, Ohio, in 1884 had, in 1907, married Lowell Mellett. He was a journalist who moved west. She was an aspiring actress who moved east, studying at the American Academy of Dramatic Arts in New York under the name Dorothy Millette, though she never explained why she changed the spelling for her stage work. It was there that she met Paul Levy (Bern). The two lived together for the next nine years, and Lowell Mellett eventually filed for divorce on the grounds of "continual abandonment." Paul then began calling her his wife and continued to do so on legal documents at least through 1920, when he made a will that named her as such.

The reason for the move to San Francisco after the sudden recovery of her mental health was logical since Dorothy had a sister there, a Violet Roddy Hessler. All of this became known, to one degree or another, to the press by Saturday, September 9, the day of Paul's funeral. Dorothy could not be found, however, and eventually it was discovered that she had committed suicide. Her body was fished from the Sacramento River on September 14. She had taken a paddle wheel vessel called the *Delta King*, jumping into the water when no one was around to see her. She was buried with a headstone listing her as Dorothy Millette Bern.

So what happened? How had Paul died? Certainly not as an adulterer because that would have given Jean, who possibly would not have cared had she known the truth in advance, a damaged reputation. And murder could never be mentioned, even if murder was the cause of Bern's death. In the end, the moguls triumphed. They created a story that was accepted as "fact" for decades.

The story went that Paul Bern had committed suicide because he was sexually inadequate. The coroner reported that his sex organs were slightly smaller than normal, though certainly adequate for him to satisfy any woman. Equally importantly, numerous women admitted that Paul did just fine in bed, Harlow included. However, there would be more public sympathy if the nation's sex symbol of the moment had married an older, mature man for his gentleness, wisdom, experience, and ability to give her pleasure. It should have been the ideal marriage and seemed to be for the pure soul Harlow was in real life, as opposed to the unwholesome women she played on the screen. Then, after saving herself body and soul for Mr. Right, she discovered on her honeymoon that Paul could not have an erection. He was humiliated when he tried to have sex with his bride. Here she was, the most erotic woman on the big screen, and he could not perform.

Suicide had been the only way out, of course. After all, he could not revel in the manhood Jean had expected. Killing himself was the only honorable exit for someone who was half a man. Eddie Mannix was quoted more forcefully. "He was impotent. He couldn't make it with Jean, so he killed himself."

Marino Bello, recognizing that his future depended upon staying in the good graces of both his stepdaughter and the moguls, agreed despite knowing better. "I knew from the beginning he was a queer little guy," he allegedly told Mannix. He also promised to take care of Jean, though not just out of personal concern. He had to convince her to remain silent about her relationship with her husband.

Oddly, Buron Fitts, the district attorney, actually wanted to be straight for once. He recognized that there was no suicide. and he personally began questioning witnesses. His actions scared Louis B. Mayer, who knew that if a crook was being honest for once in his life, he would need to keep himself one step removed from what needed to take place to protect the studio. He called the Culver City police chief, his own Whitey Hendry, and told him to bribe Fitts. Whitey was the law on the MGM lot, as well as in Culver City. His demand that the murder become a suicide, coupled with a guaranteed payoff, worked. Fitts agreed to find any cause of death Mayer desired. And Jean Harlow, for whatever reason, agreed to take on the public role of grieving widow. She would protect her career by announcing whatever cause of death Mayer told her to, even though she seemed to have truly loved her husband. She was young enough, ambitious enough, and pressured enough by the studio to let the police back off from finding a murderer and to allow the studio publicists to present a story that would preserve her career.

A second deal was reached with Coroner Frank A. Nance so that the wrong questions would not be asked of the right people. Then, the answers received would only show one conclusion: "Death by gunshot wound to the head, self-inflicted by the deceased with suicidal indent. Motive undetermined."

In the end, several questions remained because so much evidence was moved, destroyed, hidden, or not investigated. Through their research, Sam Marx, retired story editor, producer, and screenwriter at

MGM, and Joyce Vanderveen, a dancer turned writer, determined that Dorothy Millette murdered Paul Bern. The reasons are unknown, but she was mentally unbalanced, amazed by his situation in Hollywood, and probably overwhelmed with grief, anger, and shock. Whatever the motive, she pulled the trigger.

Even more intriguing is what happened to Dorothy and whether anyone instigated her murdering Paul. Some people say that Longy Zwillman had Paul killed by arranging for Dorothy to get to Paul when Jean was not around. He certainly hated Bern and would, over the years, claim he had caused Bern's death.

The problem with the theory that Zwillman arranged the murder of Bern is that it seems too risky. He would have had to designate a mentally unstable woman to make the hit. She might refuse to do it. She might talk. She might act unpredictably in ways that professional killers would not. A mob professional would not consider a mentally ill woman a safe "trigger."

Likewise, some say that Marino Bello arranged for the murder. But it's doubtful that he knew about Dorothy or could have discovered her existence. His relationship with mother and daughter was tense. He might get back in good graces with the Baby, but there were too many risks, too many unknowns.

One possibility, though, is that Zwillman was responsible for Dorothy's "suicide." She was unstable enough to kill herself after killing Paul, especially if she fantasized about being with him after death. But if she was too stable to commit suicide at that point, Zwillman might have arranged to have her killed in a manner that made it look like she had taken her own life. Or Bello could have "helped" her die at Zwillman's request after she shot Paul. Or Jean could have been at home when Millette arrived and witnessed the murder, fleeing and letting others handle the horror. Or . . .

Years later, after the publication of Sam Marx and Joyce Vanderveen's research, another twist to the story was uncovered in the files of some of the New Jersey/New York gangsters. Paul Bern was earning $75,000 a year, but due to his purchases for Harlean and continued payment for Dorothy Millette's care, he was nearly broke. Jean Harlow was earning a good living, but Paul had not married her for her future cash in the manner that her stepfather, Marino Bello, had tried to use her. As a result, Bern was in financial need, and since he was a businessman who knew the entertainment world, an arrangement was being made whereby Paul would own a business back east, presumably a nightclub, and ignore the fact that from time to time Longy Zwillman would be screwing the Baby. There was no animosity toward Paul. It was simply a matter of the pimps' changing from Bello to Bern.

The story seems crass to those who knew Paul because they liked him and saw him as a decent man. Yet, the Baby was not a decent woman. She was a slut able to separate such concepts as marriage, sex, and commitment. She would not risk her career to find the key to the loss of the man she loved any more than she would withhold sex from men who could help her reach stardom. No matter how she might feel toward others, she was a pragmatic moralist.

The most notorious period in Harlow's life was in the late 1920s, when she was single but making large sums of money. She, like many other young actors, used the House of Francis at 8439 Sunset Boulevard. The house, owned by Lee Francis, had an entrance that resembled a five-star hotel and every amenity the owner had ever wanted when she was learning the business of prostitution in Reno, Nevada, and San Francisco, California. There were prostitutes available in the house and prostitutes for outcall. The only service Francis did not offer, one available at Mae's, another exquisite location run by Billie Bennett, who offered suites and a full restaurant, was a line of prostitutes who were movie actress doubles. Billie Bennett only hired women who, through an accident of nature or surgical enhancement, looked exactly like the major film stars of the day, from Claudette Colbert to Joan Crawford to Ginger Rogers. Only Katharine Hepburn and Greta Garbo were not "duplicated," though the reason for these two exceptions seems to have been lost. However, the studios colluded with Mae's by supplying the costumes the real stars wore whenever Bennett requested them. And if, by chance, the client wanted the "actress" dressed in something that was not available, a staff of seamstresses in the basement would make it.

Harlow was known to spend her money in two ways. She rented prostitutes whom she took home with her, and she rented customers who were delighted to have the actress instead of a professional. The fact that the customer got paid for the evening instead of doing the paying himself added to the appeal.

The charge was $500 for the carryout service, 40 percent of which went to police and politicians. The remaining $300 was divided between Lee Francis and the working girl or agreeable male customer.

Clark Gable used to go the House of Francis because, as he explained, "I can always send those girls home." Gary Cooper did not, and this led to some minor problems. Both men owned identical, custom-made Duesenberg coupes. They were the only two in the world, and when Gable's was parked by the House of Francis, Cooper was likely to get teased. Eventually, Gable stopped going to the House of Francis, arranging for the women he was interested in to be sent to his dressing room on whatever set he was working on.

Jean Harlow's rentals were for rough sex, according to those who talked. What that meant to her or to them, we don't know. The knowledge adds credibility to the idea that she was capable of killing her husband during a fight. There is also no question that Harlow was one of the most promiscuous actresses to become a star in an era when image mattered more than reality.

As for Bello, Mama Jean divorced him in 1934. He married another woman soon after and remained with her until his death in 1953. Mama Jean never remarried.

Henry Bern left Los Angeles and never talked about his brother's life or death publicly. Buron Fitts, generously supported by MGM money, lost the 1940 election for district attorney, though he never revealed how much he was influenced by his relationship with that studio. Ironically, Ben Siegel, a friend of Rosselli, Luciano, Lansky, and Zwillman, gave $30,000 to Fitts' successful opponent in that same election.

Jean Harlow married briefly and unhappily a year after the murder. Her husband was Hal Rosson, a cinematographer with whom she had regularly worked for MGM. Then, at the peak of her success, but on an emotional downturn, she unexpectedly died on June 7, 1937, denying MGM the money machine they had so carefully protected. She was twenty-six years old, her death the result of a massive infection caused by botched oral surgery. She had undergone several abortions in recent years, and when she collapsed on the set of the movie *Saratoga* that May, the doctor her mother called decided she was having gall bladder trouble, should drink liquids, and go to bed. Instead, she had uremic poisoning, which the liquids made worse.

Harlow should have gone to the hospital, but her mother was a "reformed" Christian Scientist. She accepted the idea of a doctor's caring for her daughter rather than exclusively using the prayers of a healer, but she would not let Harlean go to the hospital.

Louis B. Mayer, determined to not lose money on the film, came to see Jean with Dr. Edward Jones, a studio physician who had lied about Paul Bern's death during the cover-up. Mama Jean would not tolerate Jones's presence, but on June 6, when a different doctor showed, he ignored Mama Jean's religious beliefs and rushed Harlean to Good Shepherd Hospital's Room 826, a private area where celebrities could have their abortions. Harlean had been there in the past and the familiarity seemed less stressful. However, it was too late. Her kidneys failed, and she died on June 7, 1937.

In the end, both the moguls and the mob had flexed their muscles at each other, and it had all proved an exercise in futility.

Act III

In which the greedy and the dumb make a complete mess of the studio extortion racket, and two new bad guys, Mickey Cohen and Ben Siegel, slip into town to exercise more meaningful power.

CHAPTER Eighteen

So, What Did Happen with Bioff, Browne, Schenck, and the Others?

T hey all began as street punks, the mobsters and the moguls. Most had been the equivalent of schoolyard bullies who would rather beat up a kid for 50 cents in lunch money than pull a straight score for a dollar. And in the end, each glorified his own actions while vilifying those of his fellow players in the Hollywood drama.

Willie Bioff was at the top of everyone's list as the ultimate bad boy of the motion picture world, yet even when he was caught with his hands in the mob's cookie jar, he was treated like a recalcitrant child by men who normally believed it best to treat those who cheated them by leaving no bone unbroken. This was probably not a wise decision, and it was one they corrected several years later.

The first thing that should have caused Bioff's head to be on the receiving end of a baseball bat, as would have happened if Capone had not been in jail, mentally deteriorating from untreated syphilis, was Willie's greed. Ironically, he was caught in the mob's version of a sting operation with a man with the unlikely name of Izzy Zevlin.

Izzy Zevlin was a numbers guy. He knew how to take your business and give you a profit or a loss, show you owed taxes or maybe that the government owed you. He could launder money, sure, but a lot of guys could do that. He could take it and multiply or divide it, add or subtract it, dress it up to look respectable, and dazzle the tax guys so they never looked close enough to see if it was clean or dirty. He was that kind of guy.

Willie Bioff and George Browne were playing with big numbers that screamed to be reduced through bookkeeping that was less than accurate. They'd walk into a mogul's office and come out with more cash than the average guy would see in five years, and that was without flexing muscle, showing a bulge under their jackets, or mentioning the Outfit.

The moguls called the money they paid to Bioff and Browne to prevent work stoppages and to change the work rules and benefits for the rank and file "extortion." The bad guys called this money "bribes" paid to encourage them not to act in the best interests of their members. Each side had a false sense of self-righteous innocence because each came out ahead; only the workers were hurt.

The question for the punks to answer between themselves was what to do with the cash. Bioff and Browne made very clear that the money they collected went into a strike fund to help the workers through times of crisis. But a strike fund presented a skimming problem. Stick the money in a strike fund that's open to audit and you might have to use it in the manner for which you claim it was intended. Withhold everything so it can go into your pocket and you have to justify the payment.

Then, there was the Outfit's share and maybe a few payoffs as part of the usual overhead. It could get confusing to a guy like Bioff, and when he asked Browne, the answer was usually filtered through his beer-addled mind.

That's why Frank Nitti sent Bioff Izzy Zevlin, a guy who knew from numbers, knew from cooking the books, knew from doing things with accounting that even Harry Houdini, the great magician, couldn't figure out.

Guys with more brains than Bioff and Browne, or maybe guys with a better sense of survival, would have put two and two together and figured that if Nitti sent the accountant, the accountant was Nitti's man. Not our geniuses.

When Izzy Zevlin told the two muscle-headed nitwits that he could increase their wealth with a set of double books, only one of which would be known to the Outfit, they thought it was a wonderful idea. They never thought it was a test, and so they went forth to collect more money to fill their pockets.

We need a strike insurance fund, George Browne announced to the rank and file. He invoked the names of the producers as though they were bogeymen come out from under the bed and now in charge of movies. They hated labor. They were constantly taking advantage of the rank and file when it came to pay, benefits, and hours. The only answer was to meet their hiring strength with a walkout. Not now, you understand. Maybe later, though. Maybe much later. Maybe . . .

That didn't matter. Two percent was the magic number. Two percent of everyone's gross pay. Two percent would cover a man and his family if he had to call the bluff of the moguls while standing arm in arm with his fellow union loyalists. You could almost hear the theme music swelling in loudness and tempo as Bioff and Browne made their declaration of need.

Solidarity in a crisis was what unionism was all about. Having a done deal with the producers so that everything Bioff and Browne said they would go after helped as well. Starving wives and children of out-of-work union men with no strike benefits was the kind of image the media would love. This way the men and women would be united in defense of an assault on their working conditions that would never come. And the leaders would never have to account for the money they skimmed from the strike fund if there never was a strike to spoil the plot.

The bribes from the dirty producers was split with Chicago as Nitti intended. The hard-working rank and file's 2 percent was being kept by Bioff and Browne without the knowledge of Chicago, or so they thought. After all, Izzy Zevlin had said it was going right into the invisible (to the Outfit) accounting book, that second set he was keeping for their eyes only.

Izzy was honest about where he was recording the money, just not about how many people knew there were double books. He was first and foremost the Outfit's man. He had been sent personally by Nitti.

It was Zevlin, far more than Bioff and Browne, who understood that total honesty with the men you worked for—Nitti, not B&B— meant you might reach old age or at least die of natural causes.

George Browne had the misfortune to be in Chicago when Frank Nitti saw the second set of books, the ones Izzy said no one would ever know about. Nitti took Browne into his office bathroom, the most private place available. Then, the outraged Nitti backed Browne toward a window the union leader noticed could easily accommodate his ample girth with room to spare should Nitti be planning to force him to use it as an exit.

To Browne's surprise, Nitti didn't kill him. He didn't punch him, kick him, stab him, or disembowel him. He just explained that he knew about the double books. He explained that the gravy train was over. The Outfit had been splitting the extortion/bribery/thefts fifty-fifty when everyone could trust everyone else. Now that Browne had shown what a greedy bastard he was, he and Bioff would get one-third, and the Outfit would get the remaining two-thirds.

The deal was a fair one, given the money that was coming from the assessment scam. The punks ultimately righteously pocketed more than $2.125 million for themselves out of the $6.5 million they took in. A third of that kind of money was a satisfactory haul, especially since both men were allowed to live with all their organs remaining where they had been before Nitti was apprised of the scam. Ironically, they never realized the role Zevlin played in all this. He continued to do their books and to send a proper accounting back to Chicago.

❛ ❛

These businessmen are nothing but two-bit whores with clean shirts and a shine.

> —Willie Bioff when he learned that, in 1936, the Chicago Outfit had
> sent a total of $500,000 to the Franklin Roosevelt reelection
> campaign. The money was sought by members of the Democratic
> National Committee, who were comfortable with Roosevelt
> occasionally being in bed with the mob.

❜ ❜

Joe and Nick Schenck did not sit idly by while they were being extorted for annual payments to Bioff and Browne in order to assure there would be no strikes and no intolerable pay increases. They did the numbers and realized that no matter how much they were asked to pay, the cost savings was always greater than if they had to pay fair wages. More importantly, they came to understand that no matter how successful a business venture like the film industry might become, you could always come out a little further ahead by stealing money.

The Schencks' scam was so simple it was a surprise that no one used it until entertainment crime shifted to Las Vegas and everyone followed their example. Nick Schenck took his theater receipts and removed a portion from every bag. He would take a dollar here and a dollar there, then bag the total and give it to Willie Bioff to hand carry to his brother Joe during one of Willie's trips between New York and Los Angeles. The exact amount stolen in this way is not known. It is also not known if there were other couriers. Willie made at least six trips for Nick, and it is believed that the amounts were about the same for each trip—roughly $62,500 each, with $500 from one shipment given to a grateful Willie for his expenses.

There were a variety of other deals as well. The studios long enjoyed the services of drug dealers, one of the reasons for the early war between the Chicago Outfit and Luciano's men. Bioff, acting for Chicago, arranged for each studio to have its own designated bookmaker. Willie also got into the film stock business as a way to help the moguls.

The choice of motion picture film was a serious matter in Hollywood. The quality of the on-screen image was constantly being improved. Film was becoming more light sensitive, the ability to record detail was being improved, and experimentation with color was adding a new dimension to visual storytelling.

There were two major competitors for the movie studios' business—Eastman Kodak and DuPont Chemicals, with Kodak the preferred stock at that time. However, despite its superior quality, in 1937, Willie explained to Nick Schenck, who ran the Loew's office out of New York, that there would be a conversion to Du Pont film. The longtime supplier, Jules Brulatour of Eastman Kodak, was out because Willie wanted the commission money.

Schenck had no choice but to cooperate. A year earlier, Nick had gotten into bed with Bioff and Browne during a private meeting between Willie, George, Nick, and Leo Spitz, who headed RKO. Those studio heads agreed to pay fees based on their business size to insure labor peace. Ultimately MGM, Paramount, Warner Brothers, and Fox paid $50,000 each; RKO and Columbia were given a break and told to pay only $20,000 each because of their small size. All contracts would be planned so that the studio heads benefited more than the union members, and strikes would be nonexistent. The money demanded and paid fell into two types of criminal endeavor. Bioff and Browne were committing extortion, but Schenck and Spitz were considered guilty of bribery. Everyone was dirty, just the way the Outfit liked it, and the change in film stock, which cost the studio in quality, not money, was a further price that would be paid.

Louis B. Mayer, head of Loew's Hollywood MGM operation, did not wish to make the change in film stock. He felt that Kodak's Jules Brulator had given great service with a better product for the screen. He resented that Brulator's family would suffer as well because, for the years 1937 and 1938, the 7 percent commission on selling the film stock came to $236,474. It was a huge loss.

Mayer's hostility toward making the film change following Bioff's demand earned him Willie's enmity. Bioff's reputed revenge may have been actual, or the story may have been fabricated to show Bioff's power. Whatever the case, during this time, Willie allegedly arrived at the MGM entrance only to find a security guard who did not know him and had received no indication that Bioff was expected. He was told to call Mayer, and when the guard did, Willie demanded that Mayer come personally to the gate to tell the guard off. Mayer, who was then the highest-paid executive in America, allegedly cooperated. Bioff felt that humbling so powerful a man was all the revenge he needed.

The rank and file were not forgotten during this period. Their wages were reduced from 15 to 40 percent. They assumed that the producers were putting the squeeze on them because of the Depression, never realizing they were being manipulated by their union leaders.

At the same time, Bioff and Browne thought they could muscle in on other guilds being formed. They quickly learned it was one thing to work your way slowly into power and to seduce people into believing you might be of benefit. It was quite another to have a series of actions on record that could be studied by a guild considering a merger with IATSE.

Willie Bioff did not help his image by taking advantage of the money he was earning "helping" the little guy, as he liked to claim. He built a "modest" home on eighty acres of land. Rancho Laurie, named after his wife, was furnished in the manner only a motion picture production company could achieve. Everything he owned—Louis XV furniture, oriental vases, and a magnificent library filled with books collectors lusted after but which he had neither the interest nor the ability to read—came from RKO. Leo Spitz spent at least $5,000 of the studio's money to have the purchasing department acquire whatever Willie wanted. The money was a loan of sorts. The executive was given purchasing orders and noted that Willie would repay the cost. Of course, Willie did not.

The massive house had a working garden that was used to help feed the Bioff family, employees, and numerous bodyguards. Like many of the mobsters, the house was built with holes and turrets from which guns could be fired in the event of an attack. Willie had not forgotten Tommy Maloy's death. Rancho Laurie was like a castle filled with knights and carefully placed armaments in case of a siege. One never came for Bioff—not then—but he was ready if there was a problem.

Bioff was convinced that he owned Hollywood, and the stories told about him supported this image. One involved Louis B. Mayer, a man who encouraged illegal activity on the MGM lot. In a building located in an area that would later house what was called the Thalberg Building, Mayer allowed an opium den frequented by many of the writers during their lunch hour. He allowed the studio barbershop to handle betting on college football games, using the service himself. However, he actually took a percentage of much of the criminal activity on the grounds. Frank Orsatti served as the studio bootlegger prior to the end of Prohibition, and then Mayer rewarded his willingness to give money to the mogul by helping him become an agent. Orsatti had either the best clients Mayer could provide or those who would get work in amounts disproportionate to their abilities and the likelihood that they would have been cast without connections.

Mayer also had a scam with Edwin Willis, a set decorator. Willis would spend studio money for expensive furniture designated for a movie on which Willis was the set designer, a valid expenditure and a normal cost of doing business. However, instead of storing it for future pictures or selling it with the money earned going to the corporation, Willis sold the furniture from a shop he opened on Santa Monica Boulevard. Many of the pieces were antiques purchased for period films, but no matter what the furniture, it was sold privately, with none of the money going to MGM, though a piece of the action went into Mayer's pocket.

All this was happening with Willie, the most powerful labor leader on the West Coast, not really being a union man. IATSE was run by George Browne, its elected leader. Instead, Willie had been part of the original scam when the two friends were still shaking down theater chain owners. And the power behind George Browne was the Chicago

Outfit. Willie Bioff, in the eyes of the men who mattered, was expendable.

Willie had not learned his lesson when he thought he could keep two sets of accounting books. He went a step further when he decided to keep building union power on his own by taking over the Associated Actors and Artistes of America. This was the union for vaudevillians and those vaudeville performers who also worked nightclubs. Anyone even peripherally aware of the nightclub business both before and after Prohibition knew that it was mob controlled. Both New York and Chicago dominated the clubs and their activities, and they had their own plans to merge the union with IATSE. Bioff was trying to create a side deal for himself, and he was summoned to Chicago, where he was told to stop pushing for personal power or die.

Less dangerous for Willie was his misunderstanding of Johnny Rosselli's power both in Hollywood and with the mob. He knew that Rosselli was in business with Harry Cohn of Columbia Studios, as well as being his friend, but he did not care. Willie Bioff was "the man," the person who dictated to the moguls, who could take their money at will and with impunity. He wanted Cohn's money, and to hell with Rosselli.

Willie went to see Harry Cohn after carefully negotiating payments from the heads of the other studios. Columbia was a nothing studio compared with Loew's, where Nick Schenck had ultimately paid $200,000, not just the original $50,000 requested. Harry was now being asked for "only" $25,000.

Harry called Johnny Rosselli to ask him what to do. Cohn knew how the game was played. Sometimes paying extortion was better than not. Sometimes the person trying to extort was out of line. Rosselli was so low key that no one, not even his friends, understood how well connected he was. Harry trusted Johnny's word, though, and when Rosselli told him to pay nothing to Bioff, Cohn followed Johnny's advice.

Cohn flexed the muscle he now assumed was on his side when he met with the other producers concerning the payments they were making. He explained that he would not be giving Bioff any money. He said that he had someone taking care of him.

Cohn's statement did not sit well with Rosselli. He was not named, but the producers knew who was friends with whom, and it was doubtful that anyone other than Johnny would be involved. Instead of being able to act as a friend, his presence was meant to intimidate by implying a power Cohn did not have. However, though Rosselli was annoyed, he did handle the matter.

Bioff was enough of a fool to challenge Cohn and whoever was advising him. It was November 8, 1937; Cohn was in Palm Springs relaxing when he got a call to say that Columbia had been shut down. The craft workers, cameramen, makeup artists, and others had walked off on a wildcat strike. Union pickets were in front of all entrances to the studio, and no one was giving any reason why. Harry knew. He called Johnny.

Rosselli tried to reach George Browne in Chicago since Browne could tell Bioff to stop the strike. Browne was not in, so Rosselli drove to the Hollywood IATSE office and burst in on Bioff, who had been expecting him. Willie was behind his desk, on which he had placed a revolver as a sign of his power. Rosselli was not impressed; nor did he care when Willie invoked Frank Nitti's name as justification for his actions, even though Nitti would not have wanted his name involved.

Willie Bioff was forced to call George Browne, at which time Rosselli said that the strike was ordered by Bioff for spite and was to be called off. Browne agreed, and the strike did not last the full day.

There was a second meeting, one Bioff did not expect. The night of the same day as the strike, November 8, Rosselli and Jack Dragna, the powerful local leader of organized criminal activity, drove out to see Willie in his home. The presence of the two men implied the potential for retaliatory violence Willie did not expect. They explained to Willie that he was going to accompany them to see Harry Cohn that night. Bioff knew better than to argue, and when he reached Cohn, he told the producer that the strike was off.

The problem for everyone was that the strike, not connected to a labor dispute, got attention in a company town. The state assembly had representatives in Los Angeles that week in order to look at a recent labor problem at the Metropolitan Water District. They had the power to investigate all union activity, and the Columbia problem interested them. They decided to issue a subpoena for Willie Bioff to come see them about "conditions bordering on racketeering." It was a fishing expedition that would not have gotten underway had he used more sense.

As has been noted, Willie had a sense of survival but few brains. He was making more money than he had ever imagined possible. He was also unsure what to do with it once the double books fiasco proved inappropriate.

Real organized criminals understood money laundering. They knew that a paper trail could send you to jail. However, if money went through legitimately owned cash businesses, such as race tracks and restaurants, they could declare it and pay taxes, knowing they would have no trouble.

Willie Bioff did not want to launder his money. He didn't even want to hide it under his mattress. He thought having wads of cash in his pocket made him important. He forgot that the first time he and George showed off their extortion money, the mob moved in. Until he bought Rancho Laurie in 1937, he had been paying cash and delighting in the shocked reaction of bank clerks and others, not realizing that he could be reported to the Internal Revenue Service. By the time he figured out that he needed help with his cash, law-enforcement agencies were already exploring what was happening with the unions.

Joe Schenck was the man Bioff approached for help when he needed to put $100,000 on his new home. Willie already had the money—a thousand $100 bills—and for once he decided not to impress a stranger by taking the money in an envelope to the real estate office. That was why Willie went to Joe, who was happy to write him a check for the amount in exchange for the envelope of cash. Willie was working as the man selling film stock, so when he had a Twentieth Century Fox check for so much money, it would be in line with a commission for the work being done. Although neither man realized it, the seemingly legitimate check would also prove to be one of the final pieces of evidence against both men in an investigation that would soon bring down the scammers.

The members of IATSE were not fools; nor were the members of other unions which the corrupt IATSE leadership had been trying to force them to join. Within IATSE itself was a group called the IA Progressives, who were demanding a degree of power and autonomy.

The courage of the IA Progressives was unusually strong, given factors other than the thugs they faced. First was the fact that the Great Depression had decimated jobs throughout the country. People would take any job that would help them feed themselves and their families. People who had jobs would do anything to retain them. And when the IATSE leadership controlled both who could be hired and the moguls who, in turn, had the jobs the rank and file desired, standing up to IATSE could literally mean starvation.

Willie Bioff and George Browne delighted in exercising their power over their critics within the union. They would arrange for a critic to be fired by the studio where he worked. Then, if he saw the error of his ways, he had to grovel by signing a form that had been prepared for the union leadership. It read, in part,

> I, the undersigned, an expelled member of the IATSE, who has appealed this expulsion, being cognizant of the fact that this expulsion is the result of my activities during the past three or four months, which were detrimental to the interests of the IATSE, do hereby sincerely apologize to the Alliance, its members, and particularly to the international officers, for all derogatory statements made by me against them. I am profoundly sorry now that I made these statements and committed these actions, which I admit and now realize have caused a vast amount of trouble, expense and unrest in the affairs of the Alliance and have seriously jeopardized the welfare of the Alliance and its members. I have reached the conclusion that my activities were wrong. . . . I am willing that I be placed on probationary status for a period of two years, and during this probation I agree not to be a candidate for any office, either elective or appointive, and if during this period of time I engage in any acts in violation of the constitution of my local unions or the IATSE, I agree voluntarily to surrender my membership card. I further pledge that I will be loyal to the IATSE. . . . I am grateful for this opportunity extended to me and solemnly promise that my conduct in the future will be such that the officials of the Alliance will never regret their leniency extended toward me.

The other action of Bioff and Browne that generated true loyalty was the careful use of violent force during strikes. Using the Outfit to connect them with hired muscle, they brought in strikebreakers to smash the heads of the union men, then blamed the production company moguls. The union members were certain their leaders would never beat them on a picket line they had organized. That meant that management must have hired the strikebreakers and was willing to do anything to keep the workers from getting ahead, including crippling or killing them on the picket line.

The one truth in all this, of which the rank and file was unaware, was that management was in bed with Bioff, Browne, and the Outfit. However, all truth had to be twisted on both sides to keep the money flowing.

The press was another concern in the fight against the mob take-over of the craft unions and any other unions in existence or being formed for the various trades and skills in the film industry. The *Los Angeles Times* was officially against any unions because of the potential impact on growth. The *Hollywood Reporter*, a weekday trade paper so popular that Franklin Roosevelt had copies delivered to the White House, was owned by William R. "Billy" Wilkerson. The actual circulation was small, but the influence was greater than any other publication in Los Angeles, including the rival West Coast edition of *Variety*. However, Wilkerson, who originally seemed supportive of the workers, did not publish news of the labor unrest and the studio strikes. The reason was simple—extortion by Willie Bioff to assure that he could operate with the least possible public resistance while under growing scrutiny.

The key to controlling Wilkerson lay not in his newspaper but in his famed restaurant/nightclub operations. He had run a speakeasy in New York during Prohibition and truly loved the entertainment business. His move to California enabled him both to be a publisher and to continue pursuing legitimate businesses where the public could dine in comfort. This was why, by day, he headed the Vendome, among the most popular restaurants for lunch in the region. The restaurant only served lunch, though, in part because that was the aspect of the business which made the most money and in part to free his staff to work the Trocadero at night.

The Trocadero was known for its fine food, excellent service, and outstanding entertainment. All the major stars went there, not just to be seen but genuinely to enjoy themselves. And for those who didn't care for the Trocadero or wanted a less pricey experience, there was Larue's, a restaurant that offered pasta dishes and other simpler fare.

Wilkerson's three restaurants and his popular newspaper were making him very rich, but he also knew that he was in a volatile business. He could hold his own when it came to covering the entertainment industry. *Daily Variety*, which started its Los Angeles operation after long being successful in New York, fought for the same West Coast advertising and circulation dollars, but there were enough to go around. The restaurants and nightclub, on the other hand, could suddenly lose their popularity, and he could lose much of his investment and savings before he had a chance either to restore business or to shut down completely.

Willie went to Wilkerson with an offer/threat quite similar to what had been used when Fred "Bugs" Blacker had been working for Jules Stein of MCA. It was explained that since the Outfit controlled the union employees of the restaurant, the Trocadero customers would discover there were bugs in the entrees. The Vendome would receive spoiled meat that would be served before Wilkerson could find it. And as for Larue's, the food wasn't fancy enough to worry about. Stink bombs were good enough to destroy that facility.

Wilkerson decided that his newspaper would ignore the most important news in the West Coast entertainment industry. The problem for Bioff was that Arthur Ungar was a newspaperman with only two financial interests—the New York *Daily Variety* and its sister publication, the Los Angeles *Daily Variety*. The New York paper, specializing in live theater, vaudeville, and similar entertainment, was a solid money maker and could carry any West Coast losses. At the same time, the movie industry affected so many businesses, from restaurants to stationers, that no matter what Bioff tried to do, there would always be advertisers to keep the publication afloat.

The state investigation and the *Daily Variety* coverage sparked other investigations. Louis B. Mayer may have been dishonest, but he was an honorable thief. He would never have agreed to the film-stock change had he not felt he had no other choice after the deal Nick Schenck made.

Louis and Willie threatened each other. Both were serious, Mayer having become notorious in Hollywood for his occasional fistfights that usually ended with his knocking his opponent to the ground with a single punch. But Mayer was scared when it came to the people backing Bioff and Browne. He decided to see how much he could learn about Willie, hiring private investigators, an action also taken by Robert Montgomery in his capacity as president of the Screen Actors' Guild (SAG).

The Mayer investigators seemed to cause the first wave of concern for Bioff. They were not connected with an official investigating body, law enforcement, or a newspaper, and perhaps that made them more noticeable. Whatever the case, Willie soon learned that his past was becoming known.

All the investigations into Willie Bioff revealed the interesting information that not only had he been a pimp, but he had been given a six-month sentence for perjury and pandering. Paperwork related to the sentence had been mishandled, and he had walked out of jail in either six or eight days. Thus, he still had almost twenty-three weeks to serve because there was no statute of limitations on his completing his sentence. He would soon be forced to return to serve his time, giving law enforcement a chance to further their investigation into his actions.

Two other factors both fascinated and alarmed Mayer. The pimp issue was important because of the odd moral code of the studios. Actresses could work as prostitutes, paid or as part of their six-month contracts, if they were part of the studio system. Paramount Pictures, for example, had contract players available for important out-of-town visitors, investors in films, and the like. At the same time, they insisted that the police prosecute actresses who turned tricks in such "genteel" living places for nice single girls as the Studio Club. The women were also contract employees, and the services were essentially identical. The moral outrage was over their act of freelancing. The attitude of the moguls seemed to be, "Fuck my business associates, and you're a highly regarded young actress. Fuck someone else's business associates, and you're nothing but a cheap whore."

Young women who would sell their bodies were sluts in the manner that Louis B. Mayer (accurately) perceived Jean Harlow to be. Only young women who were contract employees for the studio and "helped" their employers by "dating" important men were "proper" actresses.

A pimp was lower than the women he or she rented out. Willie Bioff could have been a murderer, and his past would have attracted less hostility. No one bothered to mention that MGM had a business charge account at the House of Francis, especially since it was listed under a false name. However, the checks were paid by Howard Strickling's office, and almost everyone who continued working past six months at least heard about it.

Willie also had a problem because of a man named Jack Zuta, a low-level "nobody" who was part of the world of the Outfit. He owned a house of prostitution where Willie had previously both tended bar and done general handyman duties. The job ended when Willie's boss was assassinated by the mob. There was suspicion of either prior knowledge on Willie's part or an awareness of who was involved, which he wisely kept to himself. Once again, it was a terrible image for the "pristine" Hollywood moguls.

The Union Has a Revolting Development

The IA Progressives were perhaps more insightful than other union members. But they were not alone. Other unions not currently affiliated with IATSE were fighting back against mob influence.

For example, IATSE had also gone after SAG, which was even more hostile to the union than the IA Progressives. It was increasingly apparent the studios were working to assure that the unions became weak, closed shops where only union men and women could work in Hollywood, yet their wages, time, and benefits would be limited.

The backlash from men and women forming other guilds was becoming stronger than expected. The writers, for example, were rebelling against the studio pay scales. Experienced writers were earning as much as $1,200 a week for their work, so the studios created a leveled writing pay scale, with junior writers making $50 a week, about the same as a newspaper reporter with a family. Yet, the junior writers had to meet the same standards and produce the same quality material as writers at higher pay scales. It was a case of unequal pay for equal work.

Further indignities occurred because the junior writers were deliberately prevented from making as much income as they could if they were treated fairly. Several of the studios liked to fire their junior writers on the Wednesday night before Thanksgiving. Then, on the following Friday morning, they would be hired back. The savings for the studios was one day's pay.

The problem was that the screen actors and writers did not feel that they were in the same category as the stagehands, technicians, and related guild members. The writers lived for screen credits, the only proof they would ever have that they worked in the film industry. But the craft guilds felt no such need. They also did not see why the screenwriters should complain about constant rewriting without adequate pay, competitive writing, or any other issue. Both professions also resented being asked to take pay cuts during the Depression while the studio executives were personally making more money than ever.

SAG recognized that IATSE was controlled by organized crime. Some of the actors had come from Chicago and were keenly aware of the intertwined interests of Bioff and Browne and the mob. Finally, actor Robert Montgomery, the new president of SAG, wanted to take a proactive stance against Bioff and Browne. The timing was right for the mob's assault on the industry to begin falling apart.

The extortion plot of Bioff, Browne, and the Outfit's leaders ultimately weakened and unraveled more quickly than it had been woven, starting in November 1937. That was when Bioff was brought before a California State Assembly committee and asked about the use of the 2 percent dues assessment and his management style. Then, on November 17, Robert Montgomery testified before the same investigating committee, telling them that the actors, writers, and directors had come together to avoid an IATSE takeover.

Despite the increasing boldness of the IATSE leadership's enemies when it came to revealing what was taking place, well-placed bribes and intimidation kept the investigations from moving forward. Bioff remained arrogant and in charge, though he made a tactical error with Louis B. Mayer. He told the mogul, when Mayer began having him investigated, "There is no room for both of us in this world, and I will be the one who stays here."

Mayer did not know if "here" meant Hollywood or Earth. The mogul did understand that he was possibly learning enough about Bioff's dirty past to bring him down, yet there was nothing that he, personally, could do with such information. He was likely to get killed before he could stop the union leader. That was why Mayer contacted investigative journalist Westbrook Pegler, who was already exploring mob influence in the labor unions around the country. Pegler's readership was in the millions, making him too high profile for a mob hit.

Pegler was a good choice. He would eventually win the Pulitzer Prize for uncovering union leadership corruption, including that of Bioff and Browne. It was Pegler, working with an old acquaintance from his days as a Chicago-based crime reporter, who discovered Bioff's conviction for having beaten a whore in 1922. The acquaintance was Lieutenant Make Mills of the Chicago police, and when they went through the files, Mills took the information and wired Bioff a warrant to finish serving his six months. The incident occurred in November 1939, when the extortion/bribery scandal was beginning to unfold.

❝

I was born in a gang neighborhood, brought up with gangsters and given a movie career by friends in the underworld. That is something no one can change, and I owe much to the many men who stayed with me when the going was rough. That's more than I can say for the unfaithful world of the motion picture industry.

—George Raft reminiscing in 1957

❞

Although he was not openly aggressive against Willie Bioff, George Raft was working against him behind the scenes. He had avoided the politics of what was happening until 1939, when he was working at Warner Brothers on the film *Each Dawn I Die*, which also starred Jimmy Cagney. Cagney had long been a labor activist concerned about studio exploitation of the stars.

Typical of the problems that caused Cagney to work to build SAG was an incident he related in *Cagney by Cagney*: Boris Karloff, a much-beloved, gentle man, who had gotten lucky as a portrayer of human and semihuman monsters, came to him to complain about his working conditions. The types of parts he played required endless hours of makeup. All actors needed makeup for the camera, but Karloff had to endure whatever was necessary to change his appearance radically, yet believably, on camera. As he explained to Cagney, "Every morning I have to report three and a half hours before work commences in order to put on these fanciful makeups. By day's end, I'm thoroughly exhausted, and then it's another hour getting the damned stuff off. Sometimes they keep me working through to eleven or twelve o'clock at night. It's terribly, terribly trying."

Cagney realized that the problem was with the moguls in general, that actors at every studio were experiencing the same pressure. Twelve-hour days were not unusual; nor was it unusual for actors to work occasionally until sunrise. Then, Cagney came across a statistic compiled by checking the work records of the actors. Many of the actors were paid extremely well per week of work but were given only an average of three-and-a-third weeks of work per year. This meant that they were constantly poor, constantly seeking work in their field, and unlikely to rebel openly. He was doing better than average himself and refused to tolerate the injustice.

Cagney fought against the SAG takeover to such a degree that Bioff began harassing his wife. Cagney would go to a guild meeting, and someone would call his home to tell his wife that he had been killed in a car accident. However, she was used to what was taking place and called the guild office to confirm that Jimmy was present.

The dangers almost got out of hand during the filming of *Each Dawn I Die*. Willie Bioff and his thugs showed up on the set with plans to hurt Jack Warner by killing one of the Warner Brothers' biggest stars in a carefully planned accident. Bioff and his thugs said nothing but were constantly checking the giant arc lamps suspended overhead. Catwalks and ladders could reach the lights, and the support cables could easily be cut.

George Raft never gave the full story of what happened that day, and Jimmy Cagney learned of only some of the details around the time of the premiere. It is certain that someone with influence over Bioff was on the set with the labor racketeer. The most likely person was Johnny Rosselli, a men affiliated with Hollywood, yet without a clearly defined role, so that he could visit sets, talk with producers, and not be mentioned since he was so familiar. Whatever the case, Bioff was told to back off from his plans.

It was only at the New York premiere of *Each Dawn I Die* that Willie Bioff, never one to keep his mouth shut, was quoted as telling Raft, "You did pretty good with *Each Dawn I Die*. You can thank me for that. I was going to take care of Cagney. We were all set to drop a lamp on him. But I got the word to lay off because you were in the picture." Since he was seen on the set, whoever told him to lay off also must have been present.

Raft was livid. He told Bioff that Jimmy Cagney was a friend and one of the finest men in Hollywood. Willie realized that Raft, who had been a gangster and was not afraid of him, was telling him that he would hurt him. It was no idle threat. Raft was serious. Willie backed off. As for Raft, the movie was such a success that Warner Brothers put him under full contract with their studio for $5,000 per week.

The Tax Man Cometh

Elmer Irey of the Internal Revenue Service opened his own investigation into Bioff and his money, an action that Willie should have anticipated, given his high lifestyle relative to his reported income. The investigation led to Irey's indicting Bioff for underestimating his 1937 tax bill by $69,000.

While the tax man, the ultimate scourge of the Outfit and their associates, went after the flash and cash of Willie Bioff, members of the IA Progressives in IATSE Local 37 were launching their own attack. They turned to labor attorney Carey McWilliams to look into Bioff, and it was McWilliams who first located the $100,000 check linking the Schenck brothers, Loew's, and MGM in the scams.

McWilliams was the man who forced the California State Assembly to begin hearings into labor racketeering in the motion picture industry, the action that led to the testimony of the SAG leadership as well. However, the hearings were a sham. The law firm of William Neblitt and William J. Jones was readily corruptible, and Jones also happened to be the state assembly speaker. He went to Louis B. Mayer privately to see if the mogul wanted to be rid of IATSE, but Mayer did not. With all the problems he was having with Bioff, he recognized what the Schenck brothers and others saw in being in bed with the IATSE leadership. There would be no real labor negotiating with the CIO. They paid bribes so as not to have to provide fair—and far more expensive—employment contracts.

Willie Bioff went even further. He was told he was being investigated, so he took $5,000 to the Jones and Neblitt law firm.

In the end, after careful deliberation, unbiased hearings, and fattened bank accounts, the state assembly rejected what went against its members' interests and said there were no problems with IATSE. Then, the assemblymen turned on Carey McWilliams, accusing him of wasting their time.

George Browne, who preferred drinking in Chicago, while Willie handled matters back in Los Angeles, now became aggressive. First, he returned to Los Angeles and ordered that the 2 percent assessment be ended on December 9, 1937. The impression that he thought he would be giving was that if he was really corrupt, he would have continued to receive the money he had been taking. Instead, his actions "proved" he must have really needed the strike fund for the battle against the producers, even though no one had ever learned where the money was going.

Next, Browne held a vote of the various union locals to see if they wanted local autonomy again. They could negotiate their own contracts. They could have an open shop. He did not tell them, however, that when the meeting of Local 37 was held in the American Legion boxing stadium, there would be a stand-up vote. The location not only held everyone who wanted to attend but was designed in such a way that Browne would be able to see everyone and know exactly how each person voted. Dissidents would find work scarce and beatings all too familiar.

The studios were looking at industrywide problems beyond labor issues. Wages were a concern, and *Variety* reported that wages were up by an average of one-third over the previous year for union workers. There was more, though. Distribution costs were also up, often by 45 percent. International markets, once a major source of revenue, were shrinking because of the impending war. The Japanese and the Germans were no longer given the unrestricted access to American movies they had been enjoying, and the lack of distribution revenue from international markets meant production had to be cut back.

Wages may have been higher, but some craft unions reported that as many as 85 percent of the workers were unemployed. The moguls did not care about how the changes were affecting the industry labor market, usually hiring the people they knew, liked, and were certain would not cause trouble. Since the IATSE leadership had long been working with them, they knew that so long as they paid Bioff, Browne, and their mob partners, there would be no unsettling labor dispute.

No matter what else was happening, however, the paper trail Bioff had been leaving was catching up to him. A grand jury was assembled in Sacramento, California, to investigate the way the state assembly pretended the mob problem did not exist in the Hollywood unions. Bioff was summoned and said that the $100,000 he received from Schenck was a personal loan deposited in a Hollywood bank, then transferred in cash to a safe deposit box.

IATSE's auditor, C. P. Cregan, was called to the stand. Cregan said that he had made out the $5,000 check that went to William Neblitt. Neblitt, when called to the stand, said that the money was for legal services of an unspecified nature. The grand jury also wanted to know how Willie Bioff had so much more money than could be accounted for by his salary.

George Browne, desperate to keep the scam going without personally paying too high a price, arranged for Bioff to drop out of the labor movement temporarily. However, because Willie had done nothing wrong, according to Browne, he was granted a year's salary by the Executive Board.

Bioff also faced the little problem of having to go to jail for his 1922 conviction, and it was while he was in prison that the 1940 IATSE international convention was again held in Louisville, Kentucky. Browne exclaimed that the union problem was Communists, not corruption. Dirty Communists were taking over the film industry. Vicious radicals were stirring up trouble for decent, patriotic union members. As for Bioff, Browne told the convention,

> Out of the clear sky came rumblings of a Grand Jury investigation authorized by the State Legislature, which was to look into legislative corruption in connection with the previous legislative Capitol Labor hearing. The aforementioned rumblings soon became a matter of fact, and shortly thereafter subpoenas were served upon your officers to appear before the California Grand Jury at Sacramento.
>
> It was not hard to see that instead of the Legislature being investigated, the I.A.T.S.E. was being investigated, and it became apparent that this was another fishing expedition to embarrass my personal representative, William Bioff, who had incurred the everlasting hatred of the open shop element for forcing the first closed shop in the leading industry in the State of California, namely that of the Motion Picture Industry.
>
> William Bioff had done the most remarkable job any man has ever done for labor against terrific odds, but what a price he and his family have had to pay that our members and their families might enjoy a better livelihood in their own pursuit of happiness.

William Bioff? Paying a price? The celebration of the life of a thug, extortionist, pimp, and all-around bad guy sounded like a funeral eulogy delivered by a member of the clergy who had never met the deceased or his family or bothered to learn anything about the life he had led.

An even more ridiculous statement came from Willie Bioff before he had to return to Illinois to finish his years' old six-month sentence. "They can't afford to let me go to jail. I've done too much for the industry in taking care of strikes, etcetera."

There was more to come, though. Joe Schenck could see what was happening with the investigations. The government wanted both to stop what was taking place and to obtain a high-profile conviction. Schenck decided to throw in with the prosecution, knowing he was going to jail, and turn evidence against Bioff and Browne for the extortion charges.

Schenck's reasoning was self-serving and ultimately successful. He knew that the government was going to convict him for failure to pay taxes and for being involved with Bioff and Browne. However, the truth was that he and several of the other studio heads were involved with labor racketeering. It was true that Willie was extorting money. It was equally true that the producers were bribing the labor leaders. They were all dirty. They were all complicit in essentially robbing the IATSE treasury and hurting the workers.

Schenck admitted to paying off IATSE, naming not only Bioff and Browne but Nick Circella. Johnny Rosselli was called separately and not linked with Schenck, but he knew that he would be going to jail. So would Bioff and Browne, who were both indicted on May 23, 1941. Circella was allowed to walk so long as he acted as a material witness.

Rosselli went to see Bioff and made clear that his name was to be kept out of the union activity as much as possible. The two men would admit to meeting only once in 1936.

The defense attorney was mob all the way through, though with the indictments in and jail a certainty for some, no one cared about his attorney's image. Sid Korshak was the best—young, a graduate of Chicago's DePaul University Law School, and a man who had worked his way through college driving for Al Capone. Capone liked him so much that he paid the youth's way through law school, ensuring for himself and the Outfit the services of a lawyer who knew the underside of their business.

Korshak quickly moved into the position of lawyer for the Outfit. There were two types of attorneys working with organized crime: the lawyer who was a part of the mob, usually a made member, and the lawyer who was independent of the organization but worked exclusively, or nearly exclusively, for the mob. He knew when he went into court that he was likely just going through the motions of presenting a case, that the outcome had been prearranged, and that he was just part of a show. That seemed to be Korshak's role, and he was paid well, living in the mob-connected Seneca Hotel in a suite that cost $10,000 a year in the 1930s.

Korshak's law practice, in 1939, was a partnership with Harry Ash in the First Ward Democratic Headquarters. Again, the building was a mob joint, where men like Curly Humphreys constantly worked to be certain that the politicians followed their interests.

Korshak had started going to Hollywood in 1935, and it was through the mob that he also fell in love. Longy Zwillman introduced him to Jean Harlow, who in turn introduced him to an actress who became his fiancé. He would spend the next several years going back and forth to Hollywood to handle legal matters for the mob, but he was their adviser, not their lawyer, in California. He never bothered to take the California bar exam and so was not eligible to practice. That did not matter, though; he was a consultant both to the mob in the Midwest and the East and to the commission, those corrupt leaders who dominated Los Angeles prior to the reform movement. He was also the link with MCA's then head, Lew Wasserman.

Korshak was arguably as straight as a lawyer for the mob could be. He had many legitimate clients not connected with organized crime. He also made certain that when he handled large money deals, he did not cheat the Internal Revenue Service.

Korshak's genius was in being totally honest. When he negotiated what was actually a bribe for the mob along the line of the payments made to Bioff and Browne for keeping labor peace, he would add a fee for his services that matched the amount normally pocketed by the extortionists. Then, he would declare the entire fee as taxable income, pay his taxes, and divide what was left with the mob. There was never a successful investigation into his activities because there was nothing illegal about his actions. The mob made almost as much money risk free because the money was clean.

Korshak was brought into the investigation of Bioff and Browne by Charles "Cherry Nose" Gioe, who lived in the same building as Korshak. He was one of the three men who ran the Outfit after Capone's downfall, and his specialty was gambling. He had been involved with what was taking place in Los Angeles prior to Bioff and Browne, and when the mob moved into the movie industry extortion racket, he fronted the money for Bioff and Browne.

There was not much that initially could be done for Bioff and Browne. The testimony was overwhelming. The head of Paramount Pictures showed himself to be a total victim. "I regarded the making of these payments to Mr. Bioff, and to such others as were associated with him in receiving these payments, as necessary to preserve my company against possible and very probable disaster."

Albert Warner told about being repeatedly forced to pay large sums of money. He said that he would be in genuine physical danger if he did not, and eventually took to using a bodyguard, though there never was an attempt on his life.

Willie Bioff was the weak part of the extortion plot. He had come to love the lifestyle he enjoyed on his eighty acres. He adored his wife. The idea of spending ten years in jail (Browne received eight and Joe Schenck, who took the fall for all the producers by letting himself be seen as the middle man, received a year and a day) was emotionally overwhelming. Then, as he considered what to do, both he and the Outfit made a mistake that would have serious repercussions for everyone.

The plan, as outlined by Korshak when they met at the Ambassador Hotel in Los Angeles two days after the indictment, was for Willie to take the fall. He was to say that he was Joe Schenck's bagman, going to jail for whatever time he was given, though with the understanding that strings would be pulled where possible to reduce the real time served.

Both Nick Schenck and Joe Kennedy had funneled hundreds of thousands of dollars to the Roosevelt campaigns on behalf of the Outfit, a fact that galled Kennedy because of his hatred for Roosevelt. But the money bought what the Outfit desired, access to individuals at high levels who were inclined to do them favors. Whether or not Franklin Roosevelt was ever directly involved is not known. However, various government officials were comfortable helping the mob when it would not embarrass them or lead to criminal charges. The mob figures who were going to jail understood this and were eventually rewarded with better prison conditions and shorter jail time.

Bioff was given $15,000 to cover legal bills when he returned to New York, and it was presumed that George Browne received a similar arrangement.

The only person who was not present to face the charges immediately was Nick Circella (Dean). He was intimately connected with the Chicago Outfit and a man who knew all that was taking place with the Hollywood extortion racket.

Nick's idea of going into hiding involved his lover, Estelle Carey.

Estelle, a beautiful blond, was originally hired to be the twenty-six game girl in Circella's Colony Club.

The twenty-six game was simple. Beautiful girls were hired to stand by a three-foot-square board, each girl at each board holding a cup containing ten dice. A man would come over, give the girl a quarter, and take the cup, emptying the dice on the board. If the score was twenty-six, an infrequent occasion given the number of dice rolled each time, he would win a free drink.

The twenty-six game girls were like the B-girls popular with night clubs a generation later. They were to talk with the players, who knew they were spending a quarter a throw to be with the girl, not to win the drink. Sometimes they would stand talking while spending quarter after quarter. The B-girl of later years would sit at a bar and let a man buy her the most expensive drink in the house; while he drank his own real drink, she would be given tea or fruit juice with the same appearance. The difference in price between the cheap and the expensive drink would be shared with the B-girl. The twenty-six game girls, by contrast, steered men into another room—the second floor in Nick's club—for high-stakes craps. The actual escort to the next room was the hostess, usually a somewhat older, more experienced, but equally beautiful woman, who had been around the block many times.

The twenty-six game girls were not prostitutes, but they understood that turning a high roller into a regular assured excellent tips and made their bosses happy. That was why the third floor of Nick's club had bedrooms that could be used for more intimate entertainment when the hostess felt it was in the club's best interest to truly keep the man happy. The sex was handled in so subtle and sophisticated a way that the men did not expect to go to bed with the hostess (or twenty-six game girl) each time he came to the club. He just knew that his presence was so appreciated that becoming a regular was an enjoyable way to spend many evenings.

Estelle Carey was a hostess and one of the best. Circella marveled at the sensual skills that enabled her to help the customers lose all their money happily. He was quoted as saying, "I once saw her steer an oil-man from Tulsa to the tables. He lost ten grand in an hour. She kept him happy all the time, and after that, whenever he came to Chicago, he wanted Estelle."

Circella was not a jealous man. He was not averse to letting her spend time with members of the Outfit, apparently proud that no matter what she did with the other men, she always came home to him. They were lovers and business associates and held one another in mutual regard. When the indictments came down because of the Hollywood extortion racket, she did not hesitate to dye her hair black and accompany him wherever he felt safe.

The first mistake was made by Bioff and Browne. Bioff was especially unnerved when he was placed in Bridewell Prison to await trial. He wanted nothing more to do with the Outfit and sent word that he was resigning. Word reached Louis Campagna, who visited Willie on behalf of Nitti and the others. He explained that resignation meant death. He might not have been a made man, but he knew too much, had been involved in too much, and should do the right thing, as would be explained by Sid Korshak.

Korshak wanted Bioff and Browne to plead guilty and be done with it. Instead, they pled innocent, meaning that a full trial would begin on October 6, 1941. Witnesses would be called, and the information obtained on the stand would affect others. The full range of the shakedowns might become known, including the activities of both sides, the studio heads and the mob-connected players.

Bioff declared himself innocent of extorting from anyone. He was a good labor leader, but maybe a little weak. That was the problem when the producers came and offered him bribes. There was no extortion.

The jury bought none of Willie and George's stories. Both were convicted in December and sentenced the following month to ten and eight years, respectively.

Circella had also been indicted, but he managed to avoid the FBI until December 1, 1941, when he was arrested. He understood that he had to plead guilty and did so, accepting an eight-year sentence on March 8, 1942.

The Chicago Outfit was falling apart, despite its efforts to let as few men as possible take the fall. In the past, they had had to worry about one man going down, such as Al Capone when he was jailed for income-tax evasion. They had carefully bribed and blackmailed everyone who seemed to matter, all the way to the head of the FBI. But there was too much working against them. Movie stars got more attention than the usual extortion victims. Hollywood was a high-profile community, and national media columnists and reporters released too many details about improper actions to ignore.

Don't Stop in the Name of the Law

J. Edgar Hoover had ordered the Justice Department to begin investigating the alleged shakedown tactics of IATSE as early as April 1939, and he did so with considerable press coverage. However, the order was given for show. There was no publicity when he called off the inquiry in May 1941.

Hoover stopped the investigation because of his personal life. He was both a homosexual and an avid gambler on horse races. Meyer Lansky and Lucky Luciano documented his habits as much as possible. Frank Costello had been helping Hoover at the track as was noted earlier. The knowledge of his homosexuality apparently came from a series of compromising photographs. They were allegedly the reason Hoover went so far as to insist that the idea of a Mafia was outrageous until the Kefauver investigations in the early 1950s brought too much information to light.

The photographs of Hoover have never been published. At least one was alleged to have been in the personal files of the late actor Peter Lawford, the brother-in-law of President Jack Kennedy, who, with his brother Bobby, hated the FBI director. However, though some claimed to have seen the photo, it was either destroyed or is in private hands, if it exists.

What matters is that Hoover knew he would be exposed at a time when to be revealed as a homosexual was to be publicly disgraced. By contrast, the little-known Alf Oftedal had nothing to hide and nothing to fear. Oftedal worked for the Intelligence Unit of the Internal Revenue Service. He did not care about Joe Schenck's payoff. He wanted him jailed for income tax evasion and brought him to trial in 1940. U.S. Attorney Mathias Correa and Prosecutor Boris Kostelanetz, who would also charge Johnny Rosselli with perjury, handled the prosecution.

Schenck told almost everything, explaining his arrangements with Bioff, Browne, and Circella. Isadore Zevlin, the IATSE bookkeeper, was indicted for perjury that October.

Circella began brooding in prison. He realized that he would probably serve all or most of his eight-year sentence and that others in the Outfit at least as involved as he was would go free. He arranged to meet with Prosecutor Kostelanetz, who later said, "He never agreed to spell everything out for us, but there was a measure of cooperation."

What happened next reflected a change in the approach the mob was using to punish those who refused to remain silent and caused problems for others. Beating or killing was inadequate unless the person's death would prevent the unwanted activity from taking place. Instead, to send the most dramatic message possible, they decided to hurt or destroy what- or whomever the individual loved most. In the case of Nick Circella, that was Estelle Carey, and the mob decided to send their message before he could testify further.

The man chosen to handle the matter was Marshall Joseph Caifano (a.k.a. John Michael Caifano, a.k.a. John Marshall, a.k.a. Michael Heale, a.k.a. Heels, a.k.a. Thomas Hynes, a.k.a. George Marini, a.k.a. Michael Monette, a.k.a. Johnie Moore, a.k.a. Joseph Rinaldi, a.k.a. Frank Roberto, a.k.a. John Roberts, a.k.a. Joe Russo, a.k.a. Joe Russell, a.k.a. Shoes, a.k.a. John Stevens). He was a Chicago mobster whose specialties included gambling, interstate fraud, burglary, and murder when necessary. He was never charged with Estelle Carey's death, but all sources connected with the Outfit knew he was the murderer.

The death could not have been more dramatic or more violent. On February 3, 1943, Caifano, under whatever name he was using that day, arrived at an apartment at 512 Addison Street on Chicago's North Side. He may have called ahead, or he may have had someone Carey would not suspect call on his behalf. All that is certain is that she was talking to her cousin on the telephone when there was a knocking at the door. Estelle explained that she was expecting someone and hung up to answer it.

The death was slow, painful, and methodical. She resisted but was no match for her assailant. Her beautiful face was slashed with a knife. She was stabbed with an ice pick. She was beaten with a blackjack, a broken whiskey bottle, and an electric iron. The violence took place in both the kitchen and the living room, the walls in both locations smeared with her hair, dyed red in her latest attempt at a disguise, and her blood.

Finally, the violence over, she was tied to a chair. Then, a flammable liquid was poured over her body and set on fire. Death, when it came, was caused by the burning.

The fire department received a call to come to the Addison Street address at 3:09 p.m. Neighbors had smelled the smoke.

So far as is known, Estelle Carey's death was the first mob hit of a woman in the history of U.S. organized crime. So shocking was the death to investigators, who were reluctant to admit the escalation of violence by the now dying Outfit, that they looked for alternative explanations. Perhaps Carey and Circella had been cheating the mob, skimming money that should have been passed on. Perhaps Carey had given Circella's address to the authorities and her death was a reprisal for his, as a result, going to jail. Or perhaps the killing was just coincidence, her killing unrelated to the mob.

The truth was much simpler. George Browne's wife was called after the murder and told that her husband, another weak link, should not reveal any information. If he did, she would be murdered and placed in a car trunk.

Nick Circella knew Estelle's murder was a message for him. He was shattered by the death and terrified by the brutality he had been shown. He knew it was time to shut up. He said nothing further to investigators. The time when he may have been any sort of help was over.

George Browne cooperated slightly but not in a way that would send anyone to jail. Willie Bioff, however, was outraged. He found Estelle's murder morally repugnant. He did not care if a man was tortured or killed. Men involved with the mob knew what they were getting into and were responsible for their choices; women and children were innocents.

Bioff went to the prosecutors, offering them whatever information they desired. He named Johnny Rosselli. He named Frank Nitti. He named Paul Ricca. He named Francis Maritote (a.k.a. Frankie Diamond), Capone's brother-in-law; Phil D'Andrea, who was Nitti's most trusted friend; Charlie "Cherry Nose" Gioe; Louis "Little New York" Campagna, who had once been Capone's bodyguard; and Louis Kaufman, a union boss who helped with the takeover of IATSE during the Kentucky gathering. Essentially, he named the power structure of the Outfit. Joe Accardo and Curly Humphreys were kept out of the prosecution and took over the operations, but they presided over a drastically reduced, far less dangerous operation.

Everyone had always known that Bioff and Browne were punks, losers, nobodies until they had thrown in with the Outfit at Frank Nitti's suggestion. Now, it was Nitti's turn to face the results of his misjudgment. His friends and business associates told him that he had brought this on the Outfit. He had let the punks gain too much knowledge and too much power with too little accountability. It was Nitti's fault.

This would not be Nitti's first trip to prison. He had hated the time he had served and did not want to go back. He was also overwhelmed with remorse for what he had done to his friends by letting the wrong men enter their world. He began drinking on March 19, 1943, the day after they were all indicted. He drank and drank, either trying to drown his sorrows or to bolster his courage. Whatever his motive, he took a bottle in one hand and a .32 caliber pistol in the other and wandered along the railroad tracks near the Illinois Central Station on Chicago's South Side. He waved the bottle when he wasn't drinking, then waved the pistol, half pointing it at anyone he saw, shouting threats too incoherent to be remembered. Then, still staggering, he waved the gun toward his head, pulled the trigger, and sent a bullet through the crown of his brown snap-brim fedora. He waved the gun again, then fired another round, again shooting a hole through his hat. A third shot was aimed slightly lower, and this time the hat was safe. Frank Nitti had blown his brains out.

What happened next, in the weeks before the October 5, 1943, trial, at which Bioff would be the star witness, surprised everyone who did not know the Outfit's reach. The good people of Chicago wanted to help the men who had extorted from them, threatened them, beaten them, stolen from them, and otherwise made their lives less pleasant than they might have been. Shopkeepers, business owners, brewers, the heads of a macaroni factory, and of course the bookmakers and other low-level mobsters all contributed cash and checks to help the indicted mob boys. The money came in small and large amounts, and every contributor was noted, putting pressure on others from the same neighborhoods who did not feel the urgency to get the mob bosses out on bail. By the time it was all counted and accounted for, $500,000 had been given to the court to free the mobsters until their trial.

The newly righteous Willie Bioff was the star of a ten-day show of truth telling. "I am just a low, uncouth person," he confessed. "I'm a low type sort of man. People of my caliber don't do nice things."

George Browne used more sense and remained relatively silent, saying only what was absolutely necessary. However, the studio heads were happy to corroborate Bioff's stories. They were mad, and they also knew that Joe Schenck, the only producer without children, had agreed to cover for them and do all the jail time. They made certain he could continue in the industry when he left prison.

Bioff's outrage worked. The men whom he had once helped get richer, while he benefited beyond his wildest imagination, were all convicted and sent to the Atlanta Penitentiary, one of the worst in the country. They let Korshak work his wonders with other lawyers and high-level officials in Washington, D.C., to get them transferred to better surroundings and released early. No one threatened Willie Bioff. No one tried to hurt Willie Bioff. They simply marked their time.

Willie Had to Die

Politics, not the mob, was the reason boyhood friends Harry Rosenzweig and Barry Goldwater came together as adults. Rosenzweig, the son of a longtime Phoenix, Arizona, jeweler, was founder of the North Central Development Company, a board member for charities and the Phoenix Art Museum, and a member of major local country clubs. When his friend Barry Goldwater decided to run for the U.S. Senate seat from Arizona in 1952, Harry ran the successful campaign. Harry was also a Republican national committeeman, Arizona GOP chairman, and the head of finance for the Maricopa County (Phoenix) Republican Committee. In 1964, he was an adviser to Goldwater's singularly unsuccessful run for the presidency against Lyndon Johnson.

During the 1952 campaign, Harry also did a favor for a man known as William Nelson. This was the new name Willie Bioff had chosen, combining his full first name with his wife's maiden name. Someone— the name of the person was never revealed—had contacted a reporter for the *Arizona Republic*, telling him that he would have a strong story if he researched Bioff's history. The reporter did, but word of the investigation into William Nelson reached Rosenzweig, who went to the publisher, Gene Pulliam, and had the story killed.

The reasons for killing the story seemed fair, especially during the time when the newspaper was strongly Republican. Rosenzweig said that Willie Bioff was a reformed man and a good citizen of Phoenix. He didn't need to be ostracized for his past.

However, years later, the reporter, a man named Jack Karie, was interviewed for, and quoted in, *The Arizona Project* about extensive corruption in Arizona. Karie said,

> A guy came up to me in the Arizona Club and told me that this guy we all knew as Bill Nelson was really this hood named Bioff. I went right out and started nosing around. It didn't take much

to verify. So I shot a couple of pictures of his house and wrote the story. It was a damn good one, too. So I'm waiting a couple of days for the story to come out. This one afternoon I stop by a liquor store, and who do I run into but this Nelson-Bioff guy. He's acting like a real smart-ass. He tells me he knows all about the story I wrote and says he's taken care of it, that it won't run. Then, he threatens me, says he has a lot of powerful friends, and I'd better stay off his ass or else. Well, I really got pissed off. I went storming into the office. I couldn't figure out how Bioff knew about the story. Sure enough, the editors are real wishy-washy when I start bitching. I finally am told that it was killed on orders of old man Pulliam.

The story did come out, however. Gene Pulliam killed it, allegedly at the request of Harry Rosenzweig, but the information was provided to Westbrook Pegler, who published it. And Willie, never one to miss an opportunity to share his wealth with others who could influence his life positively, gave Goldwater $5,000 for his campaign for the U.S. Senate, funneling the money through Rosenzweig.

Relationships became more interesting and more dangerous. Goldwater was a skilled pilot who owned his own plane. He long had flown friends around the state, including Harry. Now, his friends included William Nelson and a man named Gus Greenbaum, originally from Chicago, who had been in Phoenix since 1928 to handle gambling activities. When Las Vegas was built, he was asked by the Outfit to go to Nevada to run the Flamingo's gambling. He was later moved to the Riviera.

On November 4, 1955, Willie Bioff left his home and walked to his truck. He stepped inside, started the engine, and was blown apart by a bomb planted on behalf of the men he had sent to jail during the movie-industry extortion scandal.

Barry Goldwater at first expressed shock, claiming to have known nothing about Willie Bioff/Bill Nelson's past. Then, he said that he had known and was using Willie as a resource for investigations into labor racketeering.

Greenbaum would also come to an untimely end a few years later. On December 3, 1958, both Greenbaum and his wife were found in their apartment with their throats slit. Greenbaum had been skimming from the mob at the Riviera. He had been drinking heavily, using drugs, bedding women, and gambling extensively. He was falling apart and worried that if anyone ever took over his job, the skimming would be discovered. Apparently, the discovery was made sooner than he expected.

Although they had nothing to do with Hollywood, Barry Goldwater and his brother, Robert, were dangerous men to be connected with if you wanted to hide from the mob. The Goldwater family had a department store, which, for a while, the brothers were running. Mobster Moe Dalitz, known to be connected with both organized crime and the teamsters union, arranged for the Goldwater brothers to open a branch of their store in the Desert Inn in Las Vegas. They were the only people to have such a venture in Las Vegas at the time, and for years, questions about the life and death of both William Nelson (Bioff) and Gus Greenbaum would haunt Senator Goldwater. Rumors plagued him until his death that the killer of Bioff was Marshall Caifano, and that he had traveled to Phoenix on Goldwater's plane. Even if he did, it is certain that the senator had nothing to do with the Hollywood extortion. He, like others on the periphery of the scandal, was part of something bigger than he had anticipated when he became involved with Bioff.

Intermission 3

Okay, exhale. Take a bathroom break. Get some popcorn from our refreshment stand. Get a soft drink. We need a moment to recap.

The major assault on Hollywood, handled by the most disorganized bad guys west of Chicago, ended with jail time, retribution, torture, suicide, and murder. The Chicago mob was far from finished, but the Capone gang had been decimated, and the face of the Outfit was very different from what it had been in the 1930s. Bioff and Browne had been left alive and in charge of the union extortion racket for far too long. Even the sophisticated Johnny Rosselli had to do time.

The only mogul who went down the tubes was Joe Schenck, and he proved himself a stand-up guy for the others in the film industry. Final score—producers, one loss, mob, down by more than a dozen.

But That's Not All, Folks . . .

The Hollywood draw for the mob, the Outfit, and the independents was obvious. Bad guys have always liked Los Angeles and the film industry. Bad guys have always liked Hollywood and Beverly Hills. Bad guys have always liked naughty girls, and few industries have a higher proportion of vain, shallow, insecure, and frequently amoral women (at least when it suits their overwhelming ambitions) than the film industry. Even better for those men inclined to seek intensely erotic but otherwise meaningless relationships, either through seduction or induced by drugs and alcohol, are the Hollywood women who are "over the hill."

The term *over the hill* has quite a different meaning in Hollywood than it does in the rational world. Remember that the women coming into stardom in the 1930s and 1940s were not women at all. They were teenage girls whose facial structures and hair styles enabled them to

236

portray women twice their age. Real women, those whose beauty comes from living more than twenty-five or thirty years, developing their inner beings and their minds, honing their talents, and learning from their mistakes, were not, and frequently still are not, desirable. Today, the smart ones become screenwriters, do voice-overs, write novels, work on stage as well as in film, teach, produce, direct, and otherwise find personal satisfaction in a broad range of creative endeavors. The rest validate their existence by having sex with every male who can still get an erection without enhancers, pumps, or aphrodisiacs, and often with the men who do need those props, provided they are important enough. They may involve themselves with men who beat them because they think that that's what they deserve. They may involve themselves with men who worship the ground they walk on because they think that's what they deserve. They may involve themselves with men they can physically and verbally abuse because that keeps them in the pro-verbial catbird seat.

The women also go on "vacations," where teams of cosmetic sur-geons treat their bodies like patchwork quilts, nipping and tucking, sewing and injecting, sucking and pumping, until they have the same limited body motion and facial expression of a discount Barbie Doll knockoff from a third-world factory.

That is why the last chapters of this book will discuss not only the lingering influence of the mob in Hollywood, but also two stories of self-destructive women seduced by the mob and the tragedies that re-sulted. Out of respect for age, we will start with the older of the two, though, had she lived long enough, she undoubtedly would have em-bellished her birth date such that she would be the only woman audi-tioning for ingénue roles wearing support hose and sensible shoes.

CHAPTER Nineteen

Julia Jean, Johnny, Mickey, and Cheryl, the Romance from Hell

Nobody ever gave a damn about Julia Jean Turner, called Judy by family and friends. She was another bored kid cutting classes at Hollywood High School whenever she could. Fourteen years old, her body maturing faster than her interest in boys, she had a face that was pretty in an idealized, girl-next-door sort of way, hair that could be shaped into a variety of styles that made her look older, and no particular ambition beyond enjoying her chocolate sundae in Schwab's Drug Store one day in January 1936.

Schwab's was always the center of action and anonymity in Hollywood. There was a pharmacy and a lunch counter—everyone had those—and Leon Schwab and his three brothers let out-of-work actors hang around when they had no money. The pay phone in the lunch area served as their "office" line, and agents and producers were given the number so often by so many new actors that they had to be on to the ruse. Meals went on a tab to be paid back weekly, monthly, or whenever. Most of the actors were so grateful for a place to go until they found work that they paid the Schwabs back from their first paychecks, if not before.

The brothers had been in business for a decade when Judy started coming around. They had bought a failed drugstore and decided to follow the oldest brother's advice. Jack Schwab said that if they offered perfect, quality service, they would be successful. The formula seems trite today. It was innovative when they introduced it and amazed customers in 1936.

No purchase was too small, no service too great. Leon Schwab said that if someone called and needed a 2-cent postage stamp, he or one of the employees would deliver it to the caller's home. Actor Charles Laughton decried his inability to get a decent car during World War II, so Leon located a Cadillac, arranged the transaction, and took no money for his effort.

The food service was never intended to do more than break even because much of it was given away, or put on the "tab." A roast beef sandwich that would cost $5 for the same size and quality in other area eateries cost only 70 cents at Schwab's. Everything made a few cents profit, which paid off the unreimbursed debt. The brothers knew that the arrangement earned the loyalty of customers who, over the years, would spend large sums of money on everything from basics to expensive gift items brought back from Leon's regular buying trips to Europe.

Schwab's was also the official MGM holiday store. Louis B. Mayer let the brothers open a branch on the set, offering everything actors and crew might desire, except food and medicine. The employees had access to such a wide variety of merchandise at affordable prices that they did most or all of their holiday shopping during set breaks. Production went faster, there was less downtime, and everyone profited.

Schwab's was also the place to go when you were fourteen years old, cutting school, and didn't want to be hassled. Judy "bought" her right to sit at the counter by ordering ice cream. She was too young for a tab, yet old enough that the Schwabs and their employees left her alone.

Judy was like a lot of Midwestern transplants: her family was dysfunctional and had moved enough that she never felt anywhere was home. Wallace, Idaho, was her birthplace. Her father, Virgil Turner, like so many other men in 1921 when Judy was born, was a bootlegger with a legitimate job as an insurance salesman. He was also a skilled gambler, though no one was ever certain if he understood the cards and the dice or if he was too good a charlatan to get caught cheating. Whatever the case, the family moved to San Francisco, where in December 1930 the dice were very good to Virgil when he went out to get some Christmas spending money. He walked out of the game loaded with cash and was immediately clubbed over the head. The winnings were stolen, his corpse left in the alley by the *San Francisco Chronicle* offices.

Mildred Turner and her daughter moved to Los Angeles. Mildred was a hairdresser who quickly found work. Judy was the new kid in town, a small-town outsider whose body developed early enough that the other girls watched as she got attention that they did not.

It was Billy Wilkerson who saw Judy in Schwab's. He gave her his business card and asked her to have her mother call him at the *Hollywood Reporter* office. He explained that he thought Judy had the type of appearance that could work on screen. He never promised stardom—he didn't know if she could act—but realized she would make a perfect extra or six-month-contract girl. Her face would probably take well to the different lighting and camera angles. Her hair was of a length that could be styled to change her age and look. She had a future if she could act.*

Mildred Turner was probably flattered by the interest in her daughter. She also realized that the publisher of the *Hollywood Reporter* was not a man to use the chance to be in the movies as a sexual come-on to an impressionable teen. She was further impressed when the agent

---

*For the record, the idea that Judy Turner was first discovered in Schwab's Drug Store has been disputed. A number of writers claim that she was sitting in an ice cream parlor across from Hollywood High. Entertainment columnist Sid Skolsky was the writer who originally told the story, and he mentioned Schwab's. Later, in one of his books, he said that he had used Schwab's in the story to be nice to the brothers. They had given him a room in the back above the pharmacy to use as an office. They frequently put his meals on a tab, which he never paid. And he also had daughters who occasionally charged items to their father's tab, which again was never paid. That was why, Skolsky claimed, he mentioned Schwab's when it was really an ice cream parlor across from Hollywood High.

Years later I asked the surviving brother, Leon Schwab, by then long retired, what had really happened. He said that Wilkerson spotted the girl in his drugstore, and he added that the drugstore was so famous by then that there was no reason to seek more publicity by creating a myth. He also pointed out, as did many of her friends, that long after Judy was successful, Schwab's was a favorite hangout.

Wilkerson suggested, a man named Henry Wilson, was not only brilliant, young, and aggressive, but also a homosexual. He had no interest in the sexual side of a female client.

Wilson's efforts paid off with an extra part in David O. Selznick's *A Star Is Born.* Judy was good enough to interest director Mervyn LeRoy, who wanted to see if she could succeed. She certainly wasn't much of an actress, but she showed far more ability than would have been expected of so young a teenager with no experience other than lying her way out of school. He decided to create a star, then see how long a run she might have.

First came the name change. Judy Turner became Lana Turner, a name that sounded sexier, less like that of a girl sitting across from a boy in a high school classroom. And then came the gimmick. He gave Lana Turner boobs.

No, Lana didn't have surgery or wear tissues in her bra to give herself fullness and lift, something slightly younger girls, like Marilyn Monroe, would do. Instead, he took advantage of the prudishness of the day, avoiding any of the euphemisms for "breasts" and simply calling her "the Sweater Girl."

Every generation has its code words related to sex and sexuality. In the 1930s, call a female a "sweater girl," and every male who had passed through puberty instantly envisioned two unmistakable bulges pressing against the fabric of a form-fitting sweater, a siren's song of modesty, ripeness, and lust. There was a testosterone-driven audience for a previously unknown actress nicknamed "the Sweater Girl," even if she couldn't act. Young women were also interested in comparing their own feminine attributes with those of the new actresses, the majority of whom were teenagers when they started in the studios.

The studios were both pleased and frustrated by the way Lana Turner grew as an actress. She never was great on the screen, but she was beautiful, and her style drew men to the Sweater Girl. The coming of World War II helped as well because she, along with Betty Grable and others, were popular with the servicemen.

Lana willingly embraced the men who lusted after her. There were numerous affairs and brief marriages, including to bandleader Artie Shaw and the black singer Billy Daniels. The Daniels affair was so dangerous for her career in racist America that MGM clamped down on Lana. Publicist Johnny Meyer was assigned to work as her companion, nursemaid, and keeper. She was told that Meyer's job was to keep her happy, and he did his best. However, he knew that his primary task was to be certain that the public did not learn about Daniels.

The one marriage of her eight that mattered, to both Lana's image and the murder that soon followed, was with Steve Crane. Crane was a relative nobody, a dreamer, a man with more ambition than achievement at a time in her life when Lana was considered an MGM star. The couple had an intense affair and married on a whim in July 1942. Lana was pregnant in December, and Steve got around to divorcing his first wife in January 1943. And yes, the public could do the math, leading to a February 4 annulment and a legal March 14 marriage, after which Steve entered the U.S. Army.

After the war years, everything seemed to go downhill for Lana Turner. She and Steve Crane remained in touch with each other, not because of any residual feelings of affection but because both adored their daughter, Cheryl Crane. However, Lana was on the way down. She was old enough that the roles she wanted were going to younger actresses who had not yet learned how fickle the business could be. Steve, by contrast, was becoming quite wealthy running restaurants. Still, Lana Turner fought to get back to the top, which is why Johnny Stompanato came into her life.

Ben (Don't Call Him ''Bugsy'' to His Face or He'll Kill You) Siegel

Ben Siegel got the nickname "Bugsy" after an incident in New York in 1935. Siegel had suggested to Bo Weinberg that he take over the New York rackets then being run by Dutch Schultz. Weinberg liked the idea, but Schultz quickly got wind of the scheme. He knew that the only way to stop Bo was to kill him, and he gave the contract to Siegel.

Ben Siegel understood the work he did. You could have friendships with anyone, but if you took a job, relationships did not matter.

Siegel and Weinberg agreed to meet for dinner in Brooklyn. Siegel disdained the ritual fancy meal for an enemy about to be killed. He was waiting as Weinberg stepped out of his car. Siegel clubbed him with his pistol, then rammed a sharp knife through Weinberg's throat, killing him instantly. To prevent the discovery of the body, Siegel did what had rarely, if ever, been done in the past. He poked numerous holes in Weinberg's stomach, making them so large that when the corpse was tossed in the Hudson River, the gasses produced by a decomposing body would escape through the openings. Instead of floating to the surface as the gases expanded, the body would stay on the bottom.

The murder itself did not lead to concern about Siegel's mental state—it was what happened afterwards. He was feeling so powerful that he wanted to hurt a woman during sex. That same night, he went to see a chorus girl he knew because she was dating mobster Joe Adonis and raped her, not because he wanted to send a message but because it was the only way he could release the sexual tension he felt from the murder.

It is not known how many men in Hollywood knew the full story of the night of Bo's murder. Most people recount the incident of his cutting holes in Bo's stomach as "proof" that he was nuts. If men like George Raft did know, their acceptance of Siegel as part of their social scene says perhaps as much about their characters as Bugsy's actions did about his.

Siegel seemed to have had Johnny Rosselli's history in mind when he arrived in Hollywood, sent by friends like Meyer Lansky, fearing that rivals were going to kill him if he stayed in the East. He knew Rosselli had been an extra in the early days. Siegel felt himself superior to Johnny and a potential star. In his vanity, he even bought professional motion picture equipment, then went to a set where George Raft was making a movie. Siegel would watch Raft do a scene, then study the script and have his assistant, Moe Sedway, who later handled rackets in Arizona and Nevada for him, prepare the camera equipment. Then, Moe would film Siegel playing the same part. The professionals working on the real film would edit Siegel's as a favor, knowing who he was and having heard stories of his explosive violence. He was flattered, and when he reviewed his own performances, he always found them superior to those of professionals like his friend Raft.

Siegel also obtained money from producers he had met through Raft. He was not part of the extortion racket of either Jack Dragna, who had been operating on a small scale before Chicago muscled in, or Bioff and Browne. Instead, he suggested that if he received whatever he needed, usually $50,000 or $100,000, there would be no union trouble. The payments were not regular; nor were they big enough to lead to an investigation. The only problem they created was for Raft.

Raft was not part of the money demands; nor did he personally benefit. However, Siegel wanted to distance himself from the payments.

He had the producers make out checks to Raft, then the actor would cash them and pay Siegel. The problem was that he did not declare the checks on his income tax because the money was not for him. However, the records indicated that it was, there being no paper trail to Siegel. That was why, in 1942, Raft was told he owed the IRS $236,603 more in taxes. Allegedly, some aspect of the deal was explained, and the dollar amount was reduced.

Siegel may have seemed no different from other mob figures working their rackets in the Los Angeles area, but his explosive temper and over-the-top violence was never forgotten. George Raft discovered it in 1940 when Siegel's brother-in-law asked Raft for loans two different times. The brother-in-law, Whitey Krakower, supposedly truly wanted them to be loans, rather than "gifts," yet made no effort to repay either.

Raft wasn't certain what to think and said nothing to Ben until both men happened to be in New York. Since Whitey lived in the city, Raft asked Siegel why Krakower hadn't repaid him.

Siegel was livid. No one was going to hurt a friend of his like that. Within days, Krakower was dead on a Brooklyn street. No one was ever charged with the crime.

Siegel's influence in Los Angeles was most obvious in November 1940, when he was jailed on a nuisance charge. The reform movement had supposedly been taking place, but Siegel's jailers did not know it. Each day, the jail door would be unlocked so Ben could go to lunch with his girlfriend, Wendy Barrie. They also spent afternoons together when her schedule allowed.

Siegel's main concerns in Hollywood involved coordinating gambling operations of various types, including linking Jack Dragna's various betting parlors with the Moses Annenberg racing wire. That operation cost him $500,000 provided by the East Coast syndicate, but it netted them $8 million in the first year. He also obtained a share in the Agua Caliente racetrack partially owned by Joe Schenck.

The handsome, well-dressed Siegel impressed the studio bosses and stars. Jean Harlow became godmother to one of Siegel's two daughters. He was also close to both Louis B. Mayer and Jack Warner.

Siegel's time in Los Angeles would become better known for his gambling. In 1937, he followed Bioff and Browne by entering the union movement, focusing solely on the film extras union. It was small enough that there was no fighting over power and money and large enough that he could extort loans from studios and skim dues. However, he moved swiftly on to what he handled best, and what Luciano had tried to take over, the gambling interests.

Ben Siegel brought an Eastern sensibility to the formerly independent gambling operators, most of whom were in some way connected with the syndicate that had so long run Hollywood. He arranged a meeting of the men who owned the gambling halls, then announced his takeover. They would do business as usual. He would get a piece of the action.

Almost everyone understood that life had changed with the syndicate and the East Coast mob. Only Les Bruneman did not. Bruneman ran a number of gambling clubs in the lower part of the state and lived in the unincorporated area off of Sunset Strip, a location in the sheriff department's jurisdiction, thus controlled by the men frequently on gangsters' payrolls. He was certain he did not need to give a percentage of his business to Siegel or anyone else.

Siegel did not argue. On July 20, 1937, Les Bruneman and a blond hostess for one of his clubs were walking along Redondo Beach south of Los Angeles. Two men stepped up, aimed automatic pistols at Bruneman, and started firing. He was struck by three rounds and rushed to the hospital, where he was able to recover. She was untouched.

Bruneman felt he was home free. Siegel wasn't tough enough for his boys to kill Bruneman. He did not have to worry about anything further.

On October 25, approximately three months after he was shot, Bruneman was back in business in the Palm Springs area. He had a date again that night, with a different woman this time, and they went to dinner at The Roost, a small café.

Three men quietly came to the entrance. One man stood at the door. The other two walked over to Bruneman and fired sixteen rounds into his body. One of the workers, not understanding the nature of the hit, made the mistake of chasing the three killers. He, too, was murdered.

There was an investigation of sorts, most of it focused on Johnny Rosselli, who said he had not seen Bruneman in three years. Certainly, "eastern gangsters" were involved according to the press. However, informants in several cities provided law enforcement with information about the mob takeover of the gambling operations that had formerly been connected with the Hollywood syndicate. Both Jack Dragna and

Rosselli were named, but no one could prove anything. It was only years later, when Jimmy "the Weasel" Fratianno began talking to the feds, that he disclosed what had happened and named one of the shooters as Frank Bompensiero, then living in San Diego.

It was the Bruneman hit that radically changed politics in Los Angeles. This was the start of the reform movement.

Siegel refined his image in the months and years that followed. He was actively involved with crime, but his primary activity involved gambling and the wire services being developed to serve the bookmakers. Siegel started by wiring all of Jack Dragna's Los Angeles–area bookie joints to the national wire service operated by Moses Annenberg. He was given a relatively unlimited budget.

Siegel, rich, considered handsome, and always well dressed, became a popular escort or guest of actresses and the wealthy. In 1940, he entered into an intense affair with Virginia Hill, a beautiful mob favorite who had gone from poverty in Alabama to waitressing and nightclub jobs in Chicago, where she met members of the Outfit. She eventually became their courier for stolen merchandise, be it furs she wore when traveling, jewelry, or anything else. She could be trusted with money and valuables, knowing that the men for whom she worked helped her live in luxury. Ultimately, she was given a piece of the action when she was involved, and she was able to pass as a wealthy heiress. When she moved to Los Angeles and became involved with Siegel, she helped him establish the contacts he needed to begin smuggling drugs from Mexico. Once routes were established, millions of dollars in opium and heroin were brought across the border, then distributed throughout the United States.

Siegel's work in Hollywood was mostly in gambling. His power moves would come when he began building the Flamingo Hotel in Las Vegas. He was probably best known for his ego and his belief that he could become a movie actor. The man who was most interesting, however, the one whose actions would lead to Judy Turner's learning just what a Hollywood film career could entail for a woman, was Mickey Cohen, who worked both independently and for Siegel. He was a low-level thug who handled robberies, beatings, and other tasks for Ben Siegel when extra muscle was needed. Mostly, though, his world was gambling and extortion, and for the latter, he was the least known, yet most vicious, perpetrator in Hollywood. Instead of preying on the studios that had been complicit with Bioff and Browne, he preyed on the weakest and most vulnerable of the Hollywood professionals, the men and women either starting their careers or on their way down and fighting desperately for whatever jobs they could still obtain.

Cohen understood that Los Angeles had changed, that the police were becoming less corrupt, that any given officer could not be counted on to look the other way even if adequately bribed. That was why Cohen moved his operation to the Sunset Strip. Cohen did interact with the Los Angeles police, though. He became a trusted informant for several officers. They all knew they had no right to investigate or arrest him for his actions outside the city. However, both he and they benefited when he turned in someone who was crossing into his territory and also committing crimes within the city.

Cohen was a man who understood the relationship between sex, power, and control in ways none of the other criminals did. That was why he hired Johnny Stompanato and a number of other men with similar "talents." And it was Mickey Cohen who sent Stompanato to have a love affair with Lana Turner.

Johnny Stompanato

He had numerous names over the years—Jimmy Valentine, John Valentine, J. Hubbard, J. Holiday, and, of course, Johnny Stompanato. He was a Chicago man, a small-time, semisuccessful pimp, who frequently used the earnings from his prostitutes to pay for nights on the town with women from the Latin Quarter nightclub. However, his relationships were always limited. He liked to beat women, not on the first or second date, but after the relationship became more intimate, when the woman thought there might be some mutual affection growing between them. No one knew if he hated women and used his temper to justify what he wanted to do in the first place or if he was just a bully who would attack anyone he saw as weak when that person got in his way.

His temper and attitude toward women kept Johnny from succeeding in any of the rackets in Chicago, and he wanted to move on. The opportunity came one night when he was in Barney Ross's bar and met a man named Charlie Hubbard, an Englishman currently living in Nassau, New York. Hubbard was driving cross-country, and Johnny decided to join him on the trip to Los Angeles. He plied him with liquor, supplied him with willing women, and convinced him to take Johnny as a passenger, then to room with him upon reaching Los Angeles. Stompanato also extorted money from Hubbard, who apparently could not let his activities with Stompanato's women be known. Whatever the reason, Hubbard bankrolled Johnny until he could marry Helen Gilbert, a wealthy widow.

Johnny had no interest in being faithful, but until he married Gilbert, he did not have the money he needed to date actresses. He was handsome, and when well dressed at the "right" nightspots, he was able to spend time with Ann Miller, Kathryn Grayson, and others. Some he eventually married once he had enough of Gilbert's money to feel comfortable getting a divorce.

Stompanato did have a job with Mickey Cohen, and though he was often called Mickey's bodyguard, he wasn't. If anything, Cohen would have been insulted by the suggestion. He had been a boxer and street fighter when younger and feared no one. There were several attempts on his life, including shootings and two bombings of his home. He finally remodeled his house, placing weapons strategically, adding floodlights and multiple alarm systems, and having trusted thugs, including Stompanato, periodically watch the grounds.

Johnny Stompanato wasn't so much a hood as he was a tool for Mickey Cohen, perhaps the most successful criminal in the film industry. Cohen was a thug who made his early reputation in Chicago, Detroit, and Cleveland, before he was asked to go to California to work with Ben Siegel. The request came from several sources, including Meyer Lansky, Tony Milano, and Joe Gentile, a cross section of high-level Jewish and Italian mobsters with varying power.

Cohen was smarter than Siegel in many ways. He did not want to achieve some big score. He liked organizing gambling and other rackets from a position of safety. Los Angeles was changing. The era of wholesale corruption in the police department was over. There was no way of knowing who among the new officers might be safe to approach with a bribe and who would shut down whatever operation you were trying to protect. That was why he kept his operation along the unincorporated Sunset Strip, which was patrolled by the sheriff's office, whose deputies he was still able to influence. He worked Long Beach, Santa Monica, and Beverly Hills. Then, he learned which Los Angeles–based rivals were hurting his extortion, gambling, and upscale prostitution businesses, providing the information to friends cultivated in the Los

Angeles Police Department. The vice cops knew that Cohen was deliberately hurting others to help himself, but they did not care. They
made good cases and were able to justify working with Mickey because
all his operations were outside their jurisdiction.

Cohen had a few problems with income, but he did pay some taxes.
In 1956, for example, Mickey told the IRS that he had earned just
$1,200. In 1957 his income was just $300 more. He was apparently cash
poor due to all of his businesses, yet when he was eventually investigated by a U.S. Senate committee, his possessions indicated a somewhat larger income. His bulletproof car cost $25,000, more than eight
times the price of most luxury cars. He had sixty pairs of $60 shoes,
each costing close to the average worker's weekly pay. He also owned
275 pairs of silk lounging pajamas. As for suits, he owned three hundred—almost one for every a day of the year. He, too, was caught for his
excesses—too many "things," too little reported income—and went to
prison for tax evasion.

Cohen's most successful money-making activity involved extorting
actresses. The movie industry was trying to change its image. Studio
contracts had morals clauses that prevented an actor from keeping his
or her job if there were any violations. Essentially, this meant not getting caught drinking or taking drugs in ways and places that might
make the news. It meant not engaging in promiscuous behavior, at
least not where you would be caught.

That's not to say that anyone really cared. The studios continued
to arrange for some of their young six-month-contract players go on
"dates" with important clients. The Studio Club, an apartment where
aspiring actresses such as Marilyn Monroe lived for a time, continued
to be a place where a man could have a "date" by the hour. Usually,
stars such as Milton Berle claimed to have a "girlfriend" when referring
to an actress they saw regularly, "helping" them financially when their
careers were new. And some women chose multiple marriages rather
than admit either that they enjoyed sex or were lesbian or bisexual and
wanted to hide their orientations.

The publicists worked intensely to develop the right spin when
actors and actresses were caught in the wrong place at the wrong time.
This often meant tracking down pornographic movies made for money
when an actor had no work and needed to pay the rent. It also meant
making arrangements for marriages, stays in isolated hospitals where

they could recover from illnesses or exhaustion (i.e., abortions), and the disappearance of criminal records.

The one problem the actors and the publicists could not handle was the determined blackmailer, the person able to prove that the actor was engaged in career-destroying behavior. This was where Cohen put together his racket.

Mickey Cohen understood that actresses were human. An actress at the start of her career was often lonely, insecure, far away from the familiar, and not yet involved with the community. She was vulnerable to a handsome man who seemed to adore her for herself, not her fame or fortune, because she had neither.

A formerly successful actress who was facing the downturn of her career was also vulnerable, Mickey realized. She was insecure, not certain how long anyone would care about her, and constantly comparing her looks with those of women half her age, even though she might only have been in her mid-thirties. Again, she might find comfort in a man who seemed to adore her regardless of what was happening or had happened with her career.

Mickey's idea was to recruit several handsome men who enjoyed seducing women and were good enough actors to carry off one love affair after another. Each seduction would be filmed, photographed, or recorded without the actress's knowledge. She would be shown in compromising positions or engaged in inappropriate activities, from posing nude to having "kinky" sex. Then, the woman would be informed of what Cohen had obtained and expected to pay anything from a straight fee to a percentage of her earnings.

Marilyn Monroe was one of Cohen's victims. He assigned both Sam LoCigno and George Piscitelle to seduce her, not a difficult task because she admitted to friends that she enjoyed seeing men delight in bedding a movie star. It is not known whether Sam LoCigno had bedded her, though it was presumed he had. Piscitelle had advanced in the scheme far enough that she was seen spending the night with him in a Van Nuys Boulevard motel. Giving her a comfort zone away from her own place was probably the last step before recording her. Ironically, Cohen never realized that she was dating Jack Kennedy, the senator who would soon be president, or that those sexual encounters were being recorded through the use of wiretaps and FM transmitter microphones planted in the house of Kennedy's brother-in-law, actor Peter Lawford.

The next target for Johnny Stompanato, as scheduled by Cohen, was Ava Gardner, despite her having started a torrid affair with Frank Sinatra, who never let his marriages—his first, in this case, to Nancy—get in the way of romancing other women. Cohen wasn't concerned about the morality of cheating on your boyfriend while he is cheating on his wife. He just liked to exploit weakness and receive the blackmail money.

Johnny Stompanato began dating Ava Gardner, and he was making moves that implied he was serious about her. She was single and enjoyed casual sex as much as any man's fantasy. She would likely have married Johnny had they continued together because he was apparently fun in bed. However, Sinatra learned what was happening and was livid.

Organized criminals, whether Italian, Jewish, Irish, or from any of the other ethnic groups active during the time that Mickey Cohen dominated gambling and blackmail just outside the city, had a very specific standard when it came to manliness. A "real man" who had a problem with some other man could seek the help of a mob leader. Meyer Lansky might send an arsonist or hit man. Frank Nitti might once have provided men to administer a beating. The idea that the violence, whatever it might be, was not directly connected with the man seeking a favor was viewed as good business sense. The person who needed the work done would have an alibi, and in many instances, he would also be the alibi for someone else at another time.

The situation was different when the problem was with a woman. The mob had a double standard when it came to women. There were women to marry, women to date, and women to screw. The truly doting husbands never cheated on their wives in the cities where they lived or at least in those parts of the cities where their wives or women they knew would spot them. Men like Joe Kennedy who flaunted his girlfriends, knowing his wife would pretend he wasn't cheating because he introduced the women to one another, were rare. However the man handled his own sexual affairs was his business.

The problem came when a woman went against convention. If she had an affair when married to or when seriously dating a mobster, she had to be stopped immediately. More importantly, she had to be stopped by her husband or lover. She might need a beating. The man who was coming on to her or bedding her might need a beating. In the extreme, when a member of the mob was bedding another mobster's wife, he might need to be killed. No matter what the "crime" and no matter what the appropriate "punishment," it had to be administered by the man who originally claimed the woman. To seek help was to show weakness and be held in disdain thereafter.

Frank Sinatra fancied himself a tough guy, a friend of the mob, perhaps someone who might have had the potential to become a godfather himself, if anyone in the mob ever used that term (which they did not). The bosses always had tough guys either sitting with them in restaurants and nightclubs or positioned at the next table, carefully watching the room. These were men who protected the leader out of loyalty. They saw in him both their present success and their future careers.

Sinatra had the same type of entourage when he was out alone in the evening. The difference was that they were on his payroll. Likewise, in his early days, he would often start a fight with a heckler or drunk, then have his manager, a real tough guy named Hank Sanicola, or Hank's partner, a former athlete named Nick Sevano, handle the ensuing battle. Both could hold their own. Ironically, Mickey Cohen eventually went into business with both Hank and Frank when they invested in *Hollywood Night Life*, an entertainment weekly whose daily operations were handled by Jimmy Tarantino.

The *Hollywood Night Life* investment paid off twice. Tarantino found that many people in show business delighted in providing insider gossip. Sometimes this was meant to hurt others. Sometimes it was meant to publicize them. Whatever the case, whenever he learned career-damaging gossip, he went to the person in question, laid out what he had, and obtained money to not print. Ultimately, he took money from everyone, from studio heads to top entertainers. Eventually, enough of his victims rebelled, and he went to prison. Cohen was suspected of receiving some of the money because that would have been appropriate based on his past, though neither Hank Sanicola nor Frank Sinatra was ever believed to have known about what was taking place. Both men came through clean.

The truth about Sinatra was that he was far weaker than most people realized. His image came from befriending organized criminals who owned the nightclubs where he sought work. He also had known mobsters in New Jersey while growing up because his mother, Dolly, was connected with them. His father knew the same mobsters and had been a professional boxer in his youth before becoming a captain in the fire department.

Frank had fallen madly in love with Ava Gardner, pursuing her openly at a time when his career was failing and he had a wife and three children. Comedian Phil Silvers was also a songwriter and had written "Nancy with the Laughing Face" when Sinatra's first daughter was born. Frank had used the song as a signature piece both in his act and when he was on the radio as a way of keeping his fans loyal. They thought the song was about his wife, not his daughter, and swooned at the idea that perhaps one day, they, too, would find men who would give them "true love" like that. The affair with Gardner was potentially going to destroy his fan base and would certainly show the world that the marriage was a sham. The problem was Johnny Stompanato.

Sinatra had no idea that Stompanato didn't give a damn about Ava, even though he was ardently courting her. His job was to get her so comfortable with him that she would willingly put herself in a compromising position, which would then be recorded. Everyone knew she pursued, bedded, and dumped boyfriends like the most misogynistic of men so frequently did to women. But proof of her behavior would instantly damage, perhaps destroy, her career.

Frank knew none of the unwritten rules of the mob because Frank was mob in his mind only. He was a popular singer. He was Italian. He was raised in a home where his mother was mob connected through her services as translator, abortionist, bar owner, and politically connected as well. He was embraced by men in the mob, but he was never one of them. He might party with them, as he eventually did when he was invited to Cuba to meet with Charles Luciano during the latter's time in exile, but when the serious work took place, Frank was politely told to go elsewhere.

Sinatra was also weak, something Mickey Cohen discovered, then shared with others, effectively reducing Frank's image with everyone from Johnny Rosselli and Jack Dragna to Meyer Lansky and Frank Costello.

The problem came with Ava Gardner. Frank knew that Johnny Stompanato was moving in on his woman, and he did not like it. He did not know what to do, so he went to see Mickey Cohen, knowing that Stompanato worked for Cohen and would do anything Cohen told him. He asked Mickey to tell Johnny to leave Ava alone, and when Johnny did just that, Frank saw himself as a real man. The mob saw him as weak and ineffectual, someone who couldn't control his own woman. It was a terrible loss of face at best, yet Sinatra did not realize it.

Ava Gardner had been targeted because she was a woman on the way up. Lana Turner was targeted because she was a woman with an unknown future, someone who seemed to be going downhill, then was nominated for her first Oscar for her role in *Peyton Place*. In March 1958 Lana was in London, working on the film *Another Time, Another Place*, costarring the young Sean Connery, later to become famous as the first James Bond.

Johnny visited Lana on the set, and the two got into a violent argument during which he choked her. Lana, either scared or wanting to show him her power, went to Scotland Yard and told them that he had entered England using the alias John Steele. As a result of the violence charge and his lying to the authorities, he was forced to leave the country immediately.

Lana returned to Hollywood, contacted her publicist Betty Asher, and told her that she was going to Acapulco for a few days. She did not want anyone to know she was in Mexico so she could get some real rest.

Johnny learned what Lana was doing and met her in the hotel. He pulled a gun, put it to her head, and threatened to kill her. He stayed with her, then returned to the States, a fact discovered by a reporter for the *Los Angeles Examiner*. Stompanato may have contacted him, or the information might have come from Mickey Cohen. It was important for Lana to be known to be dating Johnny for the financial pressure to work. Certainly the headline did not help her career—*Turner Returns from Vacation with Mob Figure*. More important for both Lana's career and the blackmail was the news that she had been nominated for an Academy Award for her role in the 1957 film *Peyton Place*.

Eddie Mannix knew Stompanato and Cohen. Lana Turner had been under contract to MGM, and though she was no longer with the studio, she was one of the actresses they liked to obtain for some of their films. Mannix knew that she still had box-office appeal in the type of films MGM was making. Having her career damaged by Johnny would cost the studio future revenue. He decided to go to Cohen and tell him to stop the affair, not knowing that the affair was Cohen's idea.

Cohen compromised. He was not ready to call off the blackmail scheme, but he made certain that Johnny did not take Lana to the Academy Awards Ceremony on March 26, 1958. Instead, Lana went with her daughter, Cheryl, a nice touch for the press and a reminder of how hard Lana worked at both having a career and being a mother.

Johnny Stompanato did not appreciate any of the actions taking place. He knew his business. He knew he needed to be a more visible part of Lana's life to succeed, and she was not going to ignore him when she had to go to well-publicized events. He was waiting for her when she returned home. He told her that she would never leave him like that again, then proceeded to beat her.

The beating was a professional job meant to cause pain without leaving bruises that would be visible when she was wearing clothing. The only mark at all noticeable came when Johnny slapped Lana, accidentally striking one of her earrings, which left a small scratch on her face. The rest of the marks, invisible under clothing, came from her being punched and tossed around the room. She never cried out for fear of awakening Cheryl. She would be in pain for several days, but when dressed for the street or in costume for a film, no one would know what had happened. And, as always, her face was untouched.

This time was different for Lana, though. Johnny told her that if she ever ignored him that way again, he would kill her and her daughter. He would also disfigure her, and to emphasize the threat, he pulled out a razor and held the blade close to her face. She would lose everything she supposedly valued.

It was April Fool's Day when Lana and her daughter moved into a new home, a mansion at 730 Bedford Drive. It was an outward and visible sign of success, and Johnny arrived on April 5, Good Friday, to claim his financial future.

What happened next shows how the moguls covered their own. There are three stories about that night. One story came independently from Lana and her daughter and was the one used in court. A second story came from Lana's longtime hairdresser and friend, who eventually discussed it in the book *The Private Diary of My Life with Lana*. The third story came from Fred Otash, who was present shortly after the murder.

It is certain that Lana did not want an abrupt break with Stompanato. That struck her as too cold, too likely to trigger violence. She would ease him out instead, which is why he was helping Lana and Cheryl with the move on Good Friday.

An argument began in Lana's bedroom. Cheryl's account, likely the most accurate concerning what preceded Johnny's death, told of extensive verbal and physical violence. It actually resembled police reports concerning similar violence with other women he had blackmailed in the past.

Cheryl was a Hollywood child. She knew that career was everything. People in the movie industry only called the police when they wanted publicity, not life-or-death help. If the story would play on page 1 and not help their careers, they handled things themselves. That was why Cheryl didn't go for the telephone. Instead, she went to the kitchen and grabbed a butcher knife. (Some uncorroborated stories maintained that the knife was kept in a nightstand drawer by the bed.)

Cheryl ran back upstairs to the bedroom, knife in hand. She set the weapon on the floor and grabbed the door handle with both hands to force them to open the door and talk with her. In response, Cheryl only remembered hearing Johnny shout, "Cunt, you're dead!"

The bedroom door flew open. Apparently, either Lana or Johnny had latched or wedged the door during the violence so they could "talk" away from Cheryl. Now, Lana wanted Johnny to leave, and she heaved the door open. Cheryl saw her mother, and behind her was Johnny, his arm raised as though about to strike. Given what had come before, Cheryl was certain her mother was in danger. She grabbed the knife, held it, and started forward into the room. At the same time, according to this story, Johnny was rushing her. The two collided, the knife imbedding itself in Stompanato's chest. Or so the story went.

There was a death. The body was not going to disappear. The police needed to be called. The coroner would have to perform an autopsy. There was nothing to be gained by delaying the inevitable—except time to develop a better story than the truth to play on the hearts of the reporters.

The first call Lana made was classic Hollywood. When a matter of life or death took place, an actor had to call his or her agent or lawyer or publicist. Death was serious. Lana called her lawyer, Jerry Giesler. Then, she called her press agent. Finally, because this was going to involve Cheryl, she called Cheryl's father, Steve Crane, who would be the first person to arrive at the scene.

Having handled the crisis properly, both for professional and personal reasons, Lana called her mother and then a doctor. The doctor suggested she call an ambulance.

Suddenly, Lana froze. Little Judy Turner, the Sweater Girl, all grown up, had managed to call everyone who didn't matter to anyone living in the real world—when it came to mobsters, moguls, and movies, she was an expert. But an ambulance? She talked about how difficult it had been to dial the "0" to reach the operator. Longer numbers and more of them were no problem. But professionals outside of the films? Two hours after Johnny was killed, the Beverly Hills Police were notified, a courtesy they must have appreciated.

Lana had a new house and an image to maintain. A messy bedroom with all that pesky blood, both flecks thrown about with abandon and pools from the less than careful Stompanato, who had to die where he would stain the carpet, just would not do for company. Bath towels were grabbed, wet, and then used to clean both Stompanato's wound and the walls.

Jerry Giesler was apparently not bothered by any of this. He had defended Ben Siegel on a murder charge (and won), and he was the attorney who saved Errol Flynn from two rape charges. Those had been especially difficult because Flynn seemed to think that any girl who said yes to his sexual advances was of legal age to do what followed naturally. He shared the moguls' attitude that anyone who was of value to the movie studio could do no wrong.

Two primary witnesses were men who understood the studios, the moguls, and the cops—James Bacon, a longtime Hollywood-based columnist for the Associated Press, and Fred Otash who arrived as Giesler's personal investigator. Bacon, not recognized in all the confusion, pretended to be the coroner's assistant. Both have been interviewed over the years and the following information is all we know for certain.

First, the body was found far enough from the bedroom door that Stompanato was obviously moved. Whether this was done so he could be cleaned before the police and doctor arrived or for some other reason is not known.

The knife was in the bathroom, and the fingerprints on it were smudged. Whether it was wiped or the prints were deliberately smeared was impossible to tell. The knife would have had prints from being washed, then handled when dry and placed in whatever drawer or knife holder Lana used in the kitchen. It would have had Cheryl's prints on it. It might have had Lana's prints on it. The smudges were as likely to occur naturally as they would have if the knife had been deliberately cleaned.

Lana Turner long admitted that one of her ex-husbands had molested Cheryl. She was a rebellious teenager, emotionally troubled, apparently never counseled after the assault Lana described, and dealing with her own sexual orientation. One credible rumor, given Cheryl's psychological past, was that Johnny had her in bed, Lana walked in, and she began stabbing him. The implication was a seduction and matched the report Steve Crane received when Stompanato was being watched. However, too many questions remained. If he planned to seduce Cheryl, why do it when he was certain to get caught by Lana? She was business, the subject of future blackmail, and he was a professional unlikely to lose self-control over a teenager. And if he was trying to assault Cheryl when Lana caught him, again, why then? Why not pick a time when he was not likely be caught?

It is more likely that Lana, not Cheryl, killed Johnny. Whether the knife was in the kitchen or in the bedroom at the time she grabbed it matters little. Lana had low self-esteem at best. Her career had nearly tanked, and she was accepting violence from her so-called lover. Then, thanks to the Academy Award nomination, she was suddenly back on top. She had more self-respect. She had reason to stop tolerating what most people would have considered intolerable the first time Johnny struck her. The fight may have been over his unwillingness to get out of her life. Whether or not the threat of disfigurement to her face was real, it was undoubtedly real to Lana. Everything may have gone one step too far, and she took a knife and struck him, killing him on the bed they shared.

The greatest support for this scenario came indirectly from Beverly Hills police chief Clinton Anderson—or did it?

It is known for certain that Lana went to Chief Anderson and asked him if she could take the blame for Stompanato's death. For once in her life, she was not thinking solely of her career, though mother and daughter told the exact same story about that night. It was unlikely that this happened without their rehearsing what they would say, either on their own or with Giesler's guidance. However, the chief explained, too much evidence pointed to Cheryl—two hours after the fact, when the body had been cleaned and probably moved, various people unrelated to law enforcement had gone through the crime scene, and the knife had probably been moved. She had to be jailed and held without bond until a coroner's jury could assess what had happened. Fortunately, the ruling was justifiable homicide, which would stand no matter how cover-ups and targets for blame changed. Cheryl ultimately had to endure a series of juvenile jails, reformatories, and a mental hospital.

The other question about the story was where the death occurred. The cover was removed from the bed. Fred Otash was not allowed to see what took place because he would have been required to testify in court since he would lack Giesler's attorney-client privilege. However, Giesler allegedly said later that the cover looked like a hog had been butchered on it.

Fred Otash was also troubled by Giesler's extremely nervous reaction when asked for more details. He stressed that there was no statute of limitations on murder, and there was information that could get him into serious trouble if it came out while he was still alive. Chief Anderson was also convinced that something was changed, that something had been tampered with.

Ultimately, it did not matter. Stompanato went one potential victim too far, scaring mother and daughter to such a degree that they attacked instead of enduring further violence.

It was only Mickey Cohen who dared not let matters drop. Johnny Stompanato could not be found to have been part of the blackmail racket. Otherwise, the sheriff might have to crack down on at least some of Mickey's ventures. As a result, he encouraged Stompanato's son to file a wrongful death suit against Lana, Cheryl, and even Steve Crane. The lawsuit claimed that Cheryl was known to be emotionally disturbed. The newspapers had carried stories about her wandering Skid Row. Cheryl should have been kept under close watch for everyone's protection.

The lawsuit was combined with Cohen's efforts to characterize Stompanato as a hero who died for love. He told how Johnny, a former U.S. Marine, was a hero who had been cold-bloodedly murdered. He made certain that there was so much talk about Johnny, Lana, the movie industry, and everything else related to the story that no one thought to ask why Johnny was seducing Lana in the first place.

As for the moguls, they needed to do nothing more once the justifiable homicide verdict had been reached. Eddie Mannix was no longer defending MGM because the movie industry had changed. The public accepted a more realistic view of actresses and actors.

Still, there was one actress whom everyone tried to hold out as different. When she died in the manner of so many other actresses who became hooked on uppers and downers to handle the intensity of their work schedules and fears of aging, the public could not accept it. They needed to create a myth that would lift her out of the realm of mere mortals. Yet, the truth about the mob and Marilyn Monroe was sleazy, sordid, and simple.

CHAPTER Twenty

Marilyn, the Greatest Mob Hit That Never Was

One name. Judith Campbell. Dead years later from "natural causes" as a cop or a mob guy might look at things; cancer, the doctors said. Either way, her death came from genetics, smoking, drinking, or maybe just being SOL (shit out of luck). It didn't come from an assassin's bullet, an ice pick to the brain, a knife, poison, a car careening on a highway late at night, a bomb, a fire, or any of the other ways people help people to die.

Judy Campbell was a mob sweetheart, a good-looking brunette who knew when to say thank you for a handful of chips in Vegas— "Here, honey, enjoy yourself at the tables"—jewelry, or a night on the town in restaurants where the tips alone were more than some people earned in a week. She knew the difference between love and sex, pleasure and commitment. She knew that no matter what level they played the game at, with their clothes off, all the players were the same—like Frank, like Sam, like Jack. So, she was feted and bedded by Chicago mobster Sam Giancana, entertainer Frank Sinatra, and President Jack Kennedy, among others. And when the mob used Hollywood to establish a message system with the White House, she did her job, spoke only when spoken to, and ultimately knew too many nasty things about too many people. And Judy Campbell was allowed to live. Remember that. Judy Campbell was allowed to live.

Real life has always been simpler than our fantasies. The toughest hoods in Chicago, New Jersey, and New York couldn't figure out how to blackmail the moguls. It took a punk like Tommy Maloy to put the scam in motion. Nick and Joe Schenck responded to the mobbed-up IATSE leadership's extortion by creating a countersituation from which both sides benefited, workers be damned. And the experts said it couldn't happen.

In union there is strength. In union there is brotherhood and sisterhood. In union there is a future. But a handful of punks put the shaft to more than twelve thousand loyal, hard-working union men and women in Los Angeles alone. Willie Bioff, thug extraordinaire, said as he went to prison that the mob had taken control of 20 percent of the movie industry, and if a petty interference like being sent to prison by rackets investigators and IRS men hadn't changed things, they would have soon owned half the business.

And in real life, that most tragic of movie stars, Marilyn Monroe, was a slut, a drug abuser, and a woman so power hungry she would do anything to get her way.

The real story of Marilyn Monroe is a book in itself, not something to be related here. What matters is that she spent her life in pursuit of stardom, creating whatever myth best suited her needs.

Marilyn claimed to be an orphan, yet both her parents were alive and known to her. She claimed that her mother was severely mentally ill, yet though Marilyn's mother was in and out of hospitals, there was no family history of mental illness.

Marilyn had a distinctive walk, and though her half-sister noted that a genetic defect in the family left all the women with one leg slightly longer than the other, Marilyn's famous dip of the derriere came from shaving a portion of the heel off of one of every pair of high-heeled shoes. She stuffed her bras with tissues. And to save money when she was first a studio contract actress making $75 a week—$25 more than a reporter for the *Los Angeles Times* made to support his family comfortably—she would let men pick her up and buy her breakfast many mornings. These were mostly strangers who drove by, took her to a restaurant, then were rewarded quickly and effectively behind the closed door of her apartment.

The marriage to baseball legend Joe DiMaggio was over almost before it began. Columnist Sid Skolsky, drugstore owner Leon Schwab, and police officer (later private investigator) Fred Otash were in Sid's office in Schwab's Drug Store when Marilyn returned from her honeymoon with Joe. She came by Sid's office, a common occurrence for the two friends, and announced to the three men that she planned to marry playwright Arthur Miller. They pointed out that Miller was married, that she was just married, and, as she admitted, she had only met him briefly one time, hardly a reason to overthrow spouses.*

As for DiMaggio's devotion to Monroe and devastation at their split, the truth was that he acted the same way after his first wife divorced him, and both times he soothed the intensity of his ardor by dating an endless series of showgirls. He was also exceedingly dull outside of baseball, and allegedly the bedroom, his life devoted to receiving adulation from fans when he was in bars and clubs, reading comic books, and watching television.

Monroe, like so many actors before her, was encouraged to use uppers and downers to ensure her ability to work long hours on the set without breaks, go on promotional tours, and otherwise lead an exhausting life of "glamour." The problem was that she wanted everything that fame could bring her, and she wanted it with an intensity that belied the innocent-little-girl image.

6 6

Now I won't have to suck cock anymore.

—Marilyn Monroe, after learning that her appearance in the film *All
about Eve* assured her a pay boost and star billing for future work

In Hollywood a girl's virtue is much less important than her hairdo. You're judged by how you look, not by what you are. Hollywood's a place where they'll pay you a thousand dollars for a kiss, and fifty cents for your soul. I know, because I turned down the first offer often enough and held out for the fifty cents.

—Marilyn Monroe

, ,

Monroe was an actress of limited talent, who worked hard and achieved moderate success as a star, then faded quickly. She had a sensual presence on the screen that was most obvious in roles such as her

---

*The same story was told to me in separate conversations with Leon Schwab and Fred Otash. Sid Skolsky was dead by the time the story needed to be checked.

uncredited part in *The Asphalt Jungle* and her sexually charged starring roles in *The Seven Year Itch* and *The Misfits*. She also had an underused sense of comedy, as shown in *Some Like It Hot*. But Monroe had something more. She had the full force of the film industry publicity machine surrounding what she did, and she was arguably the most famous, though far from the most talented, actress of her day. Men sought her attention, and she delighted in numbering among her acquaintances Peter Lawford (who lost interest in having sex with her the first time he went to her apartment and found that her dog was not housebroken), through whom she met his brothers-in-law, President Jack Kennedy and Attorney General Robert Kennedy, as well as Frank Sinatra, Chicago mobster Sam Giancana, and others. Lawford was the only one with whom she was not known to have had sex.

On August 5, 1962, Marilyn Monroe died. At least everyone agrees that she is dead, unlike Elvis Presley, who regularly rises from the tabloids.

The goings-on in Hollywood, Chicago, Washington, and Havana at the time can be fairly loosely sketched to give a sense of who was doing what to whom.

1. Jack Kennedy wanted to assassinate Fidel Castro, an early example of attempted, and failed, regime change. He was encouraged because of politics—Fidel declared himself a Communist. Fidel allowed Russia to bring to Cuba missiles capable of striking Miami and other parts of the U.S. mainland, generating a crisis that almost resulted in war. Fidel was allegedly also trying to hurt Kennedy. And he was encouraged because of business—old friends of Jack's father were interested in regaining Havana so they could reestablish the gambling casinos and nightclubs that had long made the area the equivalent of Las Vegas, though with Spanish accents and legalized prostitution.

2. Sam Giancana was helping coordinate a Castro hit, including sending the young Marita Lorenz to Havana to poison the man who became her lover and the father of one of her children. She later worked for the CIA out of Miami. Information was being passed to Kennedy via Judy Campbell (later Judith Campbell Exner), both his and Giancana's bedmate. Judy had been introduced to Frank Sinatra by longtime manager and friend Nick Sevano. He enjoyed her favors, then passed her on to Jack Ken-

nedy when the three of them were in the Las Vegas Sands on February 7, 1960. Judy was a willing sex partner and had the beauty of Jacqueline Kennedy, Jack's wife. Sam Giancana had also enjoyed Judy and had been involved with the Kennedys for years, first with Joe, then working the election as a favor to Joe and Frank.

The entire relationship was convoluted. Jack thought Judy would make a nice go-between since he and Giancana were both seeing her and both were trying to be discreet. At the same time, Jack Kennedy was involved with several other women, including actresses Angie Dickenson and Marilyn Monroe. There were secret rendezvous in the Peter Lawford home, in Las Vegas hotels, and elsewhere.

Again, the full story of Monroe is too involved for a chapter. Only her death matters since rumors and myth building have turned it into a mob hit to keep her quiet about organized crime, the White House, and the attempted assassination of Fidel.

Many people knew about the relationship between Kennedy, the mob, and the various women. Some knew about Giancana. Some knew it was the Chicago mob. Some were even members of the press who looked upon the sex aspect as part of a politician's private life, not to be explored or reported. The times were different. The media had different standards.

Various Kennedy family enemies—teamster union president Jimmy Hoffa, members of the mob, rival politicians, to name a few—arranged for electronic surveillance of Jack Kennedy and some of his acquaintances. The concern was knowledge, not blackmail, though the latter had been undertaken by Giancana when Jack partied at the wrong time and place in Las Vegas. Among the recipients of the information was J. Edgar Hoover, giving him ammunition to fight off the Kennedys, who knew he was gay and wanted to oust him. Each man could blackmail the other, so Hoover stayed in his FBI director's job when Robert Kennedy wanted to replace him with Ed Parker, the Los Angeles police chief.

Quite apart from the sex and politics, Marilyn Monroe was rapidly deteriorating physically. She, along with friends like Peter Lawford, was addicted to a variety of prescription drugs. These included sleeping medications and stimulants, all originally taken in the manner the moguls had encouraged in the 1930s—to enable work, play, and sleep, regardless of the body's needs.

The problem with the addicts—and they included such stars as Judy Garland, who died in much the same way as Monroe, and Peter Lawford, who also died from the abuse his body endured—was their tolerance level. The drugs many were taking, especially the depressants they used to get to sleep, had a maximum safe dosage as well as a tolerance factor for effectiveness.

Many of the medications could not be used for long periods and still work as they had when first tried. If a 5-mg sleeping pill was adequate to give someone a night's rest, the addict would continue taking the drug longer than the normal, safe, understood prescription. Gradually, the 5 mg would stop working. The person might need 7.5 to 10 mg to get the same rest. That higher dosage would work for a while, then the dose would be raised again, the addict feeling that without the medication, normal life would be impossible.

The maximum safe dosage has nothing to do with tolerance. The person taking the drug might not feel the desired effects, but there is a limit to the amount that can be taken, no matter what the impact. For example, suppose the person taking the sleeping medication has a maximum tolerance of 25 mg. Take 25 mg, and the person is all right. Take 26 mg, and the person will die.

This was the problem for Judy Garland. She developed a tolerance for the effects of the medication she was on, but there was also a maximum dose. In her quest for rest, she exceeded the maximum dose. She never woke up.

Marilyn Monroe was on the same sleeping medication as many others in Hollywood, including Peter Lawford and Robert Kennedy. When still a U.S. Senator, Jack Kennedy and his family were regular users of medications they did not know were harmful. Some were injections from Dr. Max "Dr. Feelgood" Jacobson in New York City, who combined what apparently were vitamins with amphetamines and other substances, then injected them into Jack, Jacqueline, and many others. They thought he was helping. Instead, he became wealthy creating any number of possible problems for his rich and famous patients. He also helped prolong an era of heavy drug use by "nice" people, some of whom became so addicted to his substances or other drugs that they died.

Marilyn had deteriorated rapidly during early 1962 when, for fourteen weeks, she became less and less able to work on what would prove to be her last film, *Something's Got to Give*. She was known to be hopelessly addicted to amphetamines and barbiturates, the classic morning and evening pills for actors with heavy filming, performance, and publicity schedules. She was no different from Judy Garland, Elizabeth Taylor, and other stars who had been introduced to the same regimen when they were nearing the top. She had collapsed during her previous picture, *The Misfits*, and had been treated by Dr. Ralph Greenson, a Beverly Hills psychiatrist. She was also using alcohol in quantities that were dangerous by themselves and potentially lethal in combination with the drugs.

Ironically for someone who had worked intensely to get to the top, Marilyn was allegedly afraid of the camera. Exactly what this meant is uncertain today. In her early years, she had been a cheesecake model, being photographed at the beach and elsewhere in tight, two-piece blouse-and-shorts outfits, in bathing suits, and, at one point, in the nude. The latter was the session that became famous because one of the images was bought by a young, rebellious magazine publisher for the first issue of the magazine he called *Playboy*. Most of the images show someone relaxed, happy, and obviously enjoying the experience. But the still photographs were taken by one person in complete privacy, a radically different experience than being filmed in front of the dozens of individuals who might be on a movie set at any given time.

It is likely that the drugs were making Marilyn mildly paranoid at a time in her life when she, like so many other actresses in their thirties, was terrified of growing old. She was still a teenager when she began modeling, and though she was out of her teens when she first began working in the movies, she was still in the midst of a world where glamorous "women" were often in adolescence, mature women had not hit thirty-five, and anyone older desperately lied about her age. The physical beauty of the aging woman, as well as acting skills honed from a solid base of talent and work, meant nothing. Marilyn had taken acting lessons, hired acting coaches, and neurotically sought direction and approval from numerous people in the industry, yet she increasingly felt herself unable to function. It had been sixteen months since she last made a film when she walked on the set of *Something's Got to Give* in April 1962.

Director George Cukor, who had seen Marilyn's lack of professionalism and gradual deterioration, was livid that she had been hired. Certain basic skills are critical for an actor, including the ability to recreate a scene over and over again while changes are made or new camera angles are shot. Continuity people check everything from costumes to props to body positions, and the actors are supposed to be able to pick up lines, attitudes, and emotion at any given point in the scene. But early on, George Cukor went to the press in frustration, telling reporters that Marilyn "is so fraught with nerves she can't even match one take with the other."

Director Billy Wilder had encountered somewhat similar, though less severe, problems during *Some Like It Hot* and felt that the problem was simple. Norma Jean Baker, the woman who became Marilyn Monroe, didn't want to be a movie star anymore. She wanted a more normal life, yet she had no idea how to get out of the world she was in. She had climbed the mountain and discovered that the peak was a garbage dump with no way down.

Her insecurity had been heightened the previous December when Marilyn was reminded of her age by beauty experts hired to "save" her from the inadequacy of being herself. Hair not adequately blond? Bring in Jean Harlow's Paul Porterfield who, Longy Zwillman's locket not withstanding, had "enhanced" Harlow's look with chemicals that created what was called "hot platinum." Porterfield went to his chemistry set and mixed laundry bluing with sparkling peroxide to slowly whiten Marilyn's hair. There were hot-wax treatments and mud packs, and the Beverly Hills equivalent of Dr. Feelgood added tranquilizers and so-called vitamins to her daily "health" regimen. She was drugged, painted, and constantly reminded that she was not good enough without the help of all the experts, all the pills.

Her only friend in the midst of all this, aside from the drugs she increasingly used for self-medication, was her masseur, Ralph Roberts. He fed Marilyn cues as they worked on her script, while he also pounded on her back to relax her.

At home, there were stories of perfumed baths and other sensual experiences, but there was always something amiss. It was as though Norma Jean had to lure Marilyn Monroe from deep within someone else's mind and body. And in the midst of all this, Marilyn was being fucked—literally and figuratively.

Jack and Robert Kennedy were involved with Marilyn, and she seemed to think that one of them was going to marry her. Oddly, it was not that strange an idea.

Jack Kennedy carried the image of the good Catholic boy who married for life, had sex for procreation first and the love of his wife second, and was pure of thought in all other ways. His father helped fan rumors that Jack was likely to be led by dictates from the pope in Rome just so the idea could be challenged and a few extra liberal votes gained as a backlash against the bigots. Yet, if ever there was a male equivalent of a slut, it was the senator with ultimately successful presidential ambitions. He delightedly told "first brother-in-law" Peter Lawford that he liked to have a woman three different ways before he was done with her. He had sex with office-staff members when president. He traveled with at least one actress during the campaign. And other males in the Kennedy family were not all that different.

Pat Kennedy Lawford, Peter's first wife, was the first of the women to openly rebel against the male Kennedy infidelity. Peter claimed she was a prude about sex and life, even claiming that she kneeled by the bed to pray before intercourse. She knew too much about his affairs, yet far more was taking place than the incidents of which she was aware. The couple decided to get divorced, told Marilyn and other close, trusted friends, and postponed the split until after Jack was re-elected to a second term in office. That way the scandal would not affect his achieving a two-term presidency.

Marilyn seemed to interpret Peter and Pat's plans to mean that Jack, too, could dump his wife after the start of his second term. There was no love between Jack and Jacqueline, and if she had ever expected any (her father spent the second night of his honeymoon with another woman, and she assumed other men might do the same), she learned better when Jack was not present for the birth and tragic death of their son, Patrick.

It was while she was involved with *Something's Got to Give* that Marilyn repeatedly heard that the sex she was enjoying with the Kennedy brothers was just sex. Nobody loved her. Neither of the older two Kennedy brothers was going to marry her. Everybody may have cheated, but that had nothing to do with where Marilyn fit in their lives. She was as much a throw-away to the sons as Gloria Swanson had been to the father, Joseph P. Kennedy Sr. a generation earlier.

Sam Giancana and Frank Sinatra were in this mix, and like Charles Luciano, everyone who was mob connected made certain Marilyn was drugged for their parties. These were frequently held at the Cal-Neva Lodge, a resort partially owned by Sinatra and, illegally, by Giancana.

Presidential assignations were usually in the Lawford home. And everywhere that the president went, activated electronic listening devices were frequently hidden.

One week before Marilyn's death, in an effort to escape the stress of the movie (she was frequently late to, or missing from, the set, her work was terrible, the director wanted her fired, and others thought she needed a break to rest, calm down, and detox), she went to the Cal-Neva Lodge. There, she was given all the medication she desired, as well as intense sex play with both Sinatra and Giancana. Photographs were destroyed when it was obvious everyone had gone too far in the pursuit of "fun."

Marilyn had had enough. When she was alone in her room, she began taking pills. Then, uncertain that she wanted to die, she called the hotel operator for help. She was rushed to the hospital, where her stomach was pumped, and not for the first time. She was emotionally battered, had endured sex that was closer to rape, and was severely depressed. She needed to tell Twentieth Century Fox that she either could not make the movie or she needed time off to rest and prepare. But her career was going down the tubes. George Cukor was hostile, albeit validly, and wanted her fired if she didn't show up. And everyone was worried about the money that had already been spent on the film.

It was an old Hollywood story. It had been Judy Garland's unwritten obituary. And though mob guys were using her, this had nothing to do with organized crime. Judy Campbell was still the actress go-between for Giancana and Kennedy. The then little-known, at least to the American public, Marita Lorenz was involved with the CIA and Florida-based members of organized crime, all working covertly to overthrow Castro for the White House. And a handful of other women, believed to include actress Angie Dickinson, had heard enough pillow talk to have as strong a sense of what was taking place as some top government analysts. Marilyn was out of everybody's loop, except when someone wanted fast sex with a faded star.

The story, in brief, was a sordid one, partially overheard through planted mikes. Fred Otash had listening devices in Marilyn's home, the Lawford home, and other locations for his clients, as did others. (Most of the bugs have been uncovered over the years, usually when a house was being remodeled. They had long stopped working but confirmed the allegations that they were present.) Some of the story was overheard and recorded. Some has been told by those involved. None of the story involved conspiracies or mob hits or government cover-ups. None of it noted how sick Monroe had become.

It was August 4, 1962, and Robert Kennedy and his family had gone to San Francisco. He came down to Los Angeles on his own, the Los Angeles Police Department having been alerted to provide light cover. Chief Parker coveted the FBI director's position, and the Kennedys had long wanted to appoint him if they could get rid of Hoover. Kennedy's staff made certain that the LAPD knew when he would be in town, and a number of officers confirmed that he was and that such knowledge was normal. It just wasn't reported in the press; nor was there special security along travel routes as there was for the president and vice president. That's why there was later a myth that Robert Kennedy sneaked into the city to kill Marilyn or arrange for her death. His whereabouts were known from the time he left San Francisco until he returned.

On the day of her death, a despondent Marilyn did meet with Robert Kennedy and Peter Lawford. Lawford was having a dinner party at his home that night with a number of friends—a typical Lawford evening in which Chinese carryout was ordered, and the guests sat around eating out of the cartons. Everyone knew about Robert and Marilyn, Kennedy's wife, Ethel, was in San Francisco, and there was no problem with Monroe's coming.

Marilyn was already taking drugs and, possibly, alcohol and had an argument with Kennedy in her home. She also apparently went to bed with him that morning, then was angry for the way he was using her. The fact that she was letting herself be used was not an issue in her mind.

Before Kennedy and Lawford left, it was suggested that Marilyn take a sleeping pill, get some sleep, and come to dinner refreshed. Then, she was given one of the sleeping pills that she regularly took, and this is where the problem began.

Monroe, Kennedy, and Lawford all had prescriptions for the same dosage of the same sleeping pill, the drug of choice during that era, just as the tranquilizer Valium would become a generation later. Each of the three friends was known to keep a container at all times. And since Marilyn died of an overdose, how she took that first pill of the day (so far as anyone knows, since no one knows what she had taken earlier) affected everyone else's culpability.

If Marilyn took a pill from her prescription bottle, then died with it, and perhaps others, still in her system, there was nothing illegal about the death. This was true even if someone else opened her bottle at her request and gave her the pill. However, if the pill that killed her or one of several that combined to kill her came from a bottle carried by one of the two visitors, even though the dose was exactly the same, that person could be charged with involuntary manslaughter under California law at the time. In addition, anyone who knew about it—and the conversations were taped by at least Fred Otash, who turned the tapes over to a friend on the LAPD—could be charged as an accessory after the fact for remaining silent. This meant that unless the information about the pill that morning was kept silent, there was a chance that either the attorney general of the United States or the brother-in-law of the president and the attorney general could be charged with a felony. (Otash said that he left for Cannes when he thought his knowledge after the fact might come out, but he was never questioned or charged, and both he and Thad Brown, the LAPD officer allegedly given the tapes, are dead.)

Ultimately, Marilyn continued to take depressants that day, then talked with Peter at 5 p.m. Robert Kennedy had returned to San Francisco, but other friends were at the Lawfords and Peter wanted her to be present. She declined and continued taking depressants because her usual dose did not seem to be working. She did not realize that she was reaching the maximum dose her body could handle.

There was another call to the Lawfords at 7:30 p.m. when Marilyn's speech was slurred. Peter was convinced that Marilyn liked to overdose herself deliberately, then call to be rescued before it was too late to pump her stomach. He held up the cord, letting the receiver drop and swing freely, then shouted to his guests, "It's phone dangling time with Marilyn."

Producer Joe Naar, a longtime friend of both Peter and Marilyn, offered to go check on her, but Peter refused. He believed she was just being melodramatic. He had been through this type of experience before and was tired of it. Besides, as an addict who did not want to believe he was in danger (Peter later died from drug abuse), he said that the drugs she was on were harmless. He knew nothing about tolerance and a maximum dose before fatality.

The other danger Peter did not know about was that a drug addict's body handles routinely taken, including routinely abused, drugs differently over time. An addict's stomach becomes as accustomed to drugs regularly ingested as it is to food regularly eaten. The drugs are so rapidly digested and passed into the intestines that the true drug addict often dies with no trace of the pills in the stomach. Marilyn's autopsy confirmed this:

> The esophagus has a longitudinal folding mucosa. The stomach is almost completely empty. The volume is estimated to be no more than 20 cc. No residue of the pills is noted. A smear made from the gastric contents examined under the polarized microscope shows no refractile crystals. The mucosa shows marked congestion and submucosal petechial hemorrhage diffusely. The duodenum shows no ulcer. The contents of the duodenum are also examined under the polarized microscope and show no refractile crystals. The remainder of the small intestine shows no gross abnormality. The colon shows marked congestion and purplish discoloration.

Several coroners reviewed the autopsy report of Coroner Thomas Noguchi. The only ones who disagreed with his findings that Marilyn died of an overdose in the manner of Judy Garland, that she was not murdered, including by injection or suppository, were doctors unfamiliar with drug-addict deaths. Marilyn's death was classic.

Equally supportive of the reality of Marilyn's death were other facts. Peter had the same Hollywood syndrome as Lana Turner—too weak to do the right thing and always calling one's manager for help. In Peter's case, he called Milt Ebbins, his manager, even though Marilyn lived just four miles away and Joe Naar had offered to drive over and check on her.

Ebbins further delayed her getting real help. "You can't go over there," he told Peter according to his widow, Patricia S. Lawford. "You're the brother-in-law of the president of the United States. Your wife's away. Let me get in touch with her lawyer or doctor. They should be the ones to go over." In other words, instead of the victim of a mob hit to keep her from revealing the connection between the mob and the president, Marilyn was the victim of the peculiarities of the medications she had improperly ingested, as well as, inadvertently, of Lawford and Ebbins, fools who wouldn't call an ambulance or the police. Worse, by the time some of the people in Marilyn's life had been contacted, it was after 11 p.m. While Marilyn may or may not have still been alive, for all practical purposes, she was a dead woman. The drugs had been in her system for long enough that no amount of stomach pumping or antidote could save her.

The rumors that evolved were many. Sam Giancana arranged for men to come over some time after midnight. They taped her mouth shut (no residue or other trace evidence) and gave her a suppository that killed her (at a time when she would have been dead). An ambulance came and took her to the hospital, then returned her (she was in full livor mortis when officially found, meaning that the pooling of her blood indicated there had been no body movement). The Kennedy family ordered the hit. But Judy Campbell was left untouched and never threatened. Angie Dickinson was left untouched. Marita Lorenz was left untouched.

The list goes on. No matter what the fantasies were about the mob and the moguls, Marilyn Monroe's death was a Hollywood version of natural causes. She died of a drug overdose she never knew would be fatal.

CHAPTER Twenty-one

I'm Not Friendly with the Mob; I Just Play Someone in the White House Who Is

Hollywood changed in the 1960s. The moguls were dead, dying, or being honored with lifetime achievement awards as a reminder to clear out their desks.

Organized crime had also changed. Hollywood's unions no longer looked so interesting as sources of money. There were better worlds to conquer.

Alan Friedman, the liaison between the teamsters and the Mafia for his brother-in-law Bill Presser, his nephew Jackie Presser, and, occasionally, for Jimmy Hoffa, for whom he handled an occasional arson, beating, or similar crime, took a briefcase of money to Ronald Reagan's assistant Ed Meese. Yet, the teamsters union leadership's under-the-table support was not as influential as MCA's financial support.

It was 1951 when Ronald Reagan spent $85,000 to buy 290 acres of land in Malibu County. This was not prime property, though it was good for cattle raising. Mostly, the Reagans used it for horseback riding, weekend barbecues, and a rustic escape to the small, rather run-down house on the property.

When Reagan became the governor of California, he became beholden to Jules Stein and Taft Schreiber, principals in MCA, the conglomerate that served as agent, production company, and distribution company, the first of its kind in Hollywood. They helped him financially in a manner that looked legitimate until you saw the numbers and realized they had provided him with an indirect gift. What could be considered money to make Reagan friendly toward MCA's interests was laundered through a seemingly legitimate real estate transaction.

On December 13, 1966, Stein and Schreiber arranged for Twentieth Century Fox to buy some of the land. The deal was made through Fox Realty, a wholly owned subsidiary of the motion picture company, for 236 acres of the land. The purchase price was meant to assure that the Reagans had enough wealth to move forward in politics. The problem was that the price Fox Realty paid was $8,178. The total for 236 acres, 54 acres less than the initial $85,000 purchase for all the land, was $1.930 million. A rider on the purchase gave Fox the option to buy the remaining land for the same price.

The implication seemed to be that the land had risen in value and the rider assured that Fox would not have to pay more. The truth was that in fifteen years, the land had not increased in quality or desirability, the house had not been fixed up, and the land Reagan retained was on steep terrain.

There was no way that MCA and Fox executives would admit to buying a politician whose future looked bright. Instead, they announced that Twentieth Century Fox was moving its headquarters and studio to the property. The size may have been adequate, but not all the land was useable, and it was isolated enough to be impractical. The facts did not matter, though. There never was an interest in moving the studio other than that expressed in the false release.

Nancy Reagan was pleading poverty during this period. The couple needed money. The California governor's salary was then $40,000 a year, not enough to live on if you had been making much more on television, though it was far more than most residents of the state earned. That was why she and Ronnie were forced to sell their ranch. Of course, the implication was that the ranch was more than a weekend retreat. She also did not mention two other important facts. The appraisers for Fox Realty said that the studio should pay no more than $4,000 an acre, a price still well above the county assessment. As to the remaining acreage, a legitimate sale would have placed a maximum value of no more than $550 on each acre.

The economic seduction of a future president actually marked a change in Hollywood. Never again would the mob make a bold attempt to control the studios. Never again would there be studio heads in bed with mobsters in the manner of the past.

Not that Hollywood became a clean town. The casual perusing of contemporary celebrity publications such as *People* and *US* shows that drug use is still high, though the suppliers are no longer directly connected to New York or Chicago. Sex is still a popular medium of exchange, though in some cases it is the woman who makes the aggressive move toward the studio head, producer, or director, be that person male or female.

The morals clause has been eliminated, trampled into oblivion by changing times. Some actors have more credits in drug rehab units than they do stage and screen appearances.

Even fringe entertainment has changed. Pornography production and distribution was once the province of organized crime, often a spin-off from prostitution. Today, it is the realm of the independent entrepreneur with a camera, an Internet website, and some willing playmates. More money is being made by the mob in areas like drugs, as well as waste disposal and construction, including the use of "ghost" employees who have Social Security numbers, receive a paycheck, and pay income taxes without ever going to the job site.

Now it is the corporation that has become the bad guy in business and politics. The mob charged shockingly high interest rates, yet today a bank may charge far more for a credit card account than organized crime thought prudent when loan-sharking. The mob knew it needed a high enough payoff to bring people to its backrooms and large-scale casinos, yet such activities are either illegal or highly regulated, while state lotteries offer a far smaller return.

This is not to say, however, that just because the moguls beat the mob, organized crime doesn't continue to have influence in the film industry.

Afterword

It was the late 1960s when Detective Douglas Reid of the New York Police Department was working surveillance on the organized criminals controlling heroin importation into New York and New Jersey as part of what was then the international drug-smuggling problem known as the French Connection.

Reid and several other men were stationed in an apartment across the street from where a major drug importer and several bodyguards were living. Reid and his men took turns surveilling, sleeping, and enjoying television. They had binoculars with cameras attached, cameras with telephoto lenses, and other surveillance equipment. But many hours were spent in boredom, the men not watching the entrance and having only old movies and television shows to enjoy. Over time, as the detective shifts changed, cops went from watching television to watching the bad guys.

Reid said that they noticed that the gangsters were watching the same movies they were– films about the mob. Then, in the morning, the real gangsters would imitate whatever the "reel" gangsters had done in the film. Reid said,

> We had this lieutenant stop by one day early, and he asked, "How's it going?"
>
> I told him we knew the bad guys so well, we knew what they'd do before they did it.
>
> The Lieu thought we were putting him on. It was early in the morning, and we knew this one guy always went out at eight, so we told him to watch through the binoculars.
>
> I told him, "He's going to come out wearing a trench coat and a hat. He's going to pause under the awning and lift his collar over his neck. Then, he's going to look left, then right, then left, put his hands in his pocket and walk down the street."

So, the guy comes out, pauses, lifts his collar, looks the way I said, and walks down the street. The Lieutenant was amazed. "You really know these bad guys, Reid," said the Lieu. It was the same thing the guy did in the movie. They were watching television to learn how to be gangsters. We just saw the same movie.

A Note on Resources

I have inadvertently been researching this book for more than twenty years. Having an aversion to holding a real job, I have written for newspapers and magazines for forty-five years and have been an author since my first book was published in 1969. Along the way, I have received an unusual degree of training, from graduating from the Suburban Police Academy of the Law-Medicine Center of Case Western Reserve University to having Detective Doug Reid arrange for me to meet the key witness in the French Connection case, Jaime Cohen, in his home. Cohen was living under the Federal Witness Protection Program, and when I was called by Reid, I only knew that I was to bring my tape recorder and plenty of batteries and tape. Writing about the Mafia/teamsters connection with Allen Friedman, I was introduced to such Damon Runyon–esque characters as "Runt" and "The Jew Boy," men who linked together such seemingly disparate groups as the Mayfield Road Gang, the Purple Gang, the Jewish Combination, the mob leaders at Lucky Luciano's 1928 meeting in Cleveland, Meyer Lansky, and the men who participated in the moves on both Hollywood vice and the eventual creation of Las Vegas.

I have interviewed Gambino family members, actors, actresses, producers, directors, and backstage personnel. MGM's Sam Marx talked with me about everything from how when he directed *The Thin Man* movies for MGM, it was the first time a dog—Asta, the beloved pet of detectives Nick and Nora Charles in the stories—had gone to the bathroom essentially on camera, to what really happened to Thelma Todd. I interviewed Fred Otash for a book that was completed in rough-draft form at the time of his death and Chauncey Holt, Meyer Lansky's accountant and the man who had "talks" with Ben Siegel on behalf of the East Coast mob. I spent a week interviewing comedian and Rat Pack member Joey Bishop and was amused to watch actress Angie Dickinson compare her legs to those of Peter Lawford's widow, Patricia S. Lawford, before repositioning our chairs so that when I looked at

Angie, Patricia was outside both my direct and peripheral vision. (Opinion: Angie had better legs, both women had equally sized egos.) And there was Leon Schwab, the surviving brother of the drugstore family, who was thrilled to have someone run him down at his daughter's home, not long before his death as it turned out, to talk on the telephone about a past mostly forgotten by others.

Nick Sevano, one of Frank Sinatra's managers and the man who booked clubs owned by the Chicago and New York mobs, talked about payments and skimmings and how entertainers succeeded in the 1940s and 1950s when organized crime impacted on show business.

Always, the subject of organized crime arose. Always, we went off on a tangent during the interviews so I could be educated in the world of nightclubs, where men like Tommy Dorsey would receive a check over the table so the IRS would be happy and cash under the table. I learned about the drug business and the recording industry and, most importantly, about how everything kept coming back to Hollywood. Always, there were references to the mob and the moguls, and though the mob has a history of causing deaths by unnatural causes, the venom, the bemusement, and the fear were always reserved for the moguls. The stories about the men who ran the studios and the history of the relationship between organized crime and the movie business made me want to tell a story not previously told.

As the years passed, filing cabinets filled, cassette tapes numbered into the hundreds, notebooks filled shelf after shelf, and I kept thinking about the Hollywood stories that had never been told. Some I discussed during occasional appearances on E! Entertainment, but most were in my files, not between the covers of a single book. Finally, using old interviews and new; the voices of the long dead and the elderly but healthy; and government files acquired either as public records, such as the U.S. Senate (Kefauver) hearings into organized crime, or through Freedom of Information Act requests, I have written the story of the time when the mob tried to take over Hollywood but was not corrupt enough to succeed.

Bibliography

Altman, Diana. *Hollywood East: Louis B. Mayer and the Origins of the Studio System*. New York: Carol Publishing Group, 1992.

Anger, Kenneth. *Kenneth Anger's Hollywood Babylon II*. New York: E. P. Dutton, 1984.

Asbury, Herbert. *The Gangs of New York: An Informal History of the Underworld*. New York: Paragon House, 1990.

Barbas, Samantha. *The First Lady of Hollywood: A Biography of Louella Parsons*. Berkeley: University of California Press, 2005.

Baughman, Judith S., ed. *American Decades, 1920–1929*. New York: Gale Research, 1996.

Berg, A. Scott. *Goldwyn*. New York: Alfred A. Knopf, 1989.

Black, Gregory D. *Hollywood Censored: Morality Codes, Catholics, and the Movies*. Cambridge: Cambridge University Press, 1994.

Brashler, William. *The Don: The Life and Death of Sam Giancana*. New York: Ballantine, 1977.

Brown, Peter Harry, and Patte B. Barham. *Marilyn: The Last Take*. New York: Dutton, 1992.

Brown, Peter Harry, and Pamela Ann Brown. *The MGM Girls: Behind the Velvet Curtain*. New York: St. Martin's Press, 1983.

Brownlow, Kevin. *The Parade's Gone By . . . .* New York: Alfred A. Knopf, 1969.

———. *Hollywood: The Pioneers*. New York: Alfred A. Knopf, 1979.

Brownstein, Ronald. *The Power and the Glitter: The Hollywood-Washington Connection*. New York: Pantheon Books, 1990.

Burrough, Bryan. *Public Enemies*. New York: Penguin Press, 2004.

Cagney, Jimmy. *Cagney by Cagney*. Garden City, NY: Doubleday, 1976.

Campbell, Rodney. *The Luciano Project*. New York: McGraw-Hill, 1977.

Carey, Gary. *All the Stars in Heaven: Louis B. Mayer's MGM*. New York: E. P. Dutton, 1981.

Carpozi, George, Jr. *Frank Sinatra: Is This Man Mafia?* New York: Manor Books, 1979.

Ceplair, Larry, and Steven Englund. *The Inquisition in Hollywood: Politics in the Film Community, 1930–1960*. Garden City, NY: Anchor Press/Doubleday, 1980.

Cheshire, Maxine. *Maxine Cheshire: Reporter*. Boston: Houghton Mifflin, 1978.

Clarens, Carlos. *Crime Movies: An Illustrated History: From Griffith to the Godfather and Beyond*. New York: W. W. Norton, 1980.

Cohen, Mickey, with John Peer Nugent. *Mickey Cohen in My Own Words*. Englewood Cliffs, NJ: Prentice Hall, 1975.

Colacello, Bob. *Ronnie and Nancy: Their Path to the White House*. New York: Warner Books, 2004.

Coleman, Herbert. *The Hollywood I Knew: A Memoir: 1916–1988*. Lanham, MD: Scarecrow Press, 2003.

Cook, Fred J. *The Secret Rulers: Criminal Syndicates and How They Control the U.S. Underworld*. New York: Duell, Sloan and Pearce, 1966.

Crane, Cheryl, with Cliff Jahr. *Detour: A Hollywood Story*. New York: Arbor House/William Morris, 1987.

Crowther, Bosley. *Hollywood Rajah*. New York: Henry Holt, 1960.

———. *The Lion's Share*. New York: E. P. Dutton, 1957.

Davis, John H. *Mafia Kingfish*. New York: Signet, 1989.

De Leeuw, Hendrik. *Underworld Story: The Rise of Organized Crime and Vice Rackets in the U.S.A.* London: Neville Spearman, 1955.

Demaris, Ovid. *Captive City: Chicago in Chains*. New York: Lyle Stewart, 1969.

Dick, Bernard F. *The Merchant Prince of Poverty Row: Harry Cohn of Columbia Pictures*. Lexington: University Press of Kentucky, 1993.

Doherty, Thomas. *Pre-Code Hollywood: Sex, Immorality, and Insurrection in American Cinema, 1930–1934*. New York: Columbia University Press, 1999.

Eames, John Douglas. *The MGM Story*. New York: Crown, 1979.

Edwards, Anne. *Early Reagan: The Rise to Power*. New York: William Morrow, 1987.

Evanier, David. *Making the Wiseguys Weep*. New York: Farrar, Straus & Giroux, 1998.

Exner, Judith, as told to Ovid Demaris. *Judith Exner: My Story*. New York: Grove Press, 1977.

Eyman, Scott. *Lion of Hollywood: The Life and Legend of Louis B. Mayer*. New York: Simon & Schuster, 2005.

Farr, Finis. *Fair Enough: The Life of Westbrook Pegler*. New Rochelle, NY: Arlington House, 1975.

Feinman, Jeffrey. *Hollywood Confidential.* Chicago: Playboy Press, 1976.

Finch, Christopher, and Linda Rosenkrantz. *Gone Hollywood.* Garden City, NY: Doubleday, 1979.

Fleming, E. J. *The Fixers: Eddie Mannix, Howard Strickling and the MGM Publicity Machine.* Jefferson, NC: McFarland, 2005.

Fox, Stephen. *Blood and Power: Organized Crime in Twentieth-Century America.* New York: William Morrow, 1989.

Friedman, Allen, and Ted Schwarz. *Power and Greed: Inside the Teamsters Empire of Corruption.* New York: Franklin Watts, 1989.

Gabler, Neal. *An Empire of Their Own: How the Jews Invented Hollywood.* New York: Crown, 1988.

Gage, Nicholas. *Mafia, U.S.A.* Chicago: Playboy Press, 1972.

Gardner, Gerald. *The Censorship Papers—Movie Censorship Letters from the Hays Office, 1934 to 1968.* New York: Dodd, Mead, 1987.

Gehman, Richard. *Sinatra and His Rat Pack.* New York: Belmont Books, 1961.

Gentry, Curt. *J. Edgar Hoover: The Man and the Secrets.* New York: W. W. Norton, 1991.

Giancana, Sam, and Chuck Giancana. *Double Cross: The Explosive, Inside Story of the Mobster Who Controlled America.* New York: Warner Books, 1992.

Gibson, Barbara, and Ted Schwarz. *Rose Kennedy and Her Family: The Best and Worst of Their Lives and Times.* New York: Birch Lane Press, 1995.

Graham, Sheilah. *Confessions of a Hollywood Columnist.* New York: William Morrow, 1969.

———. *My Hollywood.* London: Michael Joseph, 1984.

Granlund, Nils Thor. *Blondes, Brunettes, and Bullets.* New York: David McKay, 1957.

Harris, Marlys J. *The Zanucks of Hollywood.* New York: Crown, 1989.

Hays, Will, Jr. *Come Home with Me Now: The Untold Story of Movie Czar Will Hays by His Son.* Indianapolis: Guild Press of Indiana, 1993.

Higham, Charles. *Merchant of Dreams: Louis B. Mayer, M.G.M. and the Secret Hollywood.* New York: Donald Fine, 1993.

Hirschhorn, Clive. *The Columbia Story.* London: Octopus Publishing, 1999.

Holt, Chauncey. *Memoirs of a Chameleon.* Unpublished autobiography.

Hunt, Irma. *The Presidents' Mistresses.* New York: McGraw-Hill, 1978.

Katcher, Leo. *The Big Bankroll: The Life and Times of Arnold Rothstein.* New York: Harper and Brothers, 1958, 1959.

Kelly, Kitty. *His Way: The Unauthorized Biography of Frank Sinatra*. New York: Bantam Books, 1986.

Kennedy, Joseph P. *The Story of the Films*. Chicago: A. W. Shaw, 1927.

Kobler, John. *Capone: The Life and World of Al Capone*. New York: G. P. Putnam's Sons, 1971.

Lawford, Patricia Seaton, with Ted Schwarz. *The Peter Lawford Story*. New York: Carroll and Graf, 1988.

Leff, Leonard J., and Jerold L. Simmons. *The Dame in the Kimono: Hollywood, Censorship, and the Production Code from the 1920s to the 1960s*. New York: Grove Weidenfeld, 1990.

Levy, Shawn. *Rat Pack Confidential*. New York: Doubleday, 1998.

Madsen, Axel. *Gloria and Joe: The Star-Crossed Love Affair of Gloria Swanson and Joe Kennedy*. New York: Arbor House, 1988.

Marx, Arthur. *Goldwyn: A Biography of the Man behind the Myth*. New York: W. W. Norton, 1976.

Marx, Samuel, and Joyce Vandervee. *Deadly Illusions: Jean Harlow and the Murder of Paul Bern*. New York: Random House, 1990.

Marx, Samuel. *Mayer and Thalberg: The Make-Believe Saints*. New York: Random House, 1975.

Matera, Dary. *John Dillinger*. New York: Carroll and Graf, 2004.

McArthur, Benjamin. *Actors and American Culture, 1880–1920*. Philadelphia: Temple University Press, 1984.

McDougal, Dennis. *The Last Mogul: Lew Wasserman, MCA, and the Hidden History of Hollywood*. New York: Da Capo Press, 2001.

Messick, Hank. *The Beauties and the Beasts: The Mob in Show Business*. New York: David McKay, 1973.

Moldea, Dan. *Dark Victory: Ronald Reagan, MCA, and the Mob*. New York: Viking, 1998.

Mosley, Leonard. *Zanuck: The Rise and Fall of Hollywood's Last Tycoon*. Boston: Little, Brown, 1984.

Munby, Jonathan. *Public Enemies, Public Heroes*. Chicago: University of Chicago Press, 1999.

Nash, Robert. *The World Encyclopedia of Organized Crime*. New York: Paragon, 1992.

Nelson, Mike, and Gene Mailes. *Hollywood's Other Blacklist: Union Struggles in the Studio System*. London: British Film Institute Publishing, 1995.

Noguchi, Thomas, MD, with Joseph DiMona. *Coroner*. New York: Simon & Schuster, 1981.

Norman, Barry. *The Story of Hollywood*. New York: NAL Books, 1987.

Offen, Ron. *Cagney*. Chicago: Regnery, 1972.

Otash, Fred. *Investigation Hollywood*. Chicago: Regnery, 1976.

Otash, Fred, with Ted Schwarz. *Marilyn, the Kennedys, and Me*. Unpublished memoir.

Parish, James Robert. *The Fox Girls*. New York: Arlington House, 1971.

Parish, James Robert, and Steven Whitney. *The George Raft File*. New York: Drake, 1973.

Parsons, Louella. *Tell It to Louella*. New York: Putnam's, 1971.

Pietrusza, David. *Rothstein: The Life, Times, and Murder of the Criminal Genius Who Fixed the 1919 World Series*. New York: Carroll and Graf, 2003.

Pilat, Oliver. *Pegler, Angry Man of the Press*. Westport, CT: Greenwood Press, 1963.

Pizzitola, Louis. *Hearst over Hollywood: Power, Passion, and Propaganda in the Movies*. New York: Columbia University Press, 2002.

Powell, Hickman. *Lucky Luciano: The Man Who Organized Crime in America*. New York: Barricade Books, 2000.

Pye, Michael. *Moguls: Inside the Business of Show Business*. New York: Holt, Rinehart and Winston, 1980.

Rappleye, Charles, and Ed Becker. *All American Mafioso: The Johnny Rosselli Story*. New York: Doubleday, 1991.

Reid, Ed. *The Grim Reapers: The Anatomy of Organized Crime in America*. Chicago: Regnery Co., 1969.

———. *Mickey Cohen: Mobster*. New York: Bantam, 1969.

Roemer, William F., Jr. *Accardo: The Genuine Godfather*. New York: Ivy Books, Ballantine, 1995.

Root, Eric, with Dale Crawford and Raymond Strait. *The Private Diary of My Life with Lana*. Beverly Hills, CA: Dove, 1996.

Rosow, Eugene. *Born to Lose: The Gangster Film in America*. New York: Oxford University Press, 1978.

Ruuth, Marianne. *Cruel City: The Dark Side of Hollywood's Rich and Famous*. Malibu, CA: Roundtable, 1991.

Schwarz, Ted. *Joseph P. Kennedy: The Mogul, the Mob, the Statesman, and the Making of an American Myth*. Hoboken, NJ: John Wiley, 2003.

Schwartz, Nancy Lynn, and Sheila Schwartz. *The Hollywood Writers' Wars*. New York: Alfred Knopf, 1982.

Sevano, Nick, and Ted Schwarz. *Sinatra: You Only Thought You Knew Him*. New York: SPI Publishing, forthcoming.

Skolsky, Sidney. *Don't Get Me Wrong—I Love Hollywood*. New York: Putnam's, 1975.

Sondern, Frederic, Jr. *Brotherhood of Evil: The Mafia*. New York: Farrar, Straus and Cudahy, 1959.

Spada, James. *Peter Lawford: The Man Who Kept the Secrets*. New York: Bantam, 1991.

Staiger, Janet. *The Studio System*. New Brunswick, NJ: Rutgers University Press, 1995.

Starr, Michael. *The Mouse in the Pack: The Joey Bishop Story*. New York: Taylor Trade, 2002.

Stenn, David. *Bombshell: The Life and Death of Jean Harlow*. New York: Doubleday, 1993.

Summers, Anthony. *Official and Confidential: The Secret Life of J. Edgar Hoover*. New York: G. P. Putnam's Sons, 1993.

Summers, Anthony. *Goddess: The Secret Lives of Marilyn Monroe*. New York: Macmillan, 1985.

Summers, Anthony, and Robbyn Swan. *Sinatra: The Life*. New York: Alfred Knopf, 2005.

Swanson, Gloria. *Swanson on Swanson: An Autobiography*. New York: Random House, 1980.

Thomas, Bob. *King Cohn: The Life and Times of Hollywood Mogul Harry Cohn*. Beverly Hills, CA: New Millennium Press, 1967 [reprint 2000].

Thomas, Tony. *The Films of Ronald Reagan*. Secaucus, NJ: Citadel Press, 1980.

Tosches, Nick. *Dino: Living High in the Dirty Business of Dreams*. New York: Doubleday, 1992.

Turner, Lana. *Lana: The Lady, the Legend, the Truth*. New York: E. P. Dutton, 1982.

Wendland, Michael F. *The Arizona Project: How a Team of Investigative Reporters Got Revenge on Deadline*. Kansas City: Sheed Andrews and McMeel, 1977.

Wills, Gary. *Reagan's America: Innocents at Home*. New York: Doubleday, 1981.

Wilson, Earl. *The Show Business Nobody Knows*. New York: Bantam, 1971.

———. *Sinatra: An Unauthorized Biography*. New York: Macmillan, 1976.

———. *Hot Times: True Tales of Hollywood and Broadway*. New York: Contemporary Books, 1984.

Wolf, George, and Joseph DiMona. *Frank Costello: Prime Minister of the Underworld*. New York: William Morrow, 1974.

Yablonsky, Lewis. *George Raft*. New York: McGraw-Hill, 1973.

Zeller, F. C. Duke. *Devil's Pact: Inside the World of the Teamsters Union*. Secaucus, NJ: Carroll, 1996.

Zukor, Adolph. *The Public Is Never Wrong*. New York: G. P. Putnam's Sons, 1953.

FBI Files

Aiuppa, Joseph

Anastasia, Albert

Bankhead, Talulah

Capone, Al

Dalitz, Morris "Moe"

Davis, Sammy, Jr.

Dillinger, John (Summary only)

Galante, Carmine

Gambino, Carlo

Genovese, Vito

Giancana, Sam

Hearst, William Randolph, Sr.

Hopper, Hedda

Kennedy, Joseph P.

Luciano, Charles "Lucky"

Mafia monograph

Monroe, Marilyn

Moran, George "Bugs"

Nitti, Frank

Otash, Fred

Parsons, Louella Oettinger

Profaci, Joseph

Raft, George

Reles, Abe

Roselli, John (*sic*)

Siegel, Bugsy

Sinatra, Frank

Spilotro, Anthony

Swanson, Gloria

Turner, Lana

Winchell, Walter

Zwillman, Abner "Longie"

Research Libraries

John F. Kennedy Library
Arizona State University, Hayden Library, Special Collections—Ted Schwarz Archives, Peter Lawford Archives
Margaret Herrick Library, Beverly Hills, California
Beverly Hills Public Library
FBI Reading Room (Freedom of Information Act files)

Index